T0178910

Introduction to Stochastic Processes and Simulation

Series Editor
Jean-Charles Pomerol

Introduction to Stochastic Processes and Simulation

Gérard-Michel Cochard

WILEY

First published 2019 in Great Britain and the United States by ISTE Ltd and John Wiley & Sons, Inc.

ISTE Ltd
27-37 St George's Road
London SW19 4EU
UK

www.iste.co.uk

John Wiley & Sons, Inc.
111 River Street
Hoboken, NJ 07030
USA

www.wiley.com

Library of Congress Control Number: 2019943763

British Library Cataloguing-in-Publication Data
A CIP record for this book is available from the British Library
ISBN 978-1-78630-484-1

Contents

Preface

For 15 years, fourth-year university (now first-year master's) students, in class and remotely, have studied the MIAGE (computer science applied to business management) course on which this book is based. The main priority of this course is to equip computer scientists with a knowledge base broad enough to be able to adapt it for different companies, administrations and organizations. It has a multidisciplinary nature, as it includes computer science, information systems, organization and management, communication, professionalism and applied mathematics. The MIAGE course is offered by 22 French universities, six of which offer a distance learning version, which is also shared by five affiliated foreign institutions. Students taking this course come from scientific or economics and management fields. Their mathematical background is not as advanced as that of a student who has studied mathematics long term. The applied mathematics concepts of the MIAGE course program focus on descriptive statistics, probabilities, data analysis, random processes and numerical simulation. The last two concepts are the subject of this book.

It is important to say from the outset that as the MIAGE course students, given their different backgrounds, have educational requirements that must be met, experienced mathematicians will not find this book to be as thorough as they may expect. Definitions and demonstrations which may deter course students have been purposefully left out. The objective is to teach students how to use methods and mathematical tools to solve problems of analysis and optimization that arise in the professional world. Therefore, it is not a case of satisfying mathematics students, but students or trainees in continuing education who do not have a full mathematics degree, but want to know how to use mathematical tools. As the word "Introduction" in the title suggests, this book attempts to get straight to the point, without complicating the presentation with overly advanced or rigorous mathematical considerations. In the bibliographical references, there are some excellent books that give very complete mathematical discussions of the issues raised. I refer the interested reader to this material. The mathematicians must forgive this approach, which may seem a little unusual to them.

This book is for a much wider audience than the MIAGE course; it is for those in initial and continuing education, at university, engineering school and management school. For this reason, in addition to conventional applications for inventory and queueing management, additional applications have been added to the initial course in areas such as equipment reliability, genetics, population dynamics, market finance and an introduction to metaheuristics.

The book has 12 chapters, which can be grouped into three parts.

Part 1 – Basic Mathematical Concepts: this part consists of reminders (hopefully) about complements in probability, covered in the first two chapters:

– Chapter 1: "Basic Reminders of Probability";

– Chapter 2: "Probabilistic Models".

The third chapter directly applies the notions of probability and probabilistic models:

– Chapter 3: "Inventory Management".

Part 2 – Stochastic Processes: in two chapters, this part sets out the fundamental notions relating to processes in which chance intervenes:

– Chapter 4: "Markov Chains";

– Chapter 5: "Markov Processes".

These two chapters are called Markov, as they are complementary. In a Markov chain, time is considered discrete, while in a Markov process, time is considered continuous.

The following chapters are devoted to applications of Markov chains and processes:

– Chapter 6: "Queueing Systems";

– Chapter 7: "Various Applications".

Queueing systems are an important area of concern in the professional world and a whole chapter is needed for them, taking as an example two basic types of queues, M/M/1 and M/M/S.

Chapter 7 contains applications for a variety of topics: reliability and availability of equipment, genetics, population dynamics with the predator–prey model, and the Brownian motion in physics and its application in market finance.

Part 3 – Simulation: theoretical calculations do not allow us to find exact results within a reasonable period of time, even with powerful computers (which are not accessible to everyone); simulation methods are an increasingly frequent recourse to obtain solutions that are closer to the sought-after solution. Given that chance is the common theme throughout the book, it is necessary to use probability and the usual laws to simulate reality in a virtual form. The basic principles are outlined in the following two chapters:

– Chapter 8: "Generator Programs";

– Chapter 9: "Principles of Simulation".

Then, we return to examples that have been theoretically covered already, and apply the simulation methods:

– Chapter 10: "Simulation of Inventory Management";

– Chapter 11: "Simulation of a Queueing Process".

Finally, the last chapter covers how to apply simulation to optimization problems, notably combinatorics:

– Chapter 12: "Optimization and Simulation".

This chapter can be considered as an introduction to metaheuristics. A summarizing review of local methods is carried out, before looking in detail at two increasingly popular methods: genetic algorithms and ant colonies.

Throughout this book, I have attempted to favor clarity and have used many examples to illustrate the use of mathematical tools and show their value. Some developments involving lengthy calculations have been presented in an appendix section within the chapter concerned, so as to not obscure the text.

The text also includes short biographical notes of scientists whose contributions to the subjects are vital. It should always be remembered that the mathematical tools presented come from their research work.

As this book introduces readers to the subject matter, I thought it useful to direct them towards basic texts, many of which are very accessible, in the bibliographical references.

As for the simulation programs, almost all of them have been built with PHP and are available to readers who want to use them for personal use. Please contact the author via email[1] with a specific request, and the programs can be sent without any rights issues. This is also a good opportunity for the author to receive readers' comments and questions, thereby establishing mutually beneficial relationships.

Finally, to conclude this foreword, I would like to thank Francis Rogard who, despite having many important duties with work, politics and family, kindly read a part of the manuscript and shared his wise comments with me.

Gérard-Michel COCHARD
July 2019

---

1 gerard-michel.cochard@u-picardie.fr.

Part 1

Basic Mathematical Concepts

1

Basic Reminders of Probability

CONCEPTS DISCUSSED IN THIS CHAPTER.– The concept of probability is at the heart of this book. It is therefore necessary to master the corresponding concepts. In principle, the reader should already have the required knowledge. However, experience shows that a reminder is always necessary to refresh knowledge which may have been learnt a while ago.

In this chapter, we will discuss the nature of chance and an empirical approach to probability, based on counting possible results from experience.

We will move on to a formal approach to probability, based on the set theory, which applies to previous experimental cases, and then a statistical definition of probability with the law of large numbers.

If the reader is proficient in these concepts, they can skip the corresponding sections.

Finally, we will end with the very important concept of composite probability, which is illustrated by a figure showing states of a system, transitions between states and graphs representative of the possible evolution of a system.

Recommended reading: [BRE 09, DEH 82, DOD 08, ENG 76, ROS 93, SAP 11].

1.1. Chance

The Larousse dictionary gives two meanings for the word "chance":

– "power regarded as the cause of apparently incidental or inexplicable events";

All figures and tables are available in color online at www.iste.co.uk/cochard/stochastic.zip.

– "unforeseen or unforeseeable circumstances, the effects of which may be favorable or unfavorable to someone".

The first definition is actually a double one:

– it introduces the concept of causality according to which an inexplicable event would nevertheless be due to an unknown cause; knowing the cause and the mechanisms that result from it, one could (theoretically) explain the inexplicable. Thus, if a passerby is hit on the head by a flowerpot that has fallen from a window after a gust of wind, it is tempting to say that this event is incidental; however, it is quite explainable. If an observer looks at the situation, he or she can indeed see that the accident is inevitable. One could even, if the problem was not so complex, explain the accident with the laws of mechanics. "Inexplicable" does not mean "chance";

– it also suggests that the cause is a power. God, maybe? Let us quote the famous answer given by Pierre-Simon de Laplace to Napoleon when asked why he did not mention the existence of God in his "*Treatise of celestial mechanics*": "Sire, I had no need of that hypothesis."

The second definition brings us to the fundamental subject of this book: can hazardous events be predicted? This question will lead to probability theory. It originates from games called "games of chance". Chevalier de Mere's bet is representative of the reflections of the time when the theory of probability was born, with Blaise Pascal and Pierre de Fermat. According to Chevalier de Mere, who had noted that as throwing a die four times had a good chance of getting a "6", it should be even more rewarding to get a double "6" by rolling 24 dice twice. Pascal showed him that his reasoning was wrong. In the first case, the probability of rolling a "6" is 0.517, while in the second case, the probability of rolling a double "6" is only 0.4911. Here, we are already calculating probability, which indicates the concept of forecasting: it does not give the definite result, but the chances of obtaining a given result.

1.2. Counting and probability

It is common when first looking at probability to take widely used examples, namely rolling a six-sided die numbered from "1" to "6", or picking out colored balls from a bag containing a certain number of balls that differ only in color, or taking cards from a deck of cards. It is very rare that a presentation on the concept of probability does not use these three examples. We will follow this custom and use these three easy-to-imagine examples, but later we will look at other examples more related to everyday life (we do not generally spend all our time playing dice, choosing balls from a bag or playing cards!).

---

1 The calculation will be carried out below (Example 1.14).

Pierre de Fermat   Blaise Pascal

Figure 1.1. *Pierre de Fermat (1601–1665) and Blaise Pascal (1623–1662) can be considered the founding fathers of the mathematical branch we call "probability calculation" today. These men exchanged letters during their research, posing problems to solve, but never met[2]*

EXAMPLE 1.1.– First, roll the die and consider our chances of getting a "5". Assuming it is a fair die (we have as many chances to get any result with such a die), we can already say that our chances of getting a "5" are the same as those of getting a "1", "2", "3", "4" or "6". This is expressed by saying that the various results are equiprobable.

As we have six possible results and only one effective result, we can say that, to get a given result, we have 1 chance in 6, which we can express by the ratio 1/6, representing the probability of having one of the possible outcomes. This ratio expresses the quotient of the number of favorable results (here 1) to the number of possible outcomes (here 6). We can then use an abbreviated notation p(result = a) = 1/6 where a is an integer between 1 and 6. The sum of all the probabilities is 6 × (1/6), so 1.

In addition, suppose that we are interested in result a. Every result that is not this one (not a) is a contrary result.

As a result, p(result = a) + p(result = not a) = 1, the sum of the probability of a result and the probability of the opposite result is equal to 1.

EXAMPLE 1.2(1).– Now let us look at the bag containing identical black and white balls. Imagine we have three black balls and two white balls. If we pick out a ball, (without looking, of course) what are our chances of getting a black ball?

---

2 The portraits of Pierre de Fermat (unknown painter) and Blaise Pascal (copy of a painting by François II Quesnel, engraved by Gérard Edelink) are from Wikimedia Commons: https://commons.wikimedia.org/wiki/Category:Pierre-de-Fermat; https://commons.wikimedia.org/wiki/Category:Blaise_Pascal.

This problem is less simple that the previous one. However, we can say that we have more chances to get a black ball than to get a white ball because there are more black balls than white balls. If we try to identify the balls in the bag using thought, we can see that there can be five possible results, of which three correspond to our expectation (picking out a black ball).

This situation is expressed by the ratio 3/5 and p(picking out a black ball) = 3/5.

Similarly, we can express the ratio 2/5, the chances of obtaining the draw of a white ball, as p(picking out a white ball) = 2/5. Here again, the probability is expressed as the ratio of the number of expected results (here 3 for the black balls and 2 for the white balls) to the number of possible results (here 5).

Note that, unlike the previous example, picking out a black ball and picking out a white ball are not equiprobable: 3/5 probability in one case, 2/5 probability in the other. Note also that the sum of the probabilities of the result of picking out a ball is 3/5 + 2/5 = 1.

EXAMPLE 1.3(1).– Let us move on to the card deck. Imagine taking 2 cards from a deck of 52 cards (13 cards of each color) and trying to estimate the odds of drawing two aces.

Let us first estimate all the possible results by naming the two cards X and Y. For the first card drawn, X, there are 52 possibilities and there are 51 cards in the deck for the second card, Y. But the roles of X and Y are interchangeable, so that in all we have $(52 \times 51)/2$ possibilities to not count the same result twice, i.e. 1,326 possible results. There are four aces in the deck, so we have four possibilities for the first ace X and more than three possibilities for the second ace Y; by exchanging the roles of X and Y, we have either $(4 \times 3)/2 = 6$ expected results, which we can easily list:

♣♥, ♣♦, ♣♠, ♥♦, ♥♠, ♦♠

So we have 6 chances out of 1,326 to obtain 2 aces, which can be expressed by the probability:

p(drawing 2 aces) = 6/1,326 = 0.00452.

Now consider the case where we do not get any aces when drawing two cards. For the first card drawn X, we have 52 – 4 = 48 possibilities (we remove the aces), and for the second card drawn, we have 52 – 4 – 1 = 47 possibilities, by interchanging the roles of X and Y, $(48 \times 47)/2 = 1,128$ possible expected results. The number of possible results being always the same, we have:

p(drawing 2 cards which are not aces) = 1,128/1,326 = 0.8506.

But there is a third possible result, which is that there is a single ace among the two cards drawn. If the first card drawn X is an ace, we have four possibilities, and for the second card Y, we have $51 - 3 = 48$ possibilities; here, there is no symmetry in X and Y, so we have $4 \times 48 = 192$ possibilities for this third possible result.

The corresponding probability is therefore:

p(drawing 2 cards with only one ace) $= 192/1,326 = 0.14479$.

The three expected results do not have the same chances of occurring. They are not equiprobable. Note that $6 + 1,128 + 192 = 1,326$, so the sum of the probabilities of the possible expected results is 1.

Figure 1.2. *Pierre-Simon de Laplace (1749–1827)*

COMMENT ON FIGURE 1.2.– *Professor, mathematician, physicist and astronomer, Laplace lived through, opportunistically, several political regimes including the Napoleonic period (he was made Count of the Empire), then the Restoration (he was named a marquis). His scientific work focused on many areas, including celestial mechanics, differential equations (he gave his name to one of them, the Laplace equation, and to a transform method, the Laplace transform, as well as to a differential operator, the Laplacian), calculus, capillary action and, of course, probability theory with the normal law and the central limit theorem. Intensely deterministic, he did not believe in chance, but in the result of various causes not yet accessible to man[3].*

---

3 The portrait of Pierre-Simon de Laplace (by Paul Guérin, 1783–1855) is from Wikimedia Commons: https://commons.wikimedia.org/wiki/Category:Pierre_Simon-Laplace.

To sum up this approach in the previous three examples:

– the procedure is to count the number of possible results (also called "possible cases") and the number of expected results (also called "favorable cases") and to report them to obtain the probability of an expected result, following the definition of Pierre-Simon de Laplace. This obviously supposes that one can count all the possible cases and all the favorable cases;

– the number of favorable cases is at most equal to the number of possible cases, which means that the probability is a positive number less than or equal to 1;

– the sum of the probabilities of the possible expected results is equal to 1. The sum of the probability of a given expected result and the probability of the opposite result is equal to 1.

For the moment, our considerations are drawn from the previous examples. Later, we will give a more exact, and therefore mathematical, definition of probability and its properties. In this case, let us look at counting methods, which are necessary to obtain probability.

Let us start with permutations of n elements and the number of permutations that can be obtained. A permutation is an ordered sequence of the n elements: the first, the second, the third…the nth. There are n possibilities to choose the first element of a permutation, there are only $n - 1$ possibilities to choose the second element and finally only one possibility remains to choose the last element of the permutation. The total number of distinct permutations is therefore:

$$P_n = n.(n - 1).(n - 2)...1 = n!$$

Thus, the number of permutations of a deck of 52 cards (which are all distinct) is 52!, an extremely large number of 8.10^{67}. The number of permutations of the four aces in the card deck is smaller: $4! = 24$.

Let us now move on to the arrangements. An arrangement is an ordered sequence of p elements taken from n elements without repetition ($p \leq n$).

An element taken alone constitutes an arrangement of order 1. Therefore, there are n arrangements of order 1 and we note $A_n^1 = n$.

To find the arrangements of order 2, we take each arrangement of order 1 whose element is the first element and put an element taken in the n, but distinct from the first, in the second position. For this second position, we have $n - 1$ choice, so the number of arrangements sought is $A_n^2 = n.(n - 1)$.

Continuing thus to the order p, we get $A_n^p = n.(n-1).(n-2)\ldots(n-p+1)$.

As $n! = [n.(n-1).(n-2)\ldots(n-p+1)].[(n-p).(n-p-1).(n-p-2)\ldots 1] = n.(n-1).(n-2)\ldots(n-p+1).(n-p)!$, gives us:

$$A_n^p = \frac{n!}{(n-p)!}$$

EXAMPLE 1.4.– So, in a 20-horse race, let us look at the number of tiers in the order (i.e. by ranking three horses in the first, second, third order), which can be written:

$$A_{20}^3 = \frac{20!}{17!} = 6{,}840$$

Finally, the combinations. A combination of p elements taken from n without repetition is simply a subset of p elements of the set of n elements. Although this definition is quite similar to the arrangement definition, there is no order here for ranking the p elements (a combination is a set). To find the number of combinations C_n^p of p elements taken from n, the previous results concerning permutations and arrangements can be used. In fact, the number of combinations of order p is the number of arrangements of order p divided by the number of permutations of order p, namely:

$$C_n^p = \frac{n!}{(n-p)!\,p!}$$

EXAMPLE 1.5.– If we come back to the 20-horse race and if we are interested now in the number of tiers in the disorder that we can make, we have:

$$C_{20}^3 = \frac{20!}{17!\,3!} = 1{,}140$$

For a reason, which we will see later, C_n^p is called the "binomial coefficient". It has many properties, among which:

PROPERTY 1.1.– $C_n^p = C_n^{n-p}$ and, in particular, $C_n^0 = C_n^n = 1$, $C_n^1 = C_n^{n-1} = n$ (remember that $0! = 1! = 1$).

PROPERTY 1.2.– $C_n^p + C_n^{p+1} = C_{n+1}^{p+1}$, property known as "Pascal's triangle"; the binomial coefficients can be set out in a triangular table where the previous relationship is shown (Table 1.1).

PROPERTY 1.3.– Development of Newton's binomial theorem (hence the name of the number of combinations):

$$(x + y)^n = \sum_{p=0}^{n} C_n^p x^{n-p} y^p$$

In particular, if $x = y = 1$, we get:

$$2^n = \sum_{p=0}^{n} C_n^p$$

		\multicolumn{9}{c}{p}								
		0	1	2	3	4	5	6	7	8
	0	1								
	1	1	1							
	2	1	2	1						
	3	1	3	3	1					
n	4	1	4	6	4	1				
	5	1	5	10	10	5	1			
	6	1	6	15	20	15	6	1		
	7	1	7	21	35	35	21	7	1	
	8	1	8	28	56	70	56	28	8	1

Table 1.1. *Pascal's triangle*

Using the previous relationships, we can find the probabilities calculated above for the standard examples of the bag and the deck of cards.

EXAMPLE 1.2(2).– Bag of balls: picking out a ball:

– number of possible cases: $C_5^1 = 5$;

– number of favorable cases of a black ball: $C_3^1 = 3$;

– number of favorable cases of a white ball: $C_2^1 = 2$.

So, p(black ball) = 3/5 and p(white ball) = 2/5.

EXAMPLE 1.3(2).– Deck of cards:

– drawing two cards; number of possible cases: $C_{52}^2 = \frac{52!}{50!2!} = 1,326$;

– drawing two aces: number of favorable cases: $C_4^2 = \frac{4!}{2!2!} = 6$, so $p(2$ aces$) = 6/1,326$;

– drawing cards which are not aces: number of favorable cases: $C_{48}^2 = \frac{48!}{46!2!} = 1\,128$, so $p(2$ cards not aces$) = 1,128/1,326$;

– drawing an ace and a card that is not an ace: number of favorable cases: $C_4^1 . C_{48}^1 = \frac{4!48!}{3!47!1!1!} = 192$, so $p($an ace and a non-ace$) = 192/1,326$.

As our approach is empirical, we must now more formally define the concept of probability.

1.3. Events and probability

Consider a nonempty set E whose elements are arbitrary. The parts of E are the sets that can be formed from the elements of E.

EXAMPLE 1.6(1).– $E = \{a, b, c, d\}$; a, b, c, d are the elements of E ; $\{a, b\}, \{c, d\}$, $\{a, b, c\}, \{b\}, E, F = \{\}$ (also written $\varnothing$) are parts of E.

All parts of E are:

– part to 0 element: $\varnothing = \{\}$;

– parts to 1 element: $\{a\}, \{b\}, \{c\}, \{d\}$;

– parts to 2 elements: $\{a, b\}, \{a, c\}, \{a, d\}, \{b, c\}, \{b, d\}, \{c, d\}$;

– parts to 3 elements: $\{a, b, c\}, \{a, b, d\}, \{a, c, d\}, \{b, c, d\}$;

– part to 4 elements: $E = \{a, b, c, d\}$.

So, there are 16 parts for E.

The set of parts of a set E is denoted $\mathscr{P}(E)$. Note that the number of elements of $\mathscr{P}(E)$ is 2^n if E has n elements.

EXAMPLE 1.6(2).– In Example 1.6(1), we consider that the different parts of E are combinations of p elements taken from the four elements of E. As a result:

– the numbers of parts to 0 elements is $C_4^0 = 1$;

– the numbers of parts to 1 element is $C_4^1 = 4$;

– the numbers of parts to 2 elements is $C_4^2 = 6$;

– the numbers of parts to 3 elements is $C_4^3 = 4$;

– the numbers of parts to 4 elements is $C_4^4 = 1$.

The total number of parts is $C_4^0 + C_4^1 + C_4^2 + C_4^3 + C_4^4 = 16$, a result that can be found with Property 1.3 of the binomial coefficient $2^4 = 16$.

Let us now call the elements of $\mathcal{P}(E)$ "events" and define an application p of $\mathcal{P}(E)$ in R (set of real numbers) satisfying the following axioms:

– axiom 1: $\forall A \in \mathcal{P}(E)\ p(A) \geq 0$;

– axiom 2: $p(E) = 1$;

– axiom 3: if $A \cap B = \emptyset$, then $p(A \cup B) = p(A) + p(B)$.

This application p is called a probability on $\mathcal{P}(E)$.

Some vocabulary: E is a certain event. $\emptyset$ is an impossible *event*. $\{a\}$, $\{b\}$, $\{c\}$ and $\{d\}$ are elementary events (we cannot make them from simpler elements).

If $A \cap B = \emptyset$, then A and B are said to be incompatible events.

If $\bar{A}$ is the complement of A, then A and $\bar{A}$ are said to be opposite.

EXAMPLE 1.6(3).– Let us go back to the previous (very well-used) example!

$\{a\}$ and $\{b, c, d\}$ are opposite, as are E and $\emptyset$ and even $\{a, b\}$ and $\{c, d\}$. $\{a\}$ and $\{b, c\}$ are incompatible, as are $\{a\}$ and $\{c\}$, and even $\{a, b\}$ and $\{c, d\}$.

It will be noted, moreover, that opposite events are incompatible, but that the reverse is not true: $\{a\}$ and $\{b, c, d\}$ are opposite so incompatible, but $\{a\}$ and $\{b, c\}$ are incompatible but not opposite.

EXAMPLE 1.7(1).– Let {x} denote the drawing of a card x in a deck of cards.

The elements of E are {ace of hearts}, {jack of diamonds}, {6 of clubs}, etc.

The "drawing a heart" event is defined, for example, by {hearts} = {ace of hearts} ∪ {2 of hearts} ∪ {3 of hearts} ∪ ... ∪ {10 of hearts} ∪ {jack of hearts} ∪ {queen of hearts} ∪ {king of hearts} = {{ace of hearts}, {2 of hearts}, {3 of hearts}, ..., {10 of hearts}, {jack of hearts}, {queen of hearts}, {king of hearts}} and is a part of E.

"Drawing a heart" and "drawing a club" are two incompatible events because {heart} ∩ {club} = ∅.

"Drawing a heart" and "drawing a club" or "drawing a diamond" or "drawing a spade" are opposite events because $\overline{\{heart\}}$ = {club} ∪ {diamond} ∪ {spade}.

Let us now give the list of the properties of probability. From the axioms of definition, we can easily draw the following conclusions by leaving it to the reader to demonstrate them.

PROPERTY 1.4.– If $A \subset B$ then $p(A) < p(B)$

PROPERTY 1.5.– $p(A) \leq 1 \quad \forall A \in \mathcal{P}(E)$

PROPERTY 1.6.– $p(\bar{A}) = 1 - p(A) \quad \forall A \in \mathcal{P}(E)$

PROPERTY 1.7.– $p(\emptyset) = 0$

PROPERTY 1.8.– $p(A \cup B) = p(A) + p(B) - p(A \cap B)$

EXAMPLE 1.7(2).– Let us go back to Example 1.7(1).

Since {heart}, {club}, {diamond} and {spade} are disjoined two by two, we have:

– p(drawing a heart) = $p(\{heart\})$ = $1 - p(\{club\} \cup \{diamond\} \cup \{spade\})$ = $1 - p(\{club\}) - p(\{diamond\}) - p(\{spade\})$;

– p(drawing any card) = 1 ;

– p(drawing a heart or a 10) = $p(\{heart\}) + p(\{10\}) - p(\{10\} \cap \{heart\})$;

but:

$p(\{\text{heart}\})$ = $p(\{\text{ace of hearts}\} \cup \{2 \text{ of hearts}\} \cup \{3 \text{ of hearts}\} \cup ... \cup \{10 \text{ of hearts}\} \cup \{\text{jack of heart}\} \cup \{\text{queen of hearts}\} \cup \{\text{king of hearts}\})$ = $p(\{\text{ace of hearts}\})$ + $p(\{2 \text{ of hearts}\})$ + $p(\{3 \text{ of hearts}\})$ + ... + $p(\{10 \text{ of hearts}\})$ + $p(\{\text{jack of hearts}\})$ + $p(\{\text{queen of hearts}\})$ + $p(\{\text{king of hearts}\})$;

and:

$p(\{10\}) = p(\{10 \text{ of hearts}\} \cup \{10 \text{ of clubs}\} \cup \{10 \text{ of diamonds}\} \cup \{10 \text{ of spades}\}) = p(\{10 \text{ of hearts}\}) + p(\{10 \text{ of clubs}\}) + p(\{10 \text{ of diamonds}\}) + p(\{10 \text{ of spades}\})$;

so that:

$p(\text{drawing a heart or a } 10) = p(\{\text{ace of hearts}\}) + p(\{2 \text{ of hearts}\}) + p(\{3 \text{ of hearts}\}) + ... + p(\{\text{jack of hearts}\}) + p(\{\text{queen of hearts}\}) + p(\{\text{king of hearts}\}) + p(\{10 \text{ of hearts}\}) + p(\{10 \text{ of clubs}\}) + p(\{10 \text{ of diamonds}\}) + p(\{10 \text{ of spades}\})$.

In general, the concept of equiprobability is of definite help. Let us come back to this concept. Elementary events are considered equiprobable if they have equal probabilities.

EXAMPLE 1.8(1).– Let us take the experience of throwing a die. As the die is not loaded, we know that all the results are equiprobable.

Therefore: $p(\{1\}) = p(\{2\}) = p(\{3\}) = p(\{4\}) = p(\{5\}) = p(\{6\})$.

EXAMPLE 1.9(1).– Let us also look at drawing a card in a card deck. As the cards are assumed to be identical in form, all possible outcomes are equiprobable:

$p(\{6 \text{ of clubs}\})$ = $p(\{3 \text{ of diamonds}\})$ = $p(\{\text{jack of hearts}\})$ = $p(\{\text{queen of spades}\})$.

In the case of equiprobable elementary events, $\forall X_i, X_j$ elementary events, $p(X_i) = p(X_j)$ so that:

$p(X_1) + p(X_2) + ... + p(X_n) = p(X_1 \cup X_2 \cup ... \cup X_n) = p(E) = 1$

hence:

$p(X_i) = 1/n$

We deduce that $\forall A \in \mathcal{R}(E)$, $A = X_1 \cup X_2 \cup ... \cup X_k$ (since the X_i are elementary).

So:

$$p(A) = p(X_1) + p(X_2) + \ldots + p(X_k) = k/n$$

This relationship, in common language, is expressed as follows: *the probability of an event is the ratio of the number of favorable cases to the number of possible cases.*

It is valid only for equiprobable events. The following examples illustrate this (very common) practical definition.

EXAMPLE 1.8(2).– Roll of a die. Elementary events are equiprobable:

$$p(\{1\}) = p(\{2\}) = p(\{3\}) = p(\{4\}) = p(\{5\}) = p(\{6\}) = 1/6$$

and, as a result, the probability of getting an odd number is:

$$p(\{odd\}) = p(\{1\}) + p(\{3\}) + p(\{5\}) = 3/6 = \frac{1}{2} = 0.5$$

EXAMPLE 1.9(2).– Drawing a card in a deck of cards. All draws are equiprobable (in an honest card game). Therefore:

$$p(\{heart\}) = 13 \times p(\{any\ card\}) = 13 \times (1/52) = \frac{1}{4}$$

An important consequence of the equiprobability schema is that the sum of probabilities for an experiment is 1. Let A, B... be the incompatible events, results of the experiment and let $n(A)$, $n(B)$... be their numbers of favorable cases (no double-counting). So, by asking:

$$n(A) + n(B) + \ldots = n$$

we have:

$$p(A) + p(B) + \ldots = n(A)/n + n(B)/n + \ldots = n/n = 1$$

The basic principle of equiprobability for elementary events can be applied in two ways:

– by counting possible cases and favorable cases. We can then use the formulas of the combinatorial analysis seen above;

– using the weak law of large numbers, which allows us to obtain, with the statistics, an approximate value of the probability. This case is explained in section 1.4.

1.4. Statistics and probability

The previous approach to the probability concept is related to counting possible events and favorable events. Counting is not always possible. Consider, for example, the INSEE (the national statistics bureau of France) survey on information and communication technologies use and electronic commerce in businesses in 2016[4]. An excerpt from this survey is given in Table 1.2.

ICT facilities/services	Actual number	Frequency
Facilities on a website	126,850	0.2826
Description of goods or services, price lists	94,244	0.2100
Ordering service or reserving products and/or services (shopping cart)	33,237	0.0740
Ability to personalize or design goods or services online	14,293	0.0318
Order tracking online	20,255	0.0451
Personalized content	21,574	0.0481
Links to access company pages on social media	53,964	0.1202
Job opportunities or applications online	41,524	0.0925
Development of a site adapted to portable devices	31,626	0.0705
Development of a site adapted to portable devices which can receive orders	11,312	0.0252
Total	448,879	1.0000

Table 1.2. *Example of a statistical study*

At the beginning of 2016, this survey focused on a sample of 12,500 active companies or businesses, employing at least 10 people (both salaried and non-salaried) in mainland France and its overseas departments. INSEE states that this sample is representative of approximately 191,000 companies. In the last column, I added the statistical frequency, which is the ratio of the number of companies for a criterion to the total number of companies meeting at least one criterion. Since this is a survey, the results are estimates that are supposed to represent the actual situation.

A valuable theorem can be used here: Bernoulli's theorem, known as the "weak law of large numbers". This law can be expressed as follows.

---

4 Available at: https://www.insee.fr.

WEAK LAW OF LARGE NUMBERS.– The weak law of large numbers tells us that for a population of large enough size of n elements, there is a probability, as close to 1 as we like, that the difference between the frequency f of the outcomes realizing the event and its probability p is smaller than any positive number ε given [HEN 09].

In other words, the statistical frequency tends towards probability when the number of elements becomes very large. We will return to this law of large numbers later, but, for the moment, we can see that the number of companies that responded is large, but not infinite. This amounts to saying that we can have an approximate value of the probability by taking the statistical frequency.

Thus, it can be said, approximately, that the probability of a company owning a website is 0.2826.

This result is not incompatible with the primary definition of probability. It does not, however, provide the exact value, but only an approximate value (the "relatively" large number of companies that responded to the survey, but there are obviously more, and it is also supposedly a representative sample).

This is another approach to the probability concept derived from statistical results.

EXAMPLE 1.10.– It can be seen that, according to a survey (imaginary) carried out on 2 million French people, the percentage of people who have a nose length greater than 6 cm is 34%. We deduce an approximate value of the probability for a French person to have a nose length greater than 6 cm: $p = 0.34$.

EXAMPLE 1.11.– Example 1.11.– In one factory, out of 1,200 mechanical parts, 60 are found to be defective. From this, we can deduce that the probability of having a defective part is $p = 60/1{,}200 = 0.05$.

Let us insist, however, once again, on the fact that this method gives us an approximate value of the probability and not the exact value, because the number of elements taken into consideration is not infinite.

1.5. Compound probability

Given set E and the set of events $\mathcal{P}(E)$, let $A, B \in \mathcal{P}(E)$ and suppose that $p(A)$ is non-zero. We write:

$$p(B|A) = p(A \cap B)/p(A)$$

We thus define a new probability, denoted $p(B|A)$ or $p(B$ if $A)$ or $p_A(B)$ and we can indeed verify that $p(B|A)$ satisfies axioms 1, 2, 3 of the definition of a probability.

It is called *conditional probability* or more exactly *conditioned by A*. We can rewrite the expression above as follows:

$p(A \cap B) = p(A).p(B|A)$

which expresses the following idea: to simultaneously have the occurrence of A and B, we must first have A (probability p(A)), then B knowing that A is already realized, which can change the context of calculating $p(B|A)$. The probabilities multiply (and are written) thus.

Note that we also have $p(A \cap B) = p(B).p(A|B)$ so that:

$p(A \cap B) = p(A).p(B|A) = p(B).p(A|B)$

from which we have the "famous" Bayes' rule (or theorem):

$$p(A|B) = \frac{p(B|A)p(A)}{p(B)}$$

EXAMPLE 1.12.– Let us take the example of the bag with black balls and white balls. Suppose we pick out a ball (which we do not put back in the bag) and then a second. What is the probability of picking out two black balls?

Apply the previous relationship:

$p(2 \text{ black balls}) = p(1 \text{ black ball}).p(1 \text{ black ball}|1 \text{ black ball}) = (3/5).(2/4) = 0.3$

Now suppose that we do the same action, but put back the ball picked out of the bag at each step:

$p(2 \text{ black balls}) = p(1 \text{ black ball}).p(1 \text{ black ball}|1 \text{ black ball}) = (3/5).(3/5) = 0.36$

EXAMPLE 1.13.– Studies of accidents give the following results:

– the probability of an accident occurring if the driver is sober is 0.001, or $p_{sober}(\text{accident}) = 0.001$;

– the probability of an accident occurring if the driver is drunk is 0.02, or $p_{drunk}(\text{accident}) = 0.02$;

– the probability of having a drunk driver is 0.01, or $p(\text{drunk}) = 0.01$.

What is the probability of having an accident with a drunk driver, $p(\text{accident}\cap\text{drunk})$?

Answer: $p(\text{accident}\cap\text{drunk}) = p(\text{drunk}).p(\text{accident}|\text{drunk}) = 0.01.0.02 = 0.0002.$

What is the probability of having a drunk driver if there is an accident, $p(\text{drunk}|\text{accident})$?

Answer: $p(\text{drunk}|\text{accident}) = p(\text{accident}\cap\text{drunk})/p(\text{accident}).$

To find the probability $p(\text{accident})$, it is necessary to draw tree diagram of events. There are four events to consider:

– drunk ∩ accident;

– drunk ∩ no accident;

– sober ∩ accident;

– sober ∩ no accident.

All probabilities are calculated with the previous rules (Figure 1.3).

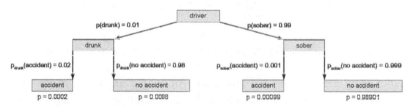

Figure 1.3. *Tree diagram of event with "driver" root*

From the results on the leaves of the preceding tree, a second tree with an "occurrence of accident" root can be built (Figure 1.4).

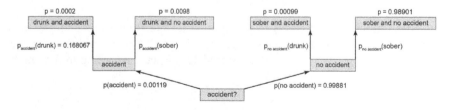

Figure 1.4. *Tree diagram of event with "accident" root*

By deduction, we obtain the probability sought.

We will define the independence of two events by the following relationship:

A and *B* are independent if and only if $p(B|A) = p(B)$

In this case, we have $p(A \cap B) = p(B).p(A)$ (as in the case of the second part of Example 1.12).

Be careful to not confuse independent events with incompatible events.

EXAMPLE 1.14.– Chevalier de Mere's problem

Chevalier de Mere thought he had more chances of getting at least a double "6" by rolling two dice 24 times than getting at least a "6" by rolling a single die 4 times. Let us calculate the probabilities of these two events:

Appearance of at least one "6" in four successive throws of a die. For the calculation, consider the opposite event – the appearance of a number that is not a "6". In a single throw, there are five in six chances to not get a "6". The corresponding probability is $p(\text{no } 6) = 5/6$. Successive throws are independent. For four throws, the probability of not getting a "6" is $\text{Prob(no 6)} = (5/6)(5/6)(5/6)(5/6)$ $= (5/6)^4$. As a result, the probability of having at least one "6" is $\text{Prob}(6) = 1 - \text{Prob(no 6)} = 1 - (5/6)^4 = 0.517\ldots$

Appearance of at least 66 in 24 successive throws of two dice. In rolling two dice, we have 35 chances out of 36 to not get a double "6". For 24 rolls of two dice, the events being independent, the probability of not getting a double "6" is $\text{Prob(no } 66) = (35/36)^{24}$. As a result, the probability of getting at least one double "6" is $\text{Prob}(66) = 1 - \text{Prob(no } 66) = 1 - (35/36)^{24} = 0.491\ldots$

Therefore, Chevalier de Mere was wrong.

1.6. Graphs, states, transitions

It is interesting (and clearer) to use graphs for compound probabilities, so we will do so below. Suppose that the studied system is initially in an initial state 0 and that it can evolve in discrete states numbered 1, 2, 3, etc. according to the graph in Figure 1.5.

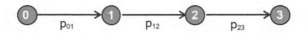

Figure 1.5. *Graph of states*

Passages from one state to another are events whose probability is indicated by the arrow indicating the transition. p_{ij} is the probability of moving from state i to state j. These probabilities are also called transition probabilities.

In this case, for the previous graph, the probability that the state moves from 0 to 3 is:

$$p_{03} = p_{01} \cdot p_{12} \cdot p_{23}$$

since the only way to move from 0 to 3 is to first move from 0 to 1, then from 1 to 2, then from 2 to 3. However, although the previous graph summarizes all the possibilities of transitions between states, it is clear that $p_{01} = 1$, $p_{12} = 1$, $p_{23} = 1$ so that it is certain to move from 0 to 3.

In fact, the previous graph is not realistic because if, for example, the system can move from state 0 to state 1 in a given period, it could also remain in state 0 (transition $0 \to 0$) during the same period.

It is therefore necessary to take into account the possibilities of remaining in the same state (note that the probability of remaining in the same state could be zero). The graph thus becomes that in Figure 1.6.

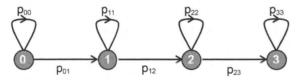

Figure 1.6. *Graph of states*

When the system is in state 0, either it moves to state 1 with probability p_{01} or it stays in state 0 with probability p_{00}. Since there are only two possibilities here, we have: $p_{00} + p_{01} = 1$.

Similarly, we would have $p_{11} + p_{12} = 1$, $p_{22} + p_{23} = 1$. Since the system in state 3 can only remain in state 3, we must have $p_{33} = 1$.

Let us now consider the case of a system that can evolve between several states as shown in the graph in Figure 1.7.

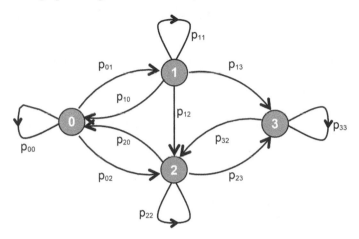

Figure 1.7. *Graph of states*

Consider state 1. Its chances to evolve are $0 \to 0$, $0 \to 1$, $0 \to 2$. Therefore, we must have $p_{00} + p_{01} + p_{02} = 1$. Similarly, we will have: $p_{11} + p_{10} + p_{12} + p_{13} = 1$, $p_{22} + p_{20} + p_{23} = 1$, $p_{33} + p_{32} = 1$.

Suppose now that we want to get the probability that the system moves from state 0 to state 3. This is not easy because there are an infinite number of paths that lead from 0 to 3. The direct paths are $0 - 1 - 3$, $0 - 1 - 2 - 3$, $0 - 2 - 3$. The less direct paths will incorporate staying in the same state, $0 - 0$, $1 - 1$, $2 - 2$, $3 - 3$ or the cycles $0 - 1 - 2 - 0$ or $0 - 1 - 3 - 2 - 0$ a number of times.

For each defined path, however, it is possible to determine the corresponding probability. For example, for the direct path $0 - 1 - 2 - 3$, we will have $p_{01}.p_{12}.p_{23}$, and for the path $0 - 1 - 2 - 2 - 3$, we will have $p_{01}.p_{12}.p_{22}.p_{23}$.

These observations lead to the following two rules:

– for a given path, the probability of traveling on the path is the product of the transition probabilities along the path (Figure 1.8);

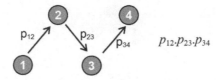

Figure 1.8. *Product of probability*

– the probability of reaching state j from state i is equal to the sum of the probabilities of the paths leading from i to j (Figure 1.9).

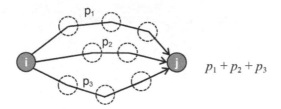

Figure 1.9. *Sum of probabilities*

EXAMPLE 1.15.– Place five identical balls in a bag, each with a letter "C", "O", "C", "O", "A". We pick out a ball, then a second (without putting the first one back).

What is the probability that the second ball bears the letter "O"?

We can consider that our system is initially in state 0 (no ball is chosen). After picking out the first ball, the system can be in several states, which can be represented by the letter: "C", "O" or "A". The final (sought-after) state is the one where the letter "O" is picked out.

We can show the evolution of the system with the graph shown in Figure 1.10, which indicates the transition probabilities.

Applying the previous rules, we obtain the probability:

$$p = \frac{2}{5} \cdot \frac{1}{2} + \frac{2}{5} \cdot \frac{1}{4} + \frac{1}{5} \cdot \frac{1}{2} = \frac{2}{5}$$

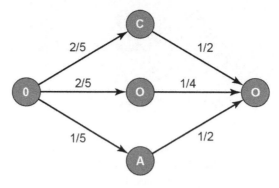

Figure 1.10. *Diagram of evolution*

2

Probabilistic Models

CONCEPTS DISCUSSED IN THIS CHAPTER.– We will begin by looking at the concept of random variables. For concrete mathematical processing, it is convenient to make a variable correspond to the occurrence of a random event. Hence, it is called a "random variable". This random variable can take discrete values or continuous values.

We will then review some common probability laws. Probability laws are functions of a random variable. We will show their main characteristics.

Finally, at the end of the chapter, we discuss stochastic processes: their definition in terms of the family of random variables according to the same probability law and their categorization.

Recommended reading: [BRE 09, PHE 77, SAP 11].

2.1. Random variables

In an experiment, we make an inventory of the results which can occur, i.e. possible events: A, B, C,..., K. We correspond the values of a variable X to these events:

– for the event A, $X = 1$;

– for the event B, $X = 2$;

– for the event C, $X = 3$;

– ...;

– for the event K, $X = n$.

All figures and tables are available in color online at www.iste.co.uk/cochard/stochastic.zip.

Such a variable, associated with a set of possible events, is called a *random variable*. The definition, for any value of X, of the corresponding probability is a *law of probability*.

EXAMPLE 2.1.– A bag contains 10 red balls, 25 green balls and 15 blue balls; all these balls are identical except in color. The experiment consists of picking out a ball. There are three possible results:

– picking out a red ball: $X = 1$, $p(X = 1) = 10/50 = 0.2$;

– picking out a green ball: $X = 2$, $p(X = 2) = 25/50 = 0.5$;

– picking out a blue ball: $X = 3$, $p(X = 3) = 15/50 = 0.3$.

And we have, of course, $p(X = 1) + p(X = 2) + p(X = 3) = 1$.

The law of probability $p(X)$ is defined above. It can be expressed by the graph in Figure 2.1.

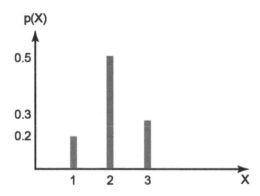

Figure 2.1. *Law of probability p(X)*

EXAMPLE 2.2.– A candidate takes an exam in which he or she must take 3 random subjects from among 20 subjects. This candidate has only revised 12 subjects. X is the number of revised subjects among the subjects taken.

The possible values of X are: $X = 0$ (poor candidate), $X = 1$, $X = 2$, $X = 3$ (lucky candidate).

To determine the law of probability, let us count the number of possible cases and the number of favorable cases (the word "favorable" does not relate to the fate of the candidate, but to the occurrence of a result):

– number of possible cases: $C_{20}^{3} = 1,140$;

– number of favorable cases for $X = 0$: $C_8^3 = 56$;

– number of favorable cases for $X = 1$: $C_{12}^1.C_8^2 = 336$;

– number of favorable cases for $X = 2$: $C_{12}^2.C_8^1 = 528$;

– number of favorable cases for $X = 3$: $C_{12}^3 = 220$.

By inference $p(X = 0) = 0.049...$, $p(X = 1) = 0.294...$, $p(X = 2) = 0.463...$, $p(X = 3) = 0.192...$

In the preceding lines, we have implicitly considered that the random variable takes discrete values. However, we can also have continuous random variables. Let us take the simple example of choosing a random point on a line segment AB (Figure 2.2).

Figure 2.2. *Choosing a random point on a line*

The choice of a point can be determined by the x-axis of the point on an axis bearing the segment. We thus define a continuous random variable $X = x$. However, we come across a serious problem: the number of favorable cases is 1, but the number of possible cases is infinite! This means that the probability sought is always zero. To avoid this issue, it is necessary to replace the concept of probability in one point by the concept of probability on an interval dx as small as we like:

$p(x)$: probability of choosing point M between x and $x + dx$

It is clear that $p(x)$ must be proportional to dx because the larger dx is, the greater the probability of finding M in this interval. This means that $p(x)$ is of the form $p(x) = f(x)dx$, where the function $f(x)$ is called *probability density*. The constraints on this function are as follows:

– $p(x) \geq 0$ so $f(x) \geq 0$;

– f is continuous on the interval (a, b);

– the sum of all the probabilities is equal to 1.

$$\int_a^b f(x)dx = 1$$

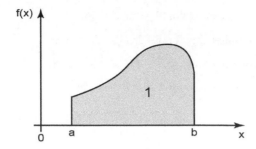

Figure 2.3. *Probability density*

It is clear, in the case of choosing a point on a segment, that $f(x) = C$ (where C is a constant), because the choice of M does not depend on its position (Figure 2.4). In this case:

$$\int_a^b Cdx = C(b-a) = 1$$

so $f(x) = \dfrac{1}{b-a}$.

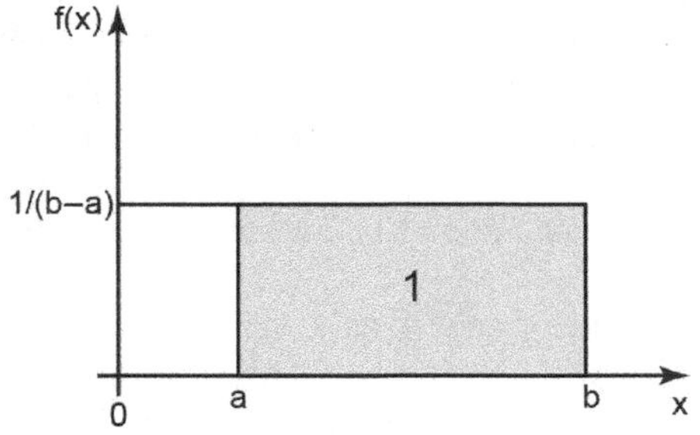

Figure 2.4. *Uniform distribution*

Figure 2.4 expresses the probability density of the *uniform distribution*. This is the simplest of the probability laws for a continuous variable. We will examine the others later on, including normal distribution (below) and exponential distribution (in a later chapter).

2.2. Mean, variance, standard deviation

Given a random variable X associated with a law of probability, we define *the mean or mathematical expectation E(X)* by:

$- E(X) = \sum_{i=1}^{n} p_i x_i$ if the variable X is discrete and takes n values x_i with $p_i = p(X = x_i)$;

$- E(X) = \int_a^b f(x) x\, dx$ if the variable X is continuous with a probability density $f(x) > 0$ on $[a, b]$.

$E(X)$ is the arithmetic mean of X weighted by the probabilities of each value. In what follows, it will sometimes be called simply m or μ.

The *variance v(X) = σ^2(X)* is defined as the mean of the squared deviations from the mean:

$- v(X) = \sigma^2(X) = \sum_{i=1}^{n} p_i \big(x_i - E(X)\big)^2$ if the variable X is discrete;

$- v(X) = \sigma^2(X) = \int_a^b f(x)\big(x - E(X)\big)^2 dx$ if the variable X is continuous.

The standard deviation $\sigma(X)$ is the square root of the variance:

$$\sigma(X) = \sqrt{v(X)}$$

The König–Huygens formula gives a useful expression for calculating the variance from the mean of the square X^2, $E(X^2)$, and the square of the mean, $E^2(X)$. We can demonstrate it in the discrete case:

$$v(X) = \sum_{i=1}^{n} p_i\big(x_i - E(X)\big)^2 = \sum_{i=1}^{n} p_i x_i^2 - 2E(X)\sum_{i=1}^{n} p_i x_i + E^2(X)\sum_{i=1}^{n} p_i$$

as:

$$\sum_{i=1}^{n} p_i x_i = E(X) \quad \text{and} \quad \sum_{i=1}^{n} p_i = 1$$

gives us:

$$v(X) = \sum_{i=1}^{n} p_i x_i^2 - E^2(X) = E(X^2) - E^2(X)$$

2.3. Some common distributions

The study of various phenomena made it possible to define probabilistic models, i.e. to derive laws of probability. We have already seen one: uniform distribution. Let us give some examples of other frequently encountered laws.

2.3.1. *Bernoulli distribution*

Bernoulli's probabilistic model or the *Bernoulli distribution* (or *binomial distribution*) is well adapted to the experiments of *successive drawing*. This law is expressed by:

$$p(X = k) = C_n^k p^k q^{n-k}$$

where p is the probability of having the expected event A and $q = 1 - p$ the probability of having the opposite event $\bar{A}$. $C_n^{\ k}$ is the binomial coefficient defined in Chapter 1:

$$C_n^k = \frac{n!}{k!\,(n - k)!}$$

We prove that the mean is $E(X) = np$ and the variance $v(X) = \sigma^2 = npq$ (see the appendix at the end of this chapter).

Figure 2.5. *Jacob Bernoulli (1654–1705) contributed to the development of probability theory by formalizing Huygens' work and contributing to the law of large numbers and the concept of a confidence interval. He belongs to a famous family that produced many scientists (including Jean and Daniel)*[1]

1 The portrait of Jacob Bernoulli (by Niklaus Bernoulli, 1662–1716) is from Wikimedia Commons: https://commons.wikimedia.org/wiki/Category:Jakob_Bernoulli.

EXAMPLE 2.3.– It is determined that the probability of arriving at a given crossing with green lights is $p = 3/5$ (so $q = 2/5$).

n successive passages are made at this intersection and X is the number of "green lights" events.

If $n = 2$, we have:

– $p(X = 0) = C_2^0 p^0 q^2 = 4/25 = 0.16$;

– $p(X = 1) = C_2^1 p^1 q^1 = 12/25 = 0.48$;

– $p(X = 2) = C_2^2 p^2 q^0 = 9/25 = 0.36$;

with a mean $E(X) = 6/5$ and a variance $v(X) = 12/25$.

If $n = 5$, we have:

– $p(X = 0) = C_5^0 p^0 q^5 = 0.01$;

– $p(X = 1) = C_5^1 p^1 q^4 = 0.07$;

– $p(X = 2) = C_5^2 p^2 q^3 = 0.23$;

– $p(X = 3) = C_5^3 p^3 q^2 = 0.35$;

– $p(X = 4) = C_5^4 p^4 q^1 = 0.26$;

– $p(X = 5) = C_5^5 p^5 q^0 = 0.08$;

with a mean $E(X) = 3$ and a variance $v(X) = 6/5$.

2.3.2. *Poisson distribution*

The *Poisson model* corresponds to the trend of the Bernoulli distribution when p is weak ($p < 0.1$) and when n is large ($n > 30$).

Its expression is:

$$p(X = k) = e^{-m} \frac{m^k}{k!}$$

where m is a parameter that corresponds to the average value of X: $E(X) = m$ (see the appendix at the end of this chapter). The variance $v(X)$ has the value m^2 (see the appendix at the end of this chapter).

Figure 2.6. *Siméon Denis Poisson (1781–1840) introduced the law that bears his name as part of work on the probabilities of judgments in the judicial field. He published nearly 400 scientific articles. His motto was: "Life is good for only two things: discovering mathematics and teaching mathematics"*[2]

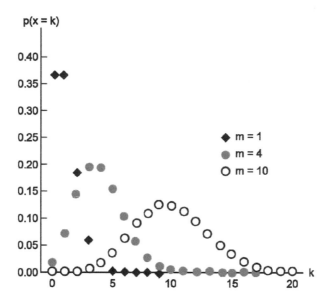

Figure 2.7. *Poisson distribution*

2 The portrait of Denis Poisson (by François Séraphin Delpech, 1778–1825), after Nicolas-Eustache Maurin (1799–1850), is from Wikimedia Commons: https://commons.wikimedia. org/wiki/Category: Siméon_Denis_Poisson.

Figure 2.7 shows the shape of some Poisson distributions.

Tables[3] are used to give the values of $p(X = k)$. Of course, you can also use a good calculator, spreadsheet or computer.

EXAMPLE 2.4.– A phenomenon follows a Poisson distribution with mean 4; let A be the expected event. What is the probability of getting A 8 times? Less than 8 times?

$- p(X = 8) = 0.0298.$

$- p(X < 8) = p(X = 0) + p(X = 1) + p(X = 2) + p(X = 3) + p(X = 4) + p(X = 5) + p(X = 6) + p(X = 7) = 0.9489.$

This last result shows that the probability that $X > 8$ is weak:

$p(X > 8) = 1 - p(X < 8) - p(X = 8) = 0.0213.$

2.3.3. Normal distribution

The *normal distribution* (or the Laplace–Gauss or *Gauss* distribution) is a law we will make much use of. It is used for a continuous random variable (not discrete, as in the two previous models).

Figure 2.8. *Carl Friedrich Gauss (1777–1855) was a true genius, simultaneously a mathematician, physicist and astronomer. Thanks to him and other scientists, probability theory has reached maturity. He left his name to the famous bell curve, which is called the "Gauss curve", representing the probability density of the normal distribution[4]*

---

3 There are many websites with the tables of common distributions. For example: https://mat.iitm. ac.in/home/vetri/public_html/statistics/poisson.pdf; http://biometria.univr.it/sesm/files/STA_ tables_poisson_MED.pdf; https://www.umass.edu/wsp/resources/poisson/.
4 The portrait of Carl Friedrich Gauss (by Christian Albrecht Jensen, 1792–1870) is from Wikimedia Commons: https://commons.wikimedia.org/wiki/Category:Carl_Friedrich_Gauß.

It is defined from the probability density:

$$f(x) = \frac{1}{\sigma\sqrt{2\pi}} e^{-\frac{(x-m)^2}{2\sigma^2}}$$

where m represents the mean and σ the standard deviation (see the appendix). This law therefore depends on two parameters, m and σ.

The shape of the density distribution (Figure 2.9) is that of the famous bell-shaped Gauss curve.

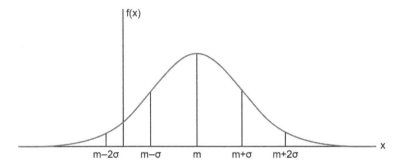

Figure 2.9. *Gauss bell curve*

The probability that $X < x_0$ is given by the expression:

$$p(X < x_0) = \int_{-\infty}^{x_0} f(x)dx$$

It corresponds to the red surface area in Figure 2.10.

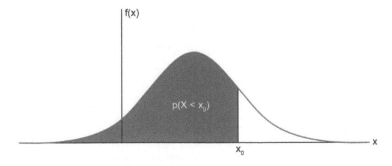

Figure 2.10. *Interpretation of $p(X < x_0)$*

Given that:

$$\int_{-\infty}^{+\infty} e^{-u^2}\, du = \sqrt{\pi}$$

we easily show that:

$$\int_{-\infty}^{+\infty} f(x)\, dx = 1$$

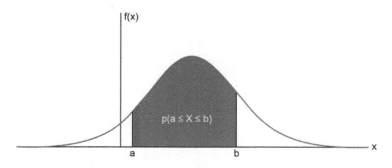

Figure 2.11. *Interpretation of p(a ≤X ≤b)*

We are often interested in the probability that the variable X is between two values a and b: prob($a \leq X \leq b$). This probability corresponds to the red surface area in Figure 2.11. We have, of course:

$$\text{prob}(a \leq X \leq b) = \text{prob}(X < b) - \text{prob}(X < a) = \int_{a}^{b} f(x)\, dx$$

Note the following special values:

– prob($m - \sigma \leq X \leq m + \sigma$) = 0.68;

– prob($m - 2\sigma \leq X \leq m + 2\sigma$) = 0.95;

– prob($m - 3\sigma \leq X \leq m + 3\sigma$) = 0.997.

It is often convenient to use the standard normal distribution ($m = 0$ and $\sigma = 1$) (Figure 2.12):

$$f_r(t) = \frac{1}{\sqrt{2\pi}}e^{-\frac{t^2}{2}}$$

Tables[5] give the values of p for the standard distribution. We go from the standard distribution (0, 1) to the normal distribution (m, σ) with the transformation:

$$t = \frac{x - m}{\sigma}$$

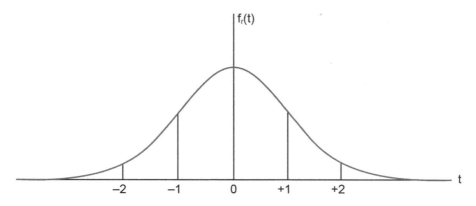

Figure 2.12. *Standard normal distribution*

EXAMPLE 2.5.– We measure the height of a workforce of 2,500 people in cm. The mean is $m = 169$ cm, and we accept that the height follows a Gaussian distribution standard deviation $\sigma = 5.6$ cm.

What is the probability that the height of an individual is less than 155 cm?

Answer: using the tables, we have: $t = (155 - 169)/5.6 = -2.5$.

Then: $p(T < -2.5) = 1 - p(T < 2.5) = 1 - 0.9938 = 0.0062$.

What is the probability that the height of an individual is greater than 172 cm?

---

5 For example: https://www.math.arizona.edu/~rsims/ma464/standardnormaltable.pdf; https://www.mathsisfun.com/data/standard-normal-distribution-table.html; https://en.wikipedia.org/wiki/Standard_normal_table.

Answer: $p(X > 172) = 1 - p(X < 172) = 1 - p(T < t)$ with $h = (172 - 169)/5.6 = 0.54$.

So using the tables, $p(X > 172) = 1 - 0.7019 = 0.2981$.

What is the probability that the height of an individual is between 160 and 178 cm?

Answer: $p(160 \leq X \leq 178) = p(X \leq 178) - p(X \leq 160)$. Let us turn to the standard distribution: $h_1 = (178 - 169)/5.6 = 1.607$ and $h_2 = (160 - 169)/5.6 = -1.607$.

From the tables:

$- p(T \leq h_1) = 0.9525;$

$- p(T \leq h_2) = p(H > h_1) = 1 - p(H \leq h_1) = 0.0475.$

So, $p(160 \leq X \leq 178) = 0.9525 - 0.0475 = 0.905$.

There are of course other usual distributions. We will see them in context in the following chapters.

2.4. Stochastic processes

Let there be a family of random variables $X(t)$ obeying the same law of probability and characterized by a real parameter t. In general, t is a time date $t \in [0, +\infty]$. Such a family is called a "stochastic process". The word "stochastic" is a scholarly word which just means "random".

We can group stochastic processes into two categories:

– the discrete time processes: t only takes discrete values, for example, $t = 0, 1, 2,\ldots, n\ldots$, and the stochastic process corresponds to the family $X(0), X(1), X(2),\ldots, X(n)\ldots$ We can, in this case, modify the notation and put t in subscript: $X_0, X_1, X_2,\ldots, X_n\ldots$;

– the continuous time processes: t continuously varies from 0 to $+\infty$. The family of $X(t)$ therefore includes an infinity of random variables.

Each variable $X(t)$ can take several possible values with a certain probability. These values represent states. The states can be discrete or continuous.

We therefore have four categories for the stochastic processes: discrete time and discrete state processes, continuous time and discrete state processes, discrete time and continuous state processes, continuous time and continuous state processes.

We are only interested in the first two categories: discrete time and discrete state processes, continuous time and discrete state processes.

EXAMPLE 2.6.– The repeated roll of a die is a stochastic process. We can number the throws from the first to the last if we throw it n times: 1, 2, 3,..., i,..., n. The result of each throw i corresponds to a random variable X_i, which can take integer values from 1 to 6 according to uniform distribution (as many chances for each number); these 6 values correspond to 6 states and the sequence of events can be represented by a figure similar to Figure 2.13.

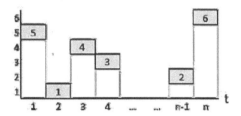

Figure 2.13. *Variation of X over time*

Here, we are dealing with a stochastic process with discrete time and discrete (and finite) states. The system will fluctuate over time between 6 states, which can be shown in a graph (Figure 2.14) with the transition probabilities corresponding to the directed arcs (all are equal to 1/6).

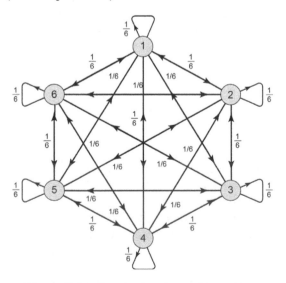

Figure 2.14. *Graph of states and transitions*

EXAMPLE 2.7.– Let us look at the number of visitors to a museum during a day. From when the museum opens ($t = 0$) to when it closes ($t = $ n), visitors arrive randomly following the same law of probability and visitors leave following the same law of probability (*a priori* different from the first).

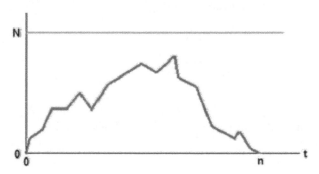

Figure 2.15. *Change in visitor numbers over time*

The change can be represented by Figure 2.15.

The time continuously varies from 0 to n: the stochastic process is in continuous time. At each moment t, $X(t)$ represents the number of visitors in the museum. The values of $X(t)$ are discrete from the value 0 (nobody in the museum) up to a maximum N (number not to be exceeded for security reasons). The states are therefore discrete.

If we number the states with the values of the numbers (from 0 to N), we can also show the states and their transitions in the graph in Figure 2.16 in the case where the increase in numbers, in each transition, is 0, 1 or –1. If this is not the case, the graph is much more complicated.

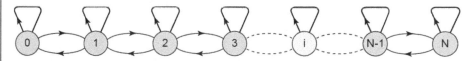

Figure 2.16. *Graph of states/transitions*

The transition probabilities clearly depend on the probability laws of the inputs and outputs.

In the next chapters, we will study some stochastic processes with discrete or continuous time and discrete states.

2.5. Appendix

2.5.1. *Calculation of the mean E(X) of the binomial distribution*

The expression to calculate is:

$$E(X) = \sum_{i=0}^{n} C_n^k \, kp^k q^{n-k} = \sum_{i=1}^{n} C_n^k \, kp^k q^{n-k}$$

with: $p + q = 1$.

To perform this calculation, let $f(z) = (pz + q)^n$ whose value is, according to the binomial formula:

$$f(z) = \sum_{k=0}^{n} C_n^k p^k z^k q^{n-k}$$

Let us derive the two expressions of $f(z)$ in relation to z:

$$np(pz + q)^{n-1} = \sum_{k=1}^{n} C_n^k \, kz^{k-1} p^k q^{n-k}$$

Taking $z = 1$ and taking into account $p + q = 1$, we quickly obtain: $E(X) = np$.

2.5.2. *Calculation of the variance v(X) of the binomial distribution*

The value to calculate is, according to Huygens' formula, $v(X) = E(X^2) - E^2(X)$. We already know $E(X)$. We still need to calculate $E(X^2)$, whose expression is:

$$E(X^2) = \sum_{i=1}^{n} C_n^k k^2 p^k q^{n-k}$$

We will use the second derivative of $f(z)$ in relation to z:

$$n(n-1)p^2(pz + q)^{n-2} = \sum_{k=1}^{n} C_n^k k(k-1)z^{k-2} p^k q^{n-k}$$

and in taking $z = 1$:

$$n(n-1)p^2 = \sum_{k=1}^{n} C_n^k (k-1) k p^k q^{n-k}$$

$$= \sum_{k=1}^{n} C_n^k k^2 p^k q^{n-k} - \sum_{k=1}^{n} C_n^k k p^k q^{n-k}$$

so that:

$$n(n-1)p^2 = E(X^2) - E(X)$$

or $E(X^2) = n(n-1)p^2 + np$

as a result:

$$v(X) = n(n-1)p^2 + np - n^2 p^2 = np(1-p) = npq$$

2.5.3. Calculation of the mean E(X) of the Poisson distribution

$$E(X) = \sum_{k=0}^{\infty} k e^{-m} \frac{m^k}{k!} = e^{-m} \frac{m}{1!} + 2e^{-m} \frac{m^2}{2!} + \cdots + k e^{-m} \frac{m^k}{k!} + \cdots$$

$$E(X) = me^{-m}\left[1 + \frac{m}{1!} + \frac{m^2}{2!} + \cdots + \frac{m^{k-1}}{(k-1)!} + \cdots\right] = me^{-m} e^{m} = m$$

2.5.4. Calculation of the variance v(X) of the Poisson distribution

$v(X) = E(X^2) - E^2(X)$. We calculate $E(X^2)$:

$$E(X^2) = \sum_{k=0}^{\infty} k^2 e^{-m} \frac{m^k}{k!} = \sum_{k=0}^{\infty} [k(k-1) + k] e^{-m} \frac{m^k}{k!}$$

$$= \sum_{k=0}^{\infty} k(k-1) e^{-m} \frac{m^k}{k!} + \sum_{k=0}^{\infty} k e^{-m} \frac{m^k}{k!}$$

The last term is none other than $E(X)$. The first term is:

$$\sum_{k=0}^{\infty} k(k-1)e^{-m}\frac{m^k}{k!} = 2e^{-m}\frac{m^2}{2!} + 6e^{-m}\frac{m^3}{3!} + \cdots + k(k-1)e^{-m}\frac{m^k}{k!} + \cdots$$

$$= m^2 e^{-m}\left(1 + \frac{m}{1!} + \cdots + \frac{m^{k-2}}{(k-2)!} + \cdots\right) = m^2 e^{-m} e^m$$

$$= m^2$$

As a result: $E(X^2) = m^2 + m$ and $v(X) = m^2 + m - m = m^2$.

2.5.5. *Calculation of the mean E(X) for the normal distribution*

$$E(X) = \frac{1}{\sigma\sqrt{2\pi}} \int_{-\infty}^{+\infty} xe^{-\frac{(x-m)^2}{2\sigma^2}}dx$$

Let us change the variable:

$$u = \frac{x-m}{\sigma\sqrt{2}}$$

and so $du = \dfrac{dx}{\sigma\sqrt{2}}$, $x = \sigma\sqrt{2}u + m$.

The integral becomes:

$$E(X) = \frac{1}{\sqrt{\pi}} \int_{-\infty}^{+\infty} (\sigma\sqrt{2}u + m)e^{-u^2}du = \frac{\sigma\sqrt{2}}{\sqrt{\pi}} \int_{-\infty}^{+\infty} ue^{-u^2}du + \frac{m}{\sqrt{\pi}} \int_{-\infty}^{+\infty} e^{-u^2}du$$

The first integral deals with an odd function. Its result is therefore 0. Furthermore:

$$\int_{-\infty}^{+\infty} e^{-u^2}du = \sqrt{\pi}$$

It appears that: $E(X) = m$.

2.5.6. *Calculation of the variance v(X) for the normal distribution*

Since $v(X) = E(X^2) - E^2(X)$ and we know $E(X)$, we still need to calculate $E(X^2)$:

$$E(X^2) = \frac{1}{\sigma\sqrt{2\pi}} \int\limits_{-\infty}^{+\infty} x^2 e^{-\frac{(x-m)^2}{2\sigma^2}} dx$$

As before, let us change the variable:

$$u = \frac{x - m}{\sigma\sqrt{2}}$$

and so $du = \dfrac{dx}{\sigma\sqrt{2}}, \; x = \sigma\sqrt{2}u + m$

which leads to:

$$E(X^2) = \frac{1}{\sqrt{\pi}} \int\limits_{-\infty}^{+\infty} \left(\sigma\sqrt{2}u + m\right)^2 e^{-u^2} du$$

$$= \frac{2\sigma^2}{\sqrt{\pi}} \int\limits_{-\infty}^{+\infty} u^2 e^{-u^2} du + \frac{2m\sigma\sqrt{2}}{\sqrt{\pi}} \int\limits_{-\infty}^{+\infty} u e^{-u^2} du$$

$$+ \frac{m^2}{\sqrt{\pi}} \int\limits_{-\infty}^{+\infty} e^{-u^2} du = I_1 + I_2 + I_3$$

The integral I_1 is known and its value is:

$$I_1 = \frac{2\sigma^2}{\sqrt{\pi}} \cdot \frac{\sqrt{\pi}}{2} = \sigma^2$$

The integral I_2 is zero, as the function to be integrated is odd.

The integral I_3 is known and its value is:

$$I_3 = \frac{m^2}{\sqrt{\pi}} \cdot \sqrt{\pi} = m^2$$

As a result, $E(X^2) = \sigma^2 + m^2$. By inference, $v(X) = \sigma^2$.

3

Inventory Management

CONCEPTS DISCUSSED IN THIS CHAPTER.– We discuss the problem of inventory management initially in a general sense, principally so we can identify the notations and clarify the definitions.

Then, we look at a very popular analytical model, Wilson's model, with three sets of assumptions: 3.1, 3.2 and 3.3.

Finally, we discuss additional considerations on the guarantee of safety and quality.

Recommended reading: [BOU 16, FAU 79, PHE 77].

3.1. General

Do you remember learning about the problem of a leaking bath in primary school? The water flows through a hole and we have to periodically open the tap to compensate for leakage. This is actually a problem of inventory management.

It is a more realistic problem in commercial enterprises that sell items to customers. These items are stored in a location so customer demand can be met. Of course, the stock has to be replenished to avoid shortages of items. There can, however, be problems if the replenishment does not arrive in time or if the quantity to be replenished is incorrectly calculated. Demand drives a virtually continuous flow stream of items. Replenishment is a generally discontinuous supply flow.

DEFINITION.– An inventory is a set of items (people, goods, etc.) stored in a warehouse, subject to an input or supply flow, and an output or flow stream.

All figures and tables are available in color online at www.iste.co.uk/cochard/stochastic.zip.

This definition is illustrated in Figure 3.1.

Supply flow   **Flow stream**
                                   (often imposed)

Figure 3.1. *Stock subject to flows*

In general, the following problems arise:

– When should replenishment be triggered?

– How much is needed for replenishment?

– What is the optimal cost of storage?

The last question is, usually, decisive.

The total storage cost depends on three factors:

$$C_T = C_E + C_R + C_P$$

where:

– C_T is the total cost;

– C_E is the stock maintenance cost (safety, insurance, immobilization, inventory, deterioration, obsolescence), which can be considered proportional to the number of items stored and the duration of storage. The holding cost per item and per unit of time will be designated by c_E (with a small c);

– C_R is the replenishment cost (discontinuous costs in general). It is considered constant in what follows for each replenishment. This cost corresponds to administrative and logistical costs;

– C_P is the shortage cost (loss of earnings). Not selling a product is a penalty, which has a price. The shortage cost per item and per unit of time will be designated by c_P (with a small c).

To solve the problems posed, two types of methods are used:

– the analytical methods: using the results of a mathematical model obtained by the calculation. We will take Wilson's model as a typical example. This model quickly reaches its limits in realistic cases. There are more complex alternatives, but, in this case, the calculations become very complicated, even irresolvable;

– simulation methods (also based on modeling reality). These methods will be explained later.

3.2. Introductory example

As an introduction to the model, consider the following situation: a store selling identical items for which demand is constant over time: Δ items per day. Assume for the moment that this demand is regular, i.e. the daily demand is constant.

Imagine that at the beginning of the year the store has an inventory Q_{max} of items to meet the annual demand (this is not realistic, but for the moment, let us suspend disbelief). Every day, the stock decreases by Δ (Figure 3.2). It reaches zero by the end of the year, which means that $Q_{max} = \Delta T$, where T is the number of days of the year (for the sake of simplicity, we will assume there are 360 days).

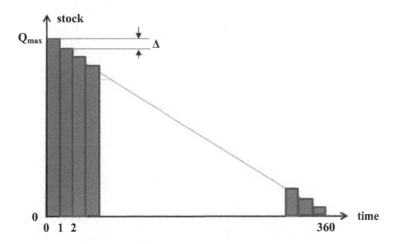

Figure 3.2. *Annual change in stock*

Imagine a sale takes place every day. The holding stock therefore decreases each day by the same amount. The quantity of items to hold on the first day is the average stock of the day $(Q_{max} + Q_{max} - \Delta)/2 = Q_{max} - \Delta/2$. On the second day, the holding stock is the average stock $(Q_{max} - \Delta + Q_{max} - 2\Delta)/2 = Q_{max} - 3\Delta/2$, on the third day, the holding stock is the average stock $(Q_{max} - 2\Delta + Q_{max} - 3\Delta)/2 = Q_{max} - 5\Delta/2,...,$ on the last day, the holding stock is $(Q_{max} - (T-1)\Delta + Q_{max} - T\Delta)/2 = Q_{max} - (2T - 1)\Delta/2$, where $T = 360$.

The sum of the items to be held over the year is therefore:

$$TQ_{max} - (\Delta/2)\,[1 + 3 + 5 + \ldots + 2T - 1] = TQ_{max} - (\Delta/2)T^2$$

$$= \Delta T^2 - \Delta T^2/2 = \Delta T^2/2$$

The holding stock is therefore $\Delta T^2/2$.

In fact, we obtain a similar result by considering that the demand is continuous (Figure 3.3): instead of having descending steps, we have a negative slope line representing regular sales: the stock is at a moment t, $q(t) = -\Delta\,t + Q_{max}$.

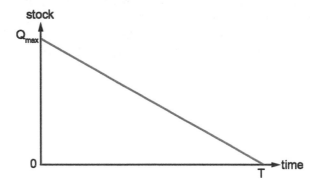

Figure 3.3. *Continuous demand*

The holding stock over the year is then the average stock $Q_{max}/2$ multiplied by the period T, i.e. $TQ_{max}/2 = \Delta T^2/2$ similar to the previous result.

Note that we find this result by calculating the integral $\int_0^T q(t)dt$.

Let us calculate the holding cost for this situation: $C_E = c_E \dfrac{\Delta T^2}{2}$.

EXAMPLE 3.1(1).– C_R = €49, c_E = €0.4, Δ = 5 items/day, T = 360 days; hence, $C_T = C_R + C_E$ = €129,649.

We can see right away that this is not a good way to manage inventory!

3.3. Wilson's model: assumptions 3.1

"Wilson's model" was established by F.W. Harris in 1915 and R.H. Wilson in 1934. It is sometimes called the EOQ (economic order quantity) model.

We will examine it under various assumptions (3.1, 3.2, 3.3), trying to get closer to a realistic situation.

ASSUMPTIONS 3.1.–

– Regular demand Δ per unit of time.

– Cyclical (i.e. periodic) supply of a constant quantity Q by periods of equal duration θ.

– No shortage: the stock is zero at the end of the period.

– No replenishment period (it is considered instantaneous).

Figure 3.4 illustrates these assumptions by showing the change in stock over time.

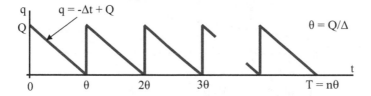

Figure 3.4. *Assumptions 3.1*

Keep in mind that the total duration is T (e.g. 360 days), but this duration is split into n periods θ to reduce holding stock (and to reduce the colossal amount obtained in the previous example). At the beginning of the period, the stock is Q, and at the end of the period, it is zero, which means that $Q = \Delta\theta$.

During a period, the average stock is $Q/2$. It is easy to deduce the cost over a period (there is no shortage):

– replenishment cost: C_R;

– holding cost: $C_E = c_E \dfrac{\theta Q}{2} = c_E \dfrac{\Delta\theta^2}{2}$.

For the total duration $T = n\theta$, we have:

$$C_T = n\left[C_R + c_E\frac{Q\theta^2}{2}\right] = \frac{T\Delta}{Q}[C_R + c_E\frac{Q^2}{2\Delta}] = C_R\frac{T\Delta}{Q} + c_E\frac{TQ}{2}$$

With this result, we see that the total cost depends only on the variable Q, the other data being fixed: $C_T = f(Q)$. In fact, it is the sum of two terms, one proportional to $1/Q$ (the replenishment cost) and the other proportional to Q (the holding cost).

Their superposition shows that there is an optimal $\tilde{Q}$ value at which the cost is minimal (Figure 3.5).

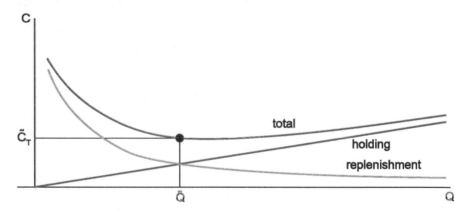

Figure 3.5. *Components of the storage cost*

To obtain this optimal value $\tilde{Q}$, calculate the derivative of $f(Q)$ and cancel it:

$$\frac{df}{dQ} = -C_R\frac{T\Delta}{Q^2} + c_E\frac{T}{2} = 0$$

hence:

$$\tilde{Q} = \sqrt{2\Delta\frac{C_R}{c_E}} \qquad \widetilde{C_T} = T\sqrt{2\Delta C_R c_E} \qquad \tilde{\theta} = \sqrt{\frac{2C_R}{\Delta c_E}}$$

EXAMPLE 3.1(2).– Use Example 3.1(1) again: $C_R = €49$, $c_E = €0.4$, $\Delta = 5$ items/day, $T = 360$ days.

We obtain:

$\tilde{Q} = 35$ items

$\widetilde{C_T} = €5,040$

$\tilde{\theta} = 7$ days

There is a clear improvement in the total cost of storage. There must be a replenishment of a quantity of 35 items every 7 days.

3.4. Wilson's model: assumptions 3.2

Suppose now that there is a stock shortage, which is a desired shortage.

ASSUMPTIONS 3.2.–

– Regular demand (Δ per unit of time).

– Predictable stock shortage for a fixed period θ_2 ($\theta_2 < \theta$).

– Cyclical supply by periods θ of quantity Q.

– No replenishment period.

It could be said that this situation is not realistic, because we are forced into a shortage towards the end of the period. However, a voluntary shortage may limit the holding cost. In any event, despite this situation being unrealistic in principle, we will study this case because it gets us ready for what follows (Wilson's model assumptions 3.3). We will see later on that there may be a reason to *want* a shortage.

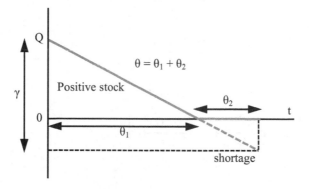

Figure 3.6. *Shortage case*

where:

- $Q = \Delta\theta_1$;
- $\gamma - Q = \Delta\theta_2$;
- $\theta_1 + \theta_2 = \theta$;
- $\theta_1 = \dfrac{Q}{\gamma}\theta$;
- $\theta_2 = \dfrac{\gamma - Q}{\gamma}\theta$.

Figure 3.6 and the corresponding calculations, based on the presence of similar triangles (proportionality of the sides), illustrate these assumptions. The quantity γ corresponds to the demand over a period.

For a period θ, there is:

– a replenishment cost C_R;

– a positive holding cost for stock. The average stock is $Q/2$; hence:

$$C_E = c_E \frac{Q\theta_1}{2} = c_E \frac{Q^2\theta}{2\gamma}$$

– a shortage cost relative to the positive average stock:

$$\frac{\gamma - Q}{2}$$

that is:

$$C_P = c_P \frac{(\gamma - Q)\theta_2}{2} = c_P \frac{(\gamma - Q)^2\theta}{2\gamma}$$

The total cost for n periods is therefore:

$$C_T = n\left[C_R + c_E \frac{Q^2}{2\gamma}\theta + c_P \frac{(\gamma - Q)^2}{2\gamma}\theta \right]$$

that is:

$$C_T = C_R \frac{T\Delta}{\gamma} + c_E \frac{TQ^2}{2\gamma} + c_P \frac{T(\gamma - Q)^2}{2\gamma} = f(Q,\gamma)$$

The total cost is now a function of two variables Q and γ. To optimize this total cost, i.e. to minimize it, it is necessary to cancel the two partial derivatives with respect to Q and with respect to γ.

$$\frac{\partial C_T}{\partial Q} = 0 \implies (c_E + c_P)Q = c_P\gamma \implies \rho\gamma = Q$$

$$\frac{\partial C_T}{\partial \gamma} = 0 \implies c_P\gamma^2 = (c_E + c_P)Q^2 + 2C_R\Delta \implies \gamma^2 - \frac{Q^2}{\rho} = 2\frac{C_R}{c_P}\Delta$$

where ρ is the shortage rate:

$$\rho = \frac{c_P}{c_E + c_P}$$

We obtain the following results:

$$\tilde{\gamma} = \sqrt{2\frac{\Delta C_R}{\rho c_E}} \quad \tilde{Q} = \sqrt{2\Delta\rho\frac{C_R}{c_E}} \quad \widetilde{C_T} = T\sqrt{2\Delta C_R c_E} \quad \tilde{\theta} = \frac{\tilde{\gamma}}{\Delta} + \sqrt{\frac{2C_R}{\rho\Delta c_E}}$$

Let us go back to the issue of "voluntary" shortage. Why would you want a shortage? A shortage may improve the total holding cost (fewer items to store).

Of course, the shortage does not only have an influence on the storage cost, but also affects the customers and therefore sales!

EXAMPLE 3.1(3).– Let us go back to 3.1(2) of the Wilson's model assumptions 3.1, where we got a total cost of €5,040. For C_R = €49, c_E = €0.4 per item and per unit of time, c_P = 4 € per item and per unit of time, Δ = 5 items per day, we will have, with the previous results of the Wilson's model assumptions 3.2:

– γ = 36.71 items per period;

– Q = 33.37 items;

– C_T = €4,805.21 (less in the case of Wilson assumptions 3.1);

– θ = 7.34 days.

The calculations of Wilson's model assumptions 3.2 anticipate those that will be carried out in the following assumptions 3.3.

3.5. Probabilistic Wilson's model: assumptions 3.3

The assumptions 3.2 of Wilson's model are modified as follows.

ASSUMPTIONS 3.3.–

– Random demand γ according to a law of probability $p(\gamma)$.

– Stock shortage possible, but not predictable.

– Cyclical supply over a period θ returning the stock to a value Q.

– Replenishment cost overlooked.

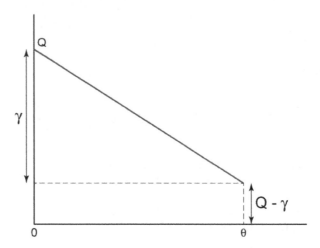

Figure 3.7. *Case without stock shortage*

Here, we overlook the replenishment cost, firstly because it will simplify the calculations (which is not really a convincing reason) and secondly because it is negligible (most of the time) compared to the cumulative cost of holding and shortage.

In a case where there is no shortage (Figure 3.7), we are more or less within the framework of the assumptions 3.1, except that the residual stock at the end of the period is positive or zero.

In the case of a shortage (Figure 3.8), we are more or less within the framework of assumption 3.2 (hence, we have studied this situation).

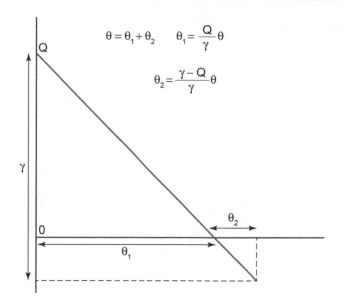

Figure 3.8. *Case without stock shortage*

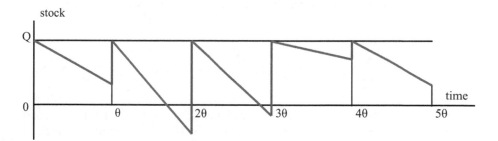

Figure 3.9. *Typical situation*

A typical situation is described in Figure 3.9.

Consider these two cases successively:

– 1st case: no stock shortage during the period θ: $\gamma \leq Q$.

The average stock is:

$$\frac{[Q + (Q - \gamma)]}{2} = Q - \frac{\gamma}{2}$$

The holding cost is:

$$c_E \left(Q - \frac{\gamma}{2} \right) p(\gamma) \theta$$

It should be noted that the result is weighted by the probability $p(\gamma)$ relative to a non-stockout;

– 2nd case: there is a stock shortage: $\gamma > Q$.

The actual average stock is $Q/2$ (during the period θ_1), so the holding cost is:

$$c_E \left(\frac{Q}{2} \right) \theta_1 p(\gamma) = c_E (\frac{Q^2}{2\gamma}) \theta p(\gamma)$$

The average shortage or average negative stock is $(\gamma - Q)/2$, so the shortage cost is:

$$c_P \frac{\gamma - Q}{2} \theta_2 p(\gamma) = c_P \frac{(\gamma - Q)^2}{2\gamma} \theta p(\gamma)$$

The total cost over the period T depends on the two cases weighted by the corresponding probability:

$$C_T(Q) = c_E \sum_{\gamma=0}^{Q} (Q - \frac{\gamma}{2}) p(\gamma) + c_E \sum_{\gamma=Q+1}^{\infty} \frac{Q^2}{2\gamma} p(\gamma) + c_P \sum_{\gamma=Q+1}^{\infty} \frac{(\gamma - Q)^2}{2\gamma} p(\gamma)$$

where we have assumed that demand increases per unit. If this is not the case and the demand increases in steps of λ (e.g. from 10 in 10), it is necessary to replace $Q + 1$ by $Q + \lambda$.

To find the optimal (the lowest) value of the cost $C_T(Q)$, we put:

$$G(Q) = (1 - \rho) \frac{C_T(Q)}{c_E}$$

which amounts to determining the value of Q for which $G(Q)$ is the minimum. In the above expression, as previously defined, ρ is the shortage rate:

$$\rho = \frac{c_P}{c_E + c_P} \quad \text{hence} \quad c_P = \frac{\rho}{1 - \rho} c_E$$

After a rather long calculation, which is explained in the appendix, $G(Q)$ is put in the following form:

$$G(Q) = QP(\gamma \leq Q) - Q\rho + \frac{Q^2}{2} \sum_{\gamma=Q+\lambda}^{\infty} \frac{p(\gamma)}{\gamma} + \frac{\rho}{2} \sum_{\gamma=0}^{\infty} \gamma p(\gamma) - \frac{1}{2} \sum_{\gamma=0}^{Q} \gamma p(\gamma)$$

By replacing Q by $Q + \lambda$, we get (see the appendix):

$$G(Q + \lambda) = G(Q) + \lambda[L(Q) - \rho] \qquad \text{where} \qquad L(Q)$$
$$= P(\gamma \leq Q) + \left(Q + \frac{\lambda}{2}\right) \sum_{\gamma=Q+\lambda}^{\infty} \frac{p(\gamma)}{\gamma}$$

Let Q_0 be the value of Q which minimizes $G(Q)$. We must then have $G(Q_0) < G(Q_0 + \lambda)$ et $G(Q_0) < G(Q_0 - \lambda)$:

$$G(Q_0 + \lambda) - G(Q_0) = \lambda[L(Q_0) - \rho] > 0$$

and similarly:

$$G(Q_0) - G(Q_0 - \lambda) = \lambda[L(Q_0 - \lambda) - \rho] < 0$$

which leads to the dual condition:

$$L(Q_0 - \lambda) < \rho < L(Q_0)$$

EXAMPLE 3.2.– Consider an inventory of identical items bought and replenished in packs of 5. The probability law of the demand is explained in Table 3.1.

γ	0	5	10	15	20	25	30 and +
$p(\gamma)$	0.1	0.1	0.2	0.3	0.2	0.1	0

Table 3.1. *Probability law of the demand*

The unit holding cost is €1 per item per day, the shortage cost is €10 per item not sold per day.

Let us use Table 3.2 to determine the optimal value of the stock.

Q	γ	$p(\gamma)$	$p(\gamma)/\gamma$	$p(\gamma \le Q)$	$\sum\limits_{\gamma=Q+5}^{30} \dfrac{p(\gamma)}{\gamma}$	$(Q+\dfrac{5}{2}) \sum\limits_{\gamma=Q+5}^{30} \dfrac{p(\gamma)}{\gamma}$	$L(Q)$
0	0	0.1	–	0.1	0.074	0.185	0.285
5	5	0.1	0.020	0.2	0.054	0.405	0.605
10	10	0.2	0.020	0.4	0.034	0.425	0.825
15	15	0.3	0.020	0.7	0.014	0.245	0.945
20	20	0.2	0.010	0.9	0.004	0.090	0.990
25	25	0.1	0.004	1	0.004	0.110	1.110
30 and +	30 and +	0.00	0.000	1	0.000	0.000	1.000

Table 3.2. *Determination of the optimal value of the stock*

The shortage rate is $\rho = 10/11 = 0.909$. By inference, $Q_0 = 15$.

This result can be found by directly calculating the total cost for each eventuality (Table 3.3). The blue zones have no shortages, the red zones have situations of shortage.

By applying the relevant relationships (weighted costs) previously seen for each situation, we find that after summing the costs corresponding to each demand, the minimum total cost corresponds to $Q_0 = 15$.

γ	$p(\gamma)$	Q 0	5	10	15	20	25	30
0	0.10	0.00	5.50	1.00	1.50	2.00	2.50	3.00
5	0.10	2.50	0.25	0.75	1.25	1.75	2.25	2.75
10	0.20	10.00	2.75	1.00	2.00	3.00	4.00	5.00
15	0.30	22.50	10.25	3.50	2.25	3.75	5.25	6.75
20	0.20	20.00	5.13	5.50	2.38	2.00	3.00	4.00
25	0.10	8.00	8.05	4.70	2.45	1.30	1.25	1.75
30	0.00		0.00	0.00	0.00	0.00	0.00	0.00
total		63.00	31.93	16.45	11.83	13.80	18.25	23.25

Table 3.3. *Examination of different cases*

3.6. Safety and quality

3.6.1. *Delivery time*

When a replenishment order is made $t_n = n\theta$, replenishment is not immediate (Figure 3.10). It arrives later, at $t'_n > t_n$ because of the delivery time.

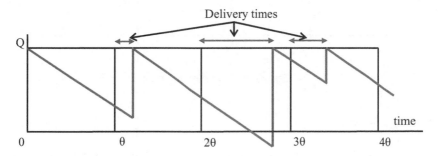

Figure 3.10. *Influence of delivery time*

We must take this into account if we want to better represent reality. However, the delivery time is not necessarily constant. It can also follow a law of probability.

In order to avoid, as far as possible, a stock shortage linked to a lengthy delivery time, we define thresholds known as minimum stock, safety stock and danger level.

3.6.2. *Minimum stock*

The minimum stock Q_m is estimated so that deliveries arrive in time to avoid a shortage.

Therefore, it corresponds, in principle, to stock when the replenishment order is made (Figure 3.11). It also depends on the demand and the delivery time.

Its estimate is empirical (but we can rely on statistics) and as there may be delays in delivery or sales acceleration, it does not guarantee the absence of non-stockouts. It just limits them.

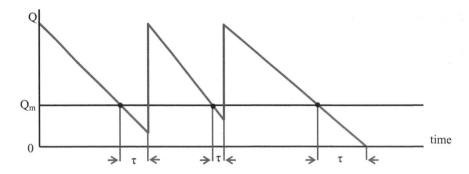

Figure 3.11. *Minimum stock*

3.6.3. *Safety stock*

For more safety, we set safety stock lower than minimum stock (Figure 3.12): this ensures that there will be fewer stock shortages (but it can still happen). The stock should not, in principle, fall below this threshold. Q_s is residual stock. One stock policy can be adopted when $Q > Q_s$ and another policy when $Q < Q_s$.

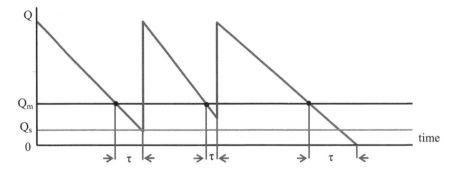

Figure 3.12. *Safety stock*

Safety stock can be defined in several ways. If there is regular demand for Δ items per unit of time and if the delivery time τ is fixed, we can take (simple geometric consideration) $Q_s = Q_m - \tau\Delta$. If this is not the case (usually more realistically), we can take $Q_s = c_s\sigma(\gamma)\sqrt{\tau}$, where γ is the demand, c_s is a safety coefficient and τ is the average delivery time.

3.6.4. *Danger level*

To be even more cautious, in order to cope with delivery delays, we define a danger level Q_a greater than Q_m such as $Q_a = Q_m + Q_s$ (Figure 3.13). We can then, for safety, trigger the replenishment order when this threshold is reached.

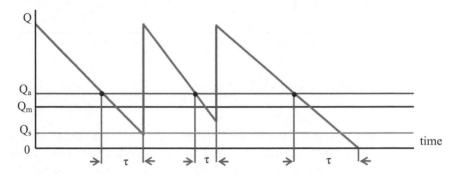

Figure 3.13. *Danger level*

3.6.5. *Quality of service*

The quality of service corresponds to the quality of the service provided to the customer so that he or she is satisfied in an optimal way.

It is defined by the relationship:

$$QS = \frac{\text{number of items provided}}{\text{number of items requested}} = 1 - \frac{\text{number of unavailable items}}{\text{number of items requested}}$$

EXAMPLE 3.3.– Consider the change in stock in Figure 3.14 where the replenishment is cyclical and instantaneous and resets the stock to its initial value (100).

Let us take a look at the demand during the period indicated:

$60 + 90 + 40 + 120 + 120 + 30 + 80 + 60 + 90 + 60 = 750$

Let us look at the shortages of items:

$20 + 20 = 40$

So the quality of service is $QS = 1 - 40/750 = 0.95$.

Figure 3.14. *Instantaneous replenishment*

However, this positive value must be tempered. It was assumed that replenishment is instantaneous, which is unrealistic. Consider that the delivery of the replenishment takes a fixed time τ (equal here to half a period). We obtain the results in Figure 3.15.

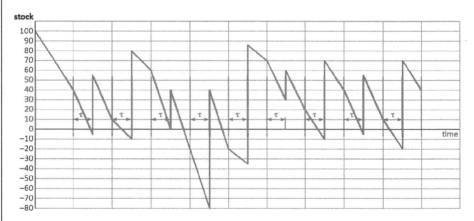

Figure 3.15. *Replenishment with fixed time*

The result is much less ideal. The demand is still the same per period, but the shortages have increased: the quality of service is now around 0.76.

To improve the situation, let us get rid of the cyclic replenishment and set a danger level $Q_a = 30$ items and replenish a constant amount of $Q_{max} - Q_a = 100 - 30 = 70$.

Keep the previous delivery time and the demand profile. We obtain the results in Figure 3.16.

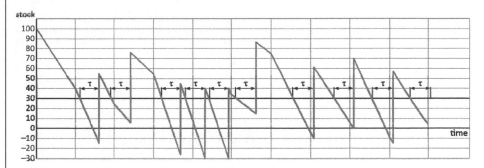

Figure 3.16. *Replenishment with danger level*

The previous results have been improved, but the shortages are not eliminated. The quality of service here is about $QS = 0.83$.

To try to improve QS, we are tempted to set a higher danger level, for example, 40. We will replenish 60 items. Keeping the other assumptions, this decision leads to the results in Figure 3.17.

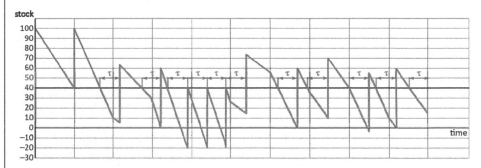

Figure 3.17. *Elevation of danger level*

The quality of service value here is about $QS = 0.91$.

We may think we are on the right track by raising the safety stock level. Let us try a security stock of 50 (and therefore a replenishment of 50 items). Keeping the other assumptions, this gives us the results in Figure 3.18.

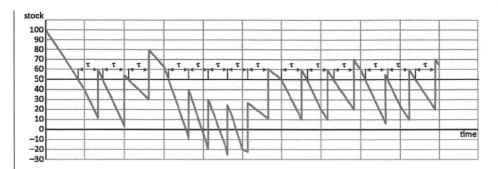

Figure 3.18. *Elevation of safety stock*

Surprisingly, the situation has not improved; it has actually deteriorated, as the quality of service drops to about $QS = 0.89$. There is an almost obvious explanation: the replenishment quantity is too low to raise the stock. On the other hand, we can see that the number of replenishments is increasing with the security stock level, which has consequences in terms of costs. There must therefore be an optimal value of the security stock.

However, if we want to improve the results in Figure 3.18, it would be enough to identify another policy for the quantity Q_R to be replenished. For example: $Q_R = Q_{max} - Q_a$ if the stock level Q is $Q \geq Q_a$ $Q_R = Q_{max} -$ demand if $Q < Q_a$.

Note that in the second case, Q_R is determined by τ units of time before replenishment.

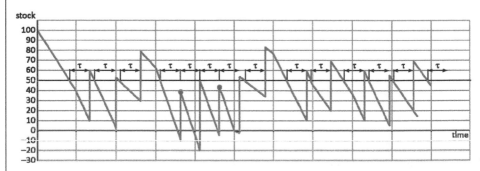

Figure 3.19. *Replenishment strategy*

The corresponding results are given in Figure 3.19. The quality of service is raised to about $QS = 0.95$.

We took an example where the demand is random. The delivery time is, in turn, fixed. In reality, the delivery time is also random.

As a result, optimization predictions are difficult to process via analytical calculation. We must use the simulation methods that we will study later.

3.7. Appendix

Let us define the search criterion for the optimal solution for the probabilistic Wilson model.

The total storage cost is:

$$C_T(Q) = c_E \sum_{\gamma=0}^{Q} \left(Q - \frac{\gamma}{2}\right) p(\gamma) + c_E \sum_{\gamma=Q+\lambda}^{\infty} \frac{Q^2}{2\gamma} p(\gamma) + c_P \sum_{\gamma=Q+\lambda}^{\infty} \frac{(\gamma - Q)^2}{2\gamma} p(\gamma)$$

Using the shortage rate:

$$\rho = \frac{c_P}{c_E + c_P} \quad \text{hence} \quad c_P = \frac{\rho}{1 - \rho} c_E$$

and the fact that:

$$\sum_{\gamma=0}^{Q} p(\gamma) = P(\gamma \leq Q) \quad \text{and} \quad \sum_{\gamma=Q+\lambda}^{\infty} p(\gamma) = 1 - \sum_{\gamma=0}^{Q} p(\gamma) = 1 - P(\gamma \leq Q)$$

$C_T(Q)$ is successively put in the form:

$$C_T(Q) = c_E \left\{ \sum_{\gamma=0}^{Q} \left(Q - \frac{\gamma}{2}\right) p(\gamma) + \sum_{\gamma=Q+\lambda}^{\infty} \frac{Q^2}{2} \frac{p(\gamma)}{\gamma} \right. $$
$$\left. + \frac{\rho}{1-\rho} \sum_{\gamma=Q+\lambda}^{\infty} \frac{(\gamma - Q)^2}{2} \frac{p(\gamma)}{\gamma} \right\}$$

$$= c_E \left\{ Q \sum_{\delta=0}^{Q} p(\gamma) - \frac{1}{2} \sum_{\gamma=0}^{Q} \gamma p(\gamma) + \frac{Q^2}{2} \sum_{\gamma=Q+\lambda}^{\infty} \frac{p(\gamma)}{\gamma} \right.$$

$$+ \frac{\rho}{2(1-\rho)} \left[\sum_{\gamma=Q+\lambda}^{\infty} \gamma p(\gamma) - 2Q \sum_{\gamma=Q+\lambda}^{\infty} p(\gamma) \right.$$

$$\left. \left. + Q^2 \sum_{\gamma=Q+\lambda}^{\infty} \frac{p(\gamma)}{\gamma} \right] \right\}$$

$$= c_E \left\{ \frac{Q}{1-\rho} P(\gamma \leq Q) - \frac{Q\rho}{1-\rho} + \frac{\rho}{2(1-\rho)} \sum_{\gamma=Q+\lambda}^{\infty} \gamma p(\gamma) - \frac{1}{2} \sum_{\gamma=0}^{Q} \gamma p(\gamma) \right.$$

$$\left. + \frac{Q^2}{2(1-\rho)} \sum_{\gamma=Q+\lambda}^{\infty} \frac{p(\gamma)}{\gamma} \right\}$$

Let us put, for simplicity:

$$G(Q) = (1-\rho) \frac{C_T(Q)}{c_E}$$

$$G(Q) = Q p(\gamma \leq Q) - Q\rho + \frac{\rho}{2} \sum_{\gamma=Q+\lambda}^{\infty} \gamma p(\gamma) - \frac{1-\rho}{2} \sum_{\gamma=0}^{Q} \gamma p(\gamma)$$

$$+ \frac{Q^2}{2} \sum_{\gamma=Q+\lambda}^{\infty} \frac{p(\gamma)}{\gamma}$$

$$= Q P(\gamma \leq Q) - Q\rho + \frac{Q^2}{2} \sum_{\gamma=Q+\lambda}^{\infty} \frac{p(\gamma)}{\gamma} + \frac{\rho}{2} \sum_{\gamma=0}^{\infty} \gamma p(\gamma) - \frac{1}{2} \sum_{\gamma=0}^{Q} \gamma p(\gamma)$$

This relationship holds for any value of Q. We therefore have notably:

$$G(Q + \lambda) = (Q + \lambda)[P(\gamma \leq Q) + P(\gamma = Q + \lambda)] - (Q + \lambda)\rho$$

$$+ \frac{(Q + \lambda)^2}{2} \left[\sum_{\gamma=Q+\lambda}^{\infty} \frac{p(\gamma)}{\gamma} - \frac{P(\gamma = Q + \lambda)}{Q + \lambda} \right]$$

$$- \frac{1}{2} \left[\sum_{\gamma=0}^{Q} \gamma p(\gamma) + (Q + \lambda) P(\gamma = Q + \lambda) \right] + \frac{\rho}{2} \sum_{\gamma=0}^{\infty} \gamma p(\gamma)$$

$$= QP(\gamma \le Q) - Q\rho + \frac{Q^2}{2} \sum_{\gamma=Q+\lambda}^{\infty} \frac{p(\gamma)}{\gamma} - \frac{1}{2} \sum_{\gamma=0}^{Q} \gamma p(\gamma) + \frac{\rho}{2} \sum_{\gamma=0}^{\infty} \gamma p(\gamma)$$

$$+ \lambda \left[P(\gamma \le Q) - \rho + Q \sum_{\gamma=Q+\lambda}^{\infty} \frac{p(\gamma)}{\gamma} + \frac{\lambda}{2} \sum_{\gamma=Q+\lambda}^{\infty} \frac{p(\gamma)}{\gamma} \right]$$

$$= G(Q) + \lambda \left[P(\gamma \le Q) + \left(Q + \frac{\lambda}{2} \right) \sum_{\gamma=Q+\lambda}^{\infty} \frac{p(\gamma)}{\gamma} - \rho \right]$$

which is:

$$G(Q + \lambda) = G(Q) + \lambda[L(Q) - \rho]$$

by putting:

$$L(Q) = P(\gamma \le Q) + \left(Q + \frac{\lambda}{2} \right) \sum_{\gamma=Q+\lambda}^{\infty} \frac{p(\gamma)}{\gamma}$$

similarly:

$$G(Q) = G(Q - \lambda) + \lambda[L(Q - \lambda) - \rho]$$

The value Q_0 which minimizes $G(Q)$ must be such that $G(Q_0) < G(Q_0 + \lambda)$ and $G(Q_0) < G(Q_0 - \lambda)$, which implies $L(Q_0) > \rho > L(Q_0 - \lambda)$.

Part 2

Stochastic Processes

4

Markov Chains

CONCEPTS DISCUSSED IN THIS CHAPTER.– Stochastic processes with discrete time and discrete states are discussed in this chapter with the additional condition of **memorylessness**.

We begin by giving useful definitions:

– Markov chains;

– probability vector;

– transition matrix.

As we have already seen, graphs are frequently used when studying stochastic processes. We will take this opportunity to provide some knowledge about graph theory.

We will then look at the case of an indefinite succession of states and thus to the problem of ergodicity conditions, learning about fixed points.

Recommended reading: [BRE 09, FAU 79, FAU 14, FOA 04, LES 14, PHE 77, RUE 89].

4.1. Markov chain concepts

Consider an evolving system. This system is assumed to go from a *defined state to a defined state*, the number of states being *finite*: E_1, E_2, E_3,..., E_m (finite continuation of discrete states). The change of state is random and we say that the process of changing state is a *stochastic* result (a scholarly word, which just means random). The system will therefore "navigate" step by step between states E_1 and

---

All figures and tables are available in color online at www.iste.co.uk/cochard/stochastic.zip.

E_m. It can clearly return to same state several times, as shown in Figure 4.1 representing the evolution of a system over time.

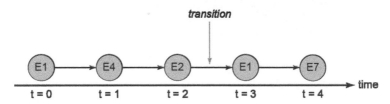

Figure 4.1. *Evolution of a system over time*

The states are characterized by the values of random variables $X(t)$, a random variable for each discrete value of time. Since time is discrete, we can write random variables with an index which highlights time: X_n for $X(t_n)$. For a pair of states i, j at a moment $t = n$, $p_{ij}(n)$ is the probability that the system in state i at the moment $t = n$ moves to state j at the moment $t = n + 1$, which means that according to the compound probabilities:

$$p_{ij}(n) = p(X_{n+1} = j \mid X_n = i, X_{n-1} = i_{n-1}, X_{n-2} = i_{n-2}, \ldots, X_0 = i_0)$$

$p_{ij}(n)$ represents the transition probability from state i to state j for the duration of $t = n$ to $t = n + 1$. It is therefore a conditional probability (the system must first be in state i at moment n, in state X_{n-1} at moment $n - 1$, etc.).

In what follows, we will make two assumptions (for the sake of simplicity):

ASSUMPTION 4.1.– The system evolves *without memory*, which means that the transition ij does not depend on the previous states of the system. It only depends on the fact that at moment n, the system is in state i. This assumption is called the Markov property, and the stochastic process is called a Markov chain. It means that:

$$p(X_{n+1} = j \mid X_n = i, X_{n-1} = i_{n-1}, X_{n-2} = i_{n-2}, \ldots, X_0 = i_0) = p(X_{n+1} = j \mid X_n = i) = p_{ij}(n)$$

ASSUMPTION 4.2.– The transition probabilities do not depend on time. So we can write:

$$p_{ij}(n) = p_{ij}$$

In other words, a translation in time does not change the transition probability. It is the same between n and $n + 1$ as between $n + k$ and $n + k + 1$. This assumption is called homogeneity. In what follows, will only look at homogeneous Markov chains.

EXAMPLE 4.1(1).– Imagine a consumer who can only buy three similar products from different brands A, B and C. We are interested in the consumer's reactions, namely: when he or she bought a product from a given brand and which brand of that product he or she will prefer at the next purchase. Assuming that these products are consumable and that the consumer does not remember the product he or she bought during the penultimate purchase, the evolution between brands A, B and C (the states) corresponds to a homogeneous Markov chain.

EXAMPLE 4.2(1).– Imagine a rabbit in an enclosure with four compartments with interconnected doors. Going through a door to move from one compartment to another is a step. Each of the compartments represents a possible state of the presence of the rabbit. In Figure 4.2, the four compartments correspond to four states: 1, 2, 3 and 4.

1	2
4	3

Figure 4.2. *The rabbit's world*

Depending on the rabbit being attracted to a particular compartment (carrots, salads, etc.), the rabbit will move from one state to another. It is assumed that the rabbit does not have a good memory and only remembers the compartment which it is in, not the compartment which it was in during its last "stay". The process of moving between compartments, with our assumptions, is a homogeneous Markov chain.

Figure 4.3. *Andrey Markov (1856–1922) was a Russian mathematician and internationally renowned scientist. He worked on probability theory and laid the foundation for research on stochastic processes. He gave his name to stochastic processes without memory, the chains and processes that bear his name*[1]

---

1 The photograph of Andrey Markov (unknown photographer) is from Wikimedia Commons: https://commons.wikimedia.org/wiki/Category:Andrey_Markov.

To describe a homogeneous Markov chain, we use two types of probability (which we have already encountered in Chapter 1):

– the probability $q_k(n)$ of finding the system in state E_k at moment n. As there are m states, there are m probabilities $q_k(n)$ ($k = 1$ à m) that we rank for convenience (and for further calculations) in a probability vector:

$$Q(n) = [q_1(n) \ q_2(n) \ q_3(n) \ ... \ q_m(n)]$$

Of course, the sum of all these probabilities is:

$$\sum_{i=1}^{m} q_i(n) = 1$$

– the probability p_{jk} of transition from state E_j to state E_k between two successive dates. These probabilities can be organized in a matrix called the *transition matrix T*. In matrix T, the rows correspond to the start states, and the columns to the arrival states:

$$T = \begin{bmatrix} p_{11} & p_{12} & \cdots & p_{1m} \\ p_{21} & p_{22} & \cdots & p_{2m} \\ \cdots & \cdots & \cdots & \cdots \\ p_{m1} & p_{m2} & \cdots & p_{mm} \end{bmatrix}$$

Starting from a given state E_j and summing all the transition probabilities of E_j to the other states, we clearly have:

$$\sum_{k=1}^{m} p_{jk} = 1$$

which means that the sum of the elements of a row of matrix T is 1. This is a characteristic of the transition matrices. This type of matrix is sometimes called a "stochastic matrix". The transition matrices have the following remarkable property:

PROPERTY 4.1.– The product of two transition matrices with the same number of rows and columns is a transition matrix.

In particular, if T is a transition matrix, T^2, T^3,..., T^n is also a transition matrix.

EXAMPLE 4.3.– Consider the following two transition matrices:

$$T = \begin{bmatrix} 0 & 1 \\ \frac{1}{2} & \frac{1}{2} \end{bmatrix} \qquad T' = \begin{bmatrix} 0 & 1 \\ 1 & 0 \end{bmatrix}$$

The remarkable property of the transition matrices can be verified: the sum of the elements of a product row is 1.

$$T.T' = \begin{bmatrix} 0 & 1 \\ \frac{1}{2} & \frac{1}{2} \end{bmatrix} \begin{bmatrix} 0 & 1 \\ 1 & 0 \end{bmatrix} = \begin{bmatrix} 1 & 0 \\ \frac{1}{2} & \frac{1}{2} \end{bmatrix}$$

$$T^2 = \begin{bmatrix} 0 & 1 \\ \frac{1}{2} & \frac{1}{2} \end{bmatrix} \begin{bmatrix} 0 & 1 \\ \frac{1}{2} & \frac{1}{2} \end{bmatrix} = \begin{bmatrix} \frac{1}{2} & \frac{1}{2} \\ \frac{1}{4} & \frac{3}{4} \end{bmatrix}$$

$$T^3 = \begin{bmatrix} \frac{1}{2} & \frac{1}{2} \\ \frac{1}{4} & \frac{3}{4} \end{bmatrix} \begin{bmatrix} 0 & 1 \\ \frac{1}{2} & \frac{1}{2} \end{bmatrix} = \begin{bmatrix} \frac{1}{4} & \frac{3}{4} \\ \frac{3}{8} & \frac{5}{8} \end{bmatrix}$$

EXAMPLE 4.1(2).– Let us take Example 4.1(1) and again suppose that the known transition probabilities are those which are shown in Figure 4.4 by taking states A, B, C and renaming them 1, 2, 3.

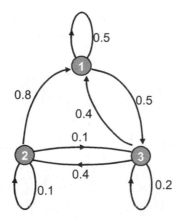

Figure 4.4. *Incomplete state/transition graph*

The sum of the transition probabilities from one state to all others must be 1, so the diagram is incomplete. The complete diagram is given in Figure 4.5 and the transition matrix is:

$$T = \begin{bmatrix} 0.5 & 0 & 0.5 \\ 0.8 & 0.1 & 0.1 \\ 0.4 & 0.4 & 0.2 \end{bmatrix}$$

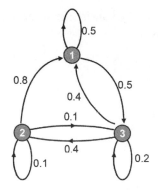

Figure 4.5. *Complete state/transition graph*

We can see that there is no opportunity to go from state 1 to state 2.

EXAMPLE 4.2(2).– Let us take another look at 4.2(1).

Represent the states as a graph with the transition probabilities (Figure 4.6) assuming that the steps consist of a compartment change:

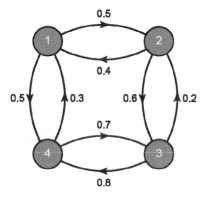

Figure 4.6. *State/transition graph*

The transition matrix is then:

$$T = \begin{bmatrix} 0 & 0.5 & 0 & 0.5 \\ 0.4 & 0 & 0.6 & 0 \\ 0 & 0.2 & 0 & 0.8 \\ 0.3 & 0 & 0.7 & 0 \end{bmatrix}$$

Of course, the transition probabilities of 1 to 3, 2 to 4, 3 to 1, 4 to 2 are zero.

EXAMPLE 4.4(1).– Let there be a system changing between 5 states, noted 1 to 5.

The transition matrix and the transition graph (Figure 4.7) are:

$$T = \begin{bmatrix} 0 & 0.4 & 0.6 & 0 & 0 \\ 0.8 & 0 & 0 & 0.2 & 0 \\ 0.9 & 0 & 0 & 0.1 & 0 \\ 0 & 0.2 & 0.5 & 0 & 0.3 \\ 0.3 & 0 & 0 & 0.7 & 0 \end{bmatrix}$$

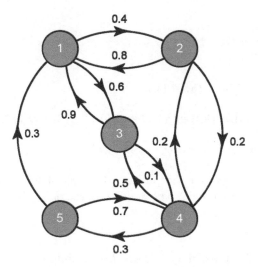

Figure 4.7. *State/transition graph*

Let us now determine the relationship between the probability vector and the transition matrix. To find the system in state E_k after step n, knowing that it was in state E_j just after step $n - 1$, we apply the result on the compound probabilities (with assumption 4.1):

$p(\text{system in } E_k \text{ in } n) = p(\text{system in } E_j \text{ in } n - 1).p_{jk}$, where $q_k(n) = q_j(n - 1).p_{jk}$

If we now consider any state of origin in n (or if we consider all the possible previous states in $n - 1$), we must sum up all the possibilities (Figure 4.8).

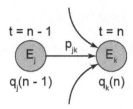

Figure 4.8. *Taking transitions to E_k into account*

$$q_k(n) = \sum_{j=1}^{m} q_j(n-1).p_{jk}$$

As a matrix, it is: $\boldsymbol{Q}(n) = \boldsymbol{Q}(n-1).\boldsymbol{T}$.

So, $\boldsymbol{Q}(1) = \boldsymbol{Q}(0).\boldsymbol{T}$, $\boldsymbol{Q}(2) = \boldsymbol{Q}(1).\boldsymbol{T} = \boldsymbol{Q}(0).\boldsymbol{T}^2$, $\boldsymbol{Q}(3) = \boldsymbol{Q}(2).\boldsymbol{T} = \boldsymbol{Q}(0).\boldsymbol{T}^3$, etc.

By recurrence, we deduce that $\boldsymbol{Q}(n) = \boldsymbol{Q}(0).\boldsymbol{T}^n$.

EXAMPLE 4.4(2).– Let us take the previous Example 4.4(1) and assume that the system is in state E_1 (certain) in 0. The probability vector in 0 is:

$\boldsymbol{Q}(0) = [1\ 0\ 0\ 0\ 0]$

To search for the probability vectors in the following steps, we apply the previous relation:

$$\boldsymbol{Q}(1) = [1 \quad 0 \quad 0 \quad 0 \quad 0]\begin{bmatrix} 0 & 0.4 & 0.6 & 0 & 0 \\ 0.8 & 0 & 0 & 0.2 & 0 \\ 0.9 & 0 & 0 & 0.1 & 0 \\ 0 & 0.2 & 0.5 & 0 & 0.3 \\ 0.3 & 0 & 0 & 0.7 & 0 \end{bmatrix} = [0 \quad 0.4 \quad 0.6 \quad 0 \quad 0]$$

$$\boldsymbol{Q}(2) = [0 \quad 0.4 \quad 0.6 \quad 0 \quad 0]\begin{bmatrix} 0 & 0.4 & 0.6 & 0 & 0 \\ 0.8 & 0 & 0 & 0.2 & 0 \\ 0.9 & 0 & 0 & 0.1 & 0 \\ 0 & 0.2 & 0.5 & 0 & 0.3 \\ 0.3 & 0 & 0 & 0.7 & 0 \end{bmatrix} = [0.86 \quad 0 \quad 0 \quad 0.14 \quad 0]$$

What happens when n goes to infinity in the relation $\boldsymbol{Q}(n) = \boldsymbol{Q}(0)\boldsymbol{T}^n$, i.e. long after the beginning of the process?

If $\boldsymbol{T}^n$ goes to a limit $\boldsymbol{T}_0$, we say that $\boldsymbol{T}$ is **ergodic** and that, in this case, $\boldsymbol{Q}(n)$ goes to a limit $\boldsymbol{Q}_0$. We will study this problem later on.

4.2. Concepts in graphs

The study of stochastic processes makes great use of graphs. Let us take a look at the world of graphs to find out more about the value of using them.

In previous graphical representations, transitions are represented by arrows and states by vertices. A graph of a stochastic process is a directed graph. Let us give a more correct definition of a directed graph.

DEFINITION.– A directed graph is a graphical representation of a connection made up of a set.

EXAMPLE 4.5(1).– Let group $E = \{a, b, c, d, e, f\}$. The directed graph in Figure 4.9 expresses the connection between the elements of E.

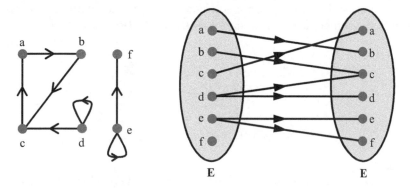

Figure 4.9. *Directed graph and connection*

Here are some other useful definitions.

DEFINITIONS.–

– A *path* is a series of arcs connecting vertex i to vertex j.

– A *circuit* is a closed path $(i = j)$.

– The *length* of a path is the number of arcs in the path.

– A *loop* is a circuit of length 1.

To any graph, we can match an *adjacency matrix*, a Boolean matrix A (containing only 0 and 1) whose elements are $a_{ij} = 1$ if an arc goes from i to j and $a_{ij} = 0$ otherwise.

EXAMPLE 4.5(2).– In Example 4.5(1), there are two loops and one circuit of length 3. It is convenient to rename the vertices of graph 1, 2, …, 6 instead of a, b, …, f. The adjacency matrix of the graph is:

$$A = \begin{bmatrix} 0 & 1 & 0 & 0 & 0 & 0 \\ 0 & 0 & 1 & 0 & 0 & 0 \\ 1 & 0 & 0 & 0 & 0 & 0 \\ 0 & 0 & 1 & 1 & 0 & 0 \\ 0 & 0 & 0 & 0 & 1 & 1 \\ 0 & 0 & 0 & 0 & 0 & 0 \end{bmatrix}$$

The adjacency matrix A clearly indicates the paths of length 1.

Let us now look for paths of length 2. If there is a path from i to j, there must be at least one vertex k as $a_{ik} = 1$ and $a_{kj} = 1$ is $a_{ik} \bullet a_{kj} = 1$ (Figure 4.10), where the sign "$\bullet$" designates logical multiplication, which, in the world of 0s and 1s, is not different from ordinary multiplication ($0 \bullet 0 = 0$, $0 \bullet 1 = 0$, $1 \bullet 0 = 0$, $1 \bullet 1 = 1$).

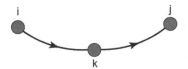

Figure 4.10. *k intermediate vertex*

To find out if there is a path of length 2 between i and j, the logical sum of all the products $a_{ik} \bullet a_{kj}$ must be carried out, i.e. for all the values of k:

$$(a_{i1} \bullet a_{1j}) \oplus (a_{i2} \bullet a_{2j}) \oplus (a_{i3} \bullet a_{3j}) \oplus ... \oplus (a_{im} \bullet a_{mj})$$

The sign "$\oplus$" indicates a logical addition in the Boolean world; it is almost analogous to ordinary addition, except that the result can only be 0 or 1 ($0 \oplus 0 = 0$, $1 \oplus 0 = 1$, $0 \oplus 1 = 1$, $1 \oplus 1 = 1$). If the result of the previous sum is 1, then there is at least one path of length 2 between i and j.

In fact, this amounts to making the matrix product $A \times A = A^2$ (with the laws $\bullet$ and $\oplus$). So, matrix A^2 indicates the presence of paths of length 2.

Similarly, using reasoning, A^3 will indicate the presence of paths of length 3 and A^n will indicate the presence of paths of length n.

EXAMPLE 4.5(3).– Let us go back to Example 4.5 (2). Let us calculate the successive powers (in the Boolean sense) of the adjacency matrix:

$$A = \begin{bmatrix} 0 & 1 & 0 & 0 & 0 & 0 \\ 0 & 0 & 1 & 0 & 0 & 0 \\ 1 & 0 & 0 & 0 & 0 & 0 \\ 0 & 0 & 1 & 1 & 0 & 0 \\ 0 & 0 & 0 & 0 & 1 & 1 \\ 0 & 0 & 0 & 0 & 0 & 0 \end{bmatrix} \quad A^2 = \begin{bmatrix} 0 & 0 & 1 & 0 & 0 & 0 \\ 1 & 0 & 0 & 0 & 0 & 0 \\ 0 & 1 & 0 & 0 & 0 & 0 \\ 1 & 0 & 1 & 1 & 0 & 0 \\ 0 & 0 & 0 & 0 & 1 & 1 \\ 0 & 0 & 0 & 0 & 0 & 0 \end{bmatrix}$$

$$A^3 = \begin{bmatrix} 1 & 0 & 0 & 0 & 0 & 0 \\ 0 & 1 & 1 & 0 & 0 & 0 \\ 0 & 0 & 1 & 0 & 0 & 0 \\ 1 & 1 & 1 & 1 & 0 & 0 \\ 0 & 0 & 0 & 0 & 1 & 1 \\ 0 & 0 & 0 & 0 & 0 & 0 \end{bmatrix} \quad A^4 = \begin{bmatrix} 0 & 1 & 0 & 0 & 0 & 0 \\ 0 & 0 & 1 & 0 & 0 & 0 \\ 1 & 0 & 0 & 0 & 0 & 0 \\ 1 & 1 & 1 & 1 & 0 & 0 \\ 0 & 0 & 0 & 0 & 1 & 1 \\ 0 & 0 & 0 & 0 & 0 & 0 \end{bmatrix}$$

$$A^5 = \begin{bmatrix} 0 & 0 & 1 & 0 & 0 & 0 \\ 1 & 0 & 0 & 0 & 0 & 0 \\ 0 & 1 & 0 & 0 & 0 & 0 \\ 1 & 1 & 1 & 1 & 0 & 0 \\ 0 & 0 & 0 & 0 & 1 & 1 \\ 0 & 0 & 0 & 0 & 0 & 0 \end{bmatrix} \quad A^6 = \begin{bmatrix} 1 & 0 & 0 & 0 & 0 & 0 \\ 0 & 1 & 1 & 0 & 0 & 0 \\ 0 & 0 & 1 & 0 & 0 & 0 \\ 1 & 1 & 1 & 1 & 0 & 0 \\ 0 & 0 & 0 & 0 & 1 & 1 \\ 0 & 0 & 0 & 0 & 0 & 0 \end{bmatrix}$$

We can see that we can stop the calculation of the powers at A^6 because $A^6 = A^3$. So, we will have $A^7 = A^4$, $A^8 = A^5$, etc.

Another benefit of the adjacency matrix is to study the connectivity of the graph, i.e. to see if from any vertex i, any vertex j can be joined. As matrices A, A^2, A^3, ... represent the existence of paths of length 1, 2, 3, ..., by doing the logical sum of these matrices, we will know if there is a path going from i to j (of any length):

$$\tilde{A} = A \oplus A^2 \oplus A^3 \oplus A^4 \oplus ...$$

EXAMPLE 4.5(4).– Let us go back to Example 4.5(3), where the calculation of $\tilde{A}$ is simple:

$$\tilde{A} = A \oplus A^2 \oplus A^3 \oplus A^4 \oplus A^5$$

$$\tilde{A} = \begin{bmatrix} 1 & 1 & 1 & 0 & 0 & 0 \\ 1 & 1 & 1 & 0 & 0 & 0 \\ 1 & 1 & 1 & 0 & 0 & 0 \\ 1 & 1 & 1 & 1 & 0 & 0 \\ 0 & 0 & 0 & 0 & 1 & 1 \\ 0 & 0 & 0 & 0 & 0 & 0 \end{bmatrix}$$

which shows that there is no path connecting certain vertices. Thus, for vertices 1, 2, 3, we cannot join vertices 4, 5, 6.

DEFINITION.– The set of vertices that can be reached from vertex i is called *transitive closure* $\Gamma(i)$ of vertex i

Vertex i is also part of $\Gamma(i)$. To be able to find the transitive closure, simply read the rows of the matrix $I \oplus \tilde{A}$ (the identity matrix I guarantees that vertex i is part of $\Gamma(i)$).

EXAMPLE 4.5(5).– In Example 4.5(4), we obtained matrix $\tilde{A}$. The matrix $I \oplus \tilde{A}$ is:

$$I \oplus \tilde{A} = \begin{bmatrix} 1 & 1 & 1 & 0 & 0 & 0 \\ 1 & 1 & 1 & 0 & 0 & 0 \\ 1 & 1 & 1 & 0 & 0 & 0 \\ 1 & 1 & 1 & 1 & 0 & 0 \\ 0 & 0 & 0 & 0 & 1 & 1 \\ 0 & 0 & 0 & 0 & 0 & 1 \end{bmatrix}$$

By inference, $\Gamma(1) = \Gamma(2) = \Gamma(3) = \{1, 2, 3\}$; $\Gamma(4) = \{1, 2, 3, 4\}$; $\Gamma(5) = \{5, 6\}$; $\Gamma(6) = \{6\}$.

Note that the form of the matrix $I \oplus \tilde{A}$ is distinctive (Figure 4.11), because it shows two sub-matrices (because the numbering of vertices was well chosen):

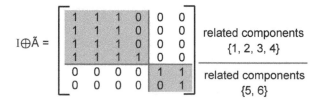

Figure 4.11. *Related components*

This form highlights two related pieces or components on the graph.

We say that two vertices i and j are communicating if these vertices are mutually accessible: there is at least one path from i to j and at least one path from j to i. The relation "is communicating with" is an equivalence relation, because it is reflexive (i is communicating with itself), symmetric (if i is communicating with j, then j is communicating with i) and transitive (if i is communicating with j and j is communicating with k, then i is communicating with k).

The equivalence classes in this relationship are divided into two classes of states:

– transient states: when we leave these states, we do not return;

– recurrent states: when we arrive at these states, we stay there.

EXAMPLE 4.5(6).– Let us go back to the previous example. Equivalence classes can "be read" directly on the $I \oplus \tilde{A}$ matrix with appropriate vertex numbering (Figure 4.12). We obtain four classes: $\{1, 2, 3\}$, $\{4\}$, $\{5\}$ and $\{6\}$.

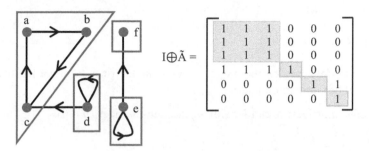

$$I \oplus \tilde{A} = \begin{bmatrix} 1 & 1 & 1 & 0 & 0 & 0 \\ 1 & 1 & 1 & 0 & 0 & 0 \\ 1 & 1 & 1 & 0 & 0 & 0 \\ 1 & 1 & 1 & 1 & 0 & 0 \\ 0 & 0 & 0 & 0 & 1 & 1 \\ 0 & 0 & 0 & 0 & 0 & 1 \end{bmatrix}$$

Figure 4.12. *Classes of states*

Classes $\{4\}$ and $\{5\}$ are classes of transient states. Classes $\{1, 2, 3\}$ and $\{6\}$ are recurrent state classes. However, these last two classes have different natures: class $\{1, 2, 3\}$ is called *periodic* (the same vertices are visited periodically), class $\{6\}$ only contains a vertex called "*absorbent*" (a change of state is impossible).

4.3. Ergodicity

DEFINITION.– T being a transition matrix, T is said to be *regular* (or *strongly ergodic*) if, from a certain power n, all the elements of T^n are *strictly positive*.

EXAMPLE 4.6.– Consider the following transition matrices:

$$T_1 = \begin{bmatrix} 0 & 1 \\ 0.6 & 0.4 \end{bmatrix} \quad T_2 = \begin{bmatrix} 0 & 0.5 & 0.5 \\ 1 & 0 & 0 \\ 0.3 & 0.3 & 0.4 \end{bmatrix} \quad T_3 = \begin{bmatrix} 1 & 0 \\ 0.6 & 0.4 \end{bmatrix}$$

Let us square them:

$$T_1^2 = \begin{bmatrix} 0.6 & 0.4 \\ 0.2 & 0.8 \end{bmatrix} \quad T_2^2 = \begin{bmatrix} 0.7 & 0.2 & 0.2 \\ 0 & 0.5 & 0.5 \\ 0.4 & 0.3 & 0.3 \end{bmatrix} \quad T_3^2 = \begin{bmatrix} 1 & 0 \\ 0.84 & 0.16 \end{bmatrix}$$

Squaring is enough to prove that T_1 is regular. For T_2^2 and T_3^2, we still have zeros. Let us continue by cubing:

$$T_2^3 = \begin{bmatrix} 0.2 & 0.4 & 0.4 \\ 0.7 & 0.2 & 0.2 \\ 0.4 & 0.3 & 0.3 \end{bmatrix} \quad T_3^3 = \begin{bmatrix} 1 & 0 \\ 0.94 & 0.06 \end{bmatrix}$$

which is enough to prove that T_2 is regular. We still have T_3, but the result of $T_3{}^n$ will always be in the following form, for $n > 0$:

$$T_3^n = \begin{bmatrix} 1 & 0 \\ a & b \end{bmatrix}$$

T_3 is therefore not regular.

We can possibly rely on the properties of some matrices to prove the regularity (or otherwise) of a transition matrix:

– reducible matrices: K and L being square sub-matrices ($n > 0$):

$$\begin{bmatrix} K & 0 \\ 0 & L \end{bmatrix}^n = \begin{bmatrix} K^n & 0 \\ 0 & L^n \end{bmatrix}$$

– periodic matrices: M and N being square sub-matrices ($n > 0$):

$$\begin{bmatrix} 0 & N \\ M & 0 \end{bmatrix}^{2n} = \begin{bmatrix} (NM)^n & 0 \\ 0 & (MN)^n \end{bmatrix} \quad \begin{bmatrix} 0 & N \\ M & 0 \end{bmatrix}^{2n+1}$$
$$= \begin{bmatrix} 0 & (NM)^n N \\ (MN)^n M & 0 \end{bmatrix}$$

– matrices with a 0 on the second diagonal:

$$\begin{bmatrix} K & 0 \\ M & L \end{bmatrix} \quad \text{or} \quad \begin{bmatrix} K & N \\ 0 & L \end{bmatrix}$$

$$\begin{bmatrix} K & 0 \\ M & L \end{bmatrix}^n = \begin{bmatrix} K^n & 0 \\ M_n & L^n \end{bmatrix} \quad \text{with} \quad \begin{cases} M_1 = M \\ M_n = M_{n-1}K + L^{n-1}M \end{cases}$$

DEFINITION.– A *fixed point* of a square matrix T is defined as the vector Q_0 such that $Q_0 T = Q_0$.

This definition also applies to transition matrices and the vector Q_0 has the structure of a probability vector (the sum of its components is 1).

With the preceding definitions of regular transitions and fixed point matrices, we can state the following fundamental theorem (given here without demonstration).

THEOREM 4.1.– If T is a regular transition matrix:

– T assumes a fixed point Q_0, which is a probability vector with strictly positive components;

– $T_0 = \lim T^n$ for n going towards infinity; T_0 has the elements of Q_0 for rows;

– Q being any probability vector, when n goes towards infinity, $\lim Q.T^n = Q_0$.

EXAMPLE 4.7(1).– A motorist changes cars every year with the following particularities: when he has a Pampa, he buys a Savanna. When he has a Savanna, he buys a Tundra. When he has a Tundra, he buys a Tundra in 50% of the cases, a Pampa in 25% of the cases and a Savanna in 25% of the cases.

Taking the makes of car as states, the process graph is shown in Figure 4.13 (Pampa = 1, Savanna = 2, Tundra = 3). Let us find out if the transition matrix is regular.

$$T = \begin{bmatrix} 0 & 1 & 0 \\ 0 & 0 & 1 \\ 0.25 & 0.25 & 0.5 \end{bmatrix} \quad T^2 = \begin{bmatrix} 0 & 0 & 1 \\ 0.25 & 0.25 & 0.5 \\ 0.125 & 0.373 & 0.5 \end{bmatrix}$$

$$T^3 = \begin{bmatrix} 0.25 & 0.25 & 0.5 \\ 0.125 & 0.375 & 0.5 \\ 0.125 & 0.25 & 0.625 \end{bmatrix}$$

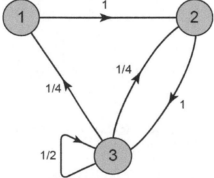

Figure 4.13. *State/transition graph*

The calculation of T^3 shows that T is regular. The fundamental theorem therefore applies; there is a fixed point:

$Q_0 = [x\ y\ z]$ with $x + y + z = 1$

The equation $Q_0 T = Q_0$ results in:

$$[x\ \ y\ \ z] \begin{bmatrix} 0 & 1 & 0 \\ 0 & 0 & 1 \\ \frac{1}{4} & \frac{1}{4} & \frac{1}{2} \end{bmatrix} = [\frac{z}{4}\ \ \ x + \frac{z}{4}\ \ \ y + \frac{z}{2}]$$

$$Q_0 T = Q_0 \quad \Longrightarrow \quad \begin{cases} x = \dfrac{z}{4} \\ y = x + \dfrac{z}{4} \\ z = y + \dfrac{z}{2} \end{cases} \quad \Longrightarrow \quad x = \dfrac{1}{7} \quad y = \dfrac{2}{7} \quad z = \dfrac{4}{7}$$

so: $T_0 = \begin{bmatrix} \dfrac{1}{7} & \dfrac{2}{7} & \dfrac{4}{7} \\ \dfrac{1}{7} & \dfrac{2}{7} & \dfrac{4}{7} \\ \dfrac{1}{7} & \dfrac{2}{7} & \dfrac{4}{7} \end{bmatrix}.$

In 2014, the motorist had a Savanna. Which car will he have in 2034 (assuming the makes still exist)?

2014 is the date $n = 0$; the probability vector is $Q(0) = [0\ 1\ 0]$. 2034 is the date $n = 20$ (considered as very far away); the probability vector is:

$$Q(20) = Q(0).T^{20} \cong Q(0).T_0 = \begin{bmatrix} 0 & 1 & 0 \end{bmatrix} \begin{bmatrix} \dfrac{1}{7} & \dfrac{2}{7} & \dfrac{4}{7} \\ \dfrac{1}{7} & \dfrac{2}{7} & \dfrac{4}{7} \\ \dfrac{1}{7} & \dfrac{2}{7} & \dfrac{4}{7} \end{bmatrix} = \begin{bmatrix} \dfrac{1}{7} & \dfrac{2}{7} & \dfrac{4}{7} \end{bmatrix}$$

He will be four times more likely to own a Tundra than a Pampa and two times more likely to own a Tundra than a Savanna.

In fact, ergodicity is related to the connectivity of the transition graph. We acknowledge the following theorem.

THEOREM 4.2.– If the number of states is discrete and finite and the graph of the transitions is strongly connected, the conclusions of Theorem 4.1 are valid.

EXAMPLE 4.7(2).– Let us check this theorem using the previous example. The number of states is discrete and finite (three states). Let us examine the graph of transitions. To verify the connectivity, we use the adjacency matrix A, which indicates the paths of length 1 (arcs of the graph of transitions). There are zeros. Calculate A^2 (which indicates the paths of length 2), then A^3 (which indicates the paths of length 3).

$$A = \begin{bmatrix} 0 & 1 & 0 \\ 0 & 0 & 1 \\ 1 & 1 & 1 \end{bmatrix} \quad A^2 = \begin{bmatrix} 0 & 0 & 1 \\ 1 & 1 & 1 \\ 1 & 1 & 1 \end{bmatrix} \quad A^3 = \begin{bmatrix} 1 & 1 & 1 \\ 1 & 1 & 1 \\ 1 & 1 & 1 \end{bmatrix}$$

We see that A^3 only has 1s, which means that, from any vertex, we can go to another vertex by a path of length at least 3. The graph is therefore strongly connected and the theorem applies: the process is ergodic.

THEOREM 4.3.– If the transition matrix T assumes the simple eigenvalue 1 and the other eigenvalues have an absolute value less than 1 (or a module less than 1 if they are complex), the conclusions of Theorem 4.1 are valid.

EXAMPLE 4.8.– Now imagine that the car purchase choices of our motorist are:

– when he owns a Pampa, he buys a Pampa in 50% of the cases and a Tundra in 50% of the cases;

– when he owns a Savanna, he buys a Pampa in 75% of the cases and a Savanna in 25% of the cases;

– when he owns a Tundra, he buys a Savanna.

The transition matrix is:

$$T = \begin{bmatrix} \frac{1}{2} & 0 & \frac{1}{2} \\ \frac{3}{4} & \frac{1}{4} & 0 \\ 0 & 1 & 0 \end{bmatrix}$$

To find the eigenvalues λ of T, we must solve the equation $\det(T - \lambda I) = 0$, where I is the identity matrix. So, we have:

$$\begin{vmatrix} \frac{1}{2} - \lambda & 0 & \frac{1}{2} \\ \frac{3}{4} & \frac{1}{4} - \lambda & 0 \\ 0 & 1 & -\lambda \end{vmatrix} = -\lambda \left(\frac{1}{2} - \lambda\right)\left(\frac{1}{4} - \lambda\right) + \frac{3}{8} = 0$$

which leads to the equation $8\lambda^3 - 6\lambda^2 + \lambda - 3 = 0$.

We can immediately see that $\lambda = 1$ is the root of this equation. As a result, we can factorize the first member:

$$(\lambda - 1)(8\lambda^2 + 2\lambda + 3) = 0$$

The term of the second degree has the roots ½ and –¾, whose absolute values are less than 1. According to Theorem 4.3, the transition matrix is ergodic.

Its fixed point is $Q_0 = [6/13 \quad 4/13 \quad 3/13]$.

4.4. Random paths

A random path is a homogeneous Markov chain in which a transition can only take place between two neighboring states:

$$p_{ij} \neq 0 \text{ if } j = i - 1 \text{ or } j = i + 1$$

Figure 4.14 illustrates the graph of transitions of a random path.

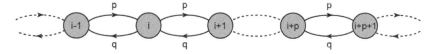

Figure 4.14. *States/transitions graph of a random path*

Of course, we have $p + q = 1$. This graph can have 0 and m ends. In the case where these ends are not absorbent, we have $p_{01} = p_{m, m-1} = 1$.

To illustrate these particular Markov chains, let us take two well-known examples.

EXAMPLE 4.9.– The drunkard's walk.

Suppose a drunkard is going from street lamp to street lamp in a road that is straight. The drunkard goes from one street lamp to the next with a ½ probability and returns to the previous street lamp with a ½ probability.

The street lamps materialize the states of the drunkard. They can be numbered 0, 1, 2,..., m.

The drunkard starts from a street lamp 1, 2 or 3 and stops when he reaches either street lamp 0 or street lamp 4. Suppose for simplicity that $m = 4$. Figure 4.15 represents the graph of transitions.

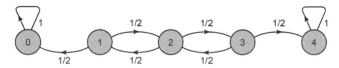

Figure 4.15. *The drunkard's walk*

States 0 and 4 are called "absorbent".

Let us look for the probability $P(i)$ that the drunkard, being in an i *interior* state (street lamps 1, 2 or 3), goes to state 0 (street lamp 0). In general, the drunkard must go from street lamp to street lamp until he reaches street lamp 0, which means that:

$$P(i) = \sum_{j=0}^{4} p_{ij} P(j)$$

We have $P(0) = 1$ (case of certainty) and $P(4) = 0$ (case of impossibility). The p_{ij} are worth ½ for the values $j = i + 1$ and $j = i - 1$ and 0 for the other values ($i = 1, 2, 3$), which gives:

$$P(i) = \frac{1}{2}[P(i - 1) + P(i + 1)] \qquad (i = 1, 2, 3)$$

From this relation, we draw:

$$P(1) = \frac{1}{2}[P(0) + P(2)] = \frac{1}{2}[1 + P(2)]$$

$$P(2) = \frac{1}{2}[P(1) + P(3)]$$

$$P(3) = \frac{1}{2}[P(2) + P(4)] = \frac{1}{2}P(2)$$

From these three relations, we easily deduce:

$$P(1) = \frac{3}{4} \quad P(2) = \frac{1}{2} \quad P(3) = \frac{1}{4}$$

By designating P'(i) as the probability that the drunkard arrives at the street lamp 4, we will naturally have:

$$P'(1) = \frac{1}{4} \qquad P'(2) = \frac{1}{2} \qquad P'(3) = \frac{3}{4}$$

since P(i)+P'(i) = 1.

Let us now consider the average number of steps (a step being a passage from a street lamp to a neighboring street lamp) when the drunkard is at street lamp i to get to street lamp 0 or to street lamp 4. Let N_i be the random variable corresponding to the number of steps necessary to reach the street lamp i and $\bar{N}_i$ its mean value: $\bar{N}_i = E(N_i)$.

If a street lamp j is close to the street light i, we have $N_i = 1 + N_j$, which is one step from i to j then N_j steps to reach the lamp posts at the ends. Moreover, since j is close to i, we must have $j = i + 1$ or $j = i - 1$, so that:

$$N_i = 1 + p_{i,i-1}N_{i-1} + p_{i,i+1}N_{i+1} = 1 + \frac{1}{2}[N_{i-1} + N_{i+1}]$$

hence:

$$\overline{N}_i = 1 + \frac{1}{2}[\overline{N}_{i-1} + \overline{N}_{i+1}]$$

We know that $\overline{N}_0 = \overline{N}_4 = 0$, so the previous relation gives us the system:

$$\overline{N}_1 = 1 + \frac{1}{2}\overline{N}_2 \qquad \overline{N}_2 = 1 + \frac{1}{2}[\overline{N}_1 + \overline{N}_3] \qquad \overline{N}_3 = \frac{1}{2}\overline{N}_2$$

which leads to: $\overline{N}_1 = 3$; $\overline{N}_2 = 4$; $\overline{N}_3 = 3$.

EXAMPLE 4.10.– The risk-all game.

A player performs a series of "all or nothing" games. In each game, he has the probability p of winning and the probability q of losing ($p + q = 1$). If he wins, he receives \$1. If he loses, he loses \$1. The series of games stops when his gain is zero or equal to 4.

We can look at the probability of having a zero gain or a gain of \$4 and also the average number of games that we can identify as the average duration of the game.

The player's states can be represented by his gain G whose possible values at a given moment are 0, 1, 2, 3 and 4, i.e. five states.

Suppose the player starts the game with a win of \$1. This problem bears some resemblance to the previous problem of the drunkard's walk, since the gain can only, when changing state, increase by 1 or decrease by 1. The graph of transitions is the same as that in Figure 4.15. As a result, the probability of winning is $P'(1) = \frac{1}{4}$ by taking the notation of the previous example and assuming $p = q = 1/2$.

Suppose now that the player starts the game with \$0 and looks for the probability $P'(0)$ of winning, i.e. going from state 0 to state 4. Strictly speaking, the graph of transitions is here different (Figure 4.16).

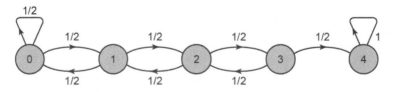

Figure 4.16. *The risk-all game*

By repeating the previous reasonings:

$P'(0) = pP'(1)$ // we can only go from 0 to 1 if we want to win.

$P'(1) = pP'(2$ // we can only go from 1 to 2 if we want to win.

$P'(2) = pP'(3) + qP'(1)$ // returning to 1 does not mean that we will lose.

$P'(3) = pP'(4) + qP'(2)$ // returning to 2 does not mean that we will lose.

$P'(4) = 1$ // if we are at 4, we have won.

Solving this system of equations yields the value of $P'(0)$:

$$P'(0) = \frac{p^4}{p^2+q^2}$$

where we used the fact that $1 = (p+q)^2 = p^2 + q^2 + 2qp$.

For $p = q = \frac{1}{2}$, we obtain $P'(0) = 1/8$.

EXAMPLE 4.11.– Random walk on the edges of a cube.

Consider the following problem: a cube of 1 side unit of length, of which one of the vertices, O, is at the origin of the coordinates (Figure 4.17).

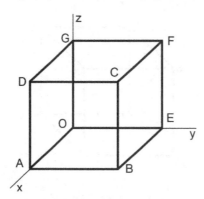

Figure 4.17. *Random walk on a cube*

Imagine a random walk of one unit in one of three dimensions, where you can go from one vertex to another neighboring one, with probabilities p_1, p_2, p_3:

– the probability of moving parallel to the Ox axis is p_1;

– the probability of moving parallel to the Oy axis is p_2;

– the probability of moving parallel to the Oz axis is p_3.

We assume that the transition from one vertex to another does not depend on which transitions have occurred previously.

We will obviously note that $p_1 + p_2 + p_3 = 1$.

We are interested in calculating the probability of randomly moving from vertex A (x_A, y_A, z_A) to vertex B (x_B, y_B, z_B).

We could consider that the states correspond to the vertices of the cube. There would be eight states.

Suppose then that the three probabilities are each equal to 1/3. In this case, taking into account the symmetry of the cube and the probabilities, the number of states can be reduced to 4. We renumber them 1, 2, 3, 4 (Figure 4.18).

The transitions between vertices can be represented by a graph relating to a Markov chain (Figure 4.19).

We want to calculate the average number of steps to go, randomly, from vertex 1 to vertex 4. The random walk stops at 4. This state is absorbent.

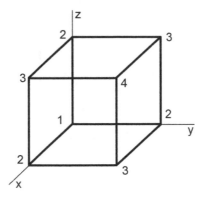

Figure 4.18. *The states*

From vertex 1, we can only go to 2. So $p_{12} = 1$. From vertex 2, we have two possibilities to go to 3 and only one to go to 1: $p_{23} = 2/3$ and $p_{21} = 1/3$. From vertex 3, we have two possibilities to go to 2 and only 1 possibility to go to 4: $p_{32} = 2/3$ and

$p_{34} = 1/3$. From vertex 4, we cannot go anywhere, as it is the end vertex. We can put $p_{44} = 1$, hence the transition matrix T and the graph of the transitions in Figure 4.19.

$$T = \begin{bmatrix} 0 & 1 & 0 & 0 \\ \frac{1}{3} & 0 & \frac{2}{3} & 0 \\ 0 & \frac{2}{3} & 0 & \frac{1}{3} \\ 0 & 0 & 0 & 1 \end{bmatrix}$$

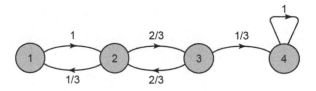

Figure 4.19. *Random walk on the cube*

The matrix T is not regular, but it does not mean that we cannot reach vertex 4 from vertex 1. To go from 1 to 4, the most direct path is $1 - 2 - 3 - 4$, which corresponds to three steps and the probability $1 \times \frac{2}{3} \times \frac{1}{3} = \frac{2}{9}$.

However, we can also oscillate between 1 and 2 and also between 2 and 3.

5

Markov Processes

CONCEPTS DISCUSSED IN THIS CHAPTER.– This chapter deals with the study of Markov processes, the equivalents of Markov chains when time is considered continuous and all states remain discrete.

We will first begin by giving a precise definition of a Markov process and then study a special case: the Poisson process.

In the following section, we will look into the probability law that governs the time intervals separating two consecutive events of a Poisson process: exponential distribution. The relationship between Poisson distribution and exponential distribution will be examined.

Then we will study the general case of a birth process and a death process.

We will end with the study of the conjugation of the two preceding processes when they are in equilibrium, i.e. self-regulating, which is called the birth and death process.

The results obtained in this chapter will be used in the following chapter on queueing systems.

Recommended reading: [ENG 76, FAU 79, FOA 04, LES 14, RUE 89].

5.1. The concept of Markov processes

In *Markov chains*, time is considered discrete: it takes countable values. When time is considered continuous, the corresponding process is called a *Markov process*.

In both cases, Markov chains and processes, all the states taken by a system remain discrete: $E_1, E_2,..., E_m,...$, finite or infinite.

Let $X(t)$ be a random variable taking the value i when the system is in state E_i at moment t. $X(t)$ defines a Markov process if the following assumption is satisfied.

ASSUMPTION 5.1(1).– The process is "memoryless".

This means that the probability of moving from state E_i where it was at moment t to state E_j at moment $t + \tau$ does not depend on the history of the process, but only on the present state. This property is already the property of the Markov chains.

It is expressed here, for a transition E_i to E_j, by:

$$\text{prob}(X(t + \tau) = j \mid X(u) = \text{any value for } 0 \le u < t, X(t) = i)$$

$$= \text{prob}(X(t + \tau) = j \mid X(t) = i)$$

which means that the values of $X(u)$ for u including between 0 and t do not matter. Here, it only depends on states E_i and E_j and the dates of residence in these states.

In general, we are mainly focusing on homogeneous Markov processes, as we have already used them for Markov chains, i.e. verifying assumption 5.2.

ASSUMPTION 5.2(1).– A process defined by a random variable $X(t)$ is homogeneous if the transition E_i to E_j does not depend on date t.

More precisely:

$$\text{prob}(X(t + \tau) = j \mid X(t) = i) = p_{ij}(\tau)$$

As this expression indicates, the transition probability depends only on states E_i and E_j and the **time interval** τ, but not the date t. We could still write it by taking $t = 0$:

$$\text{prob}(X(\tau) = j \mid X(0) = i) = p_{ij}(\tau)$$

Another way of expressing it is stating that a translation in time does not change the probability of transition.

Of course, we always have the relation:

$$\sum_j p_{ij}(\tau) = 1$$

A homogeneous Markov process verifies the Chapman–Kolmogorov equation:

$$p_{ij}(\tau_1 + \tau_2) = \sum_k p_{ik}(\tau_1)p_{kj}(\tau_2)$$

Indeed (Figure 5.1):

$$p_{ij}(\tau_1 + \tau_2) = prob(X(\tau_1 + \tau_2) = j \mid X(0) = i)$$
$$= \sum_k prob(X(\tau_1 + \tau_2) = j \text{ and } X(\tau_1) = k \mid X(0) = i)$$

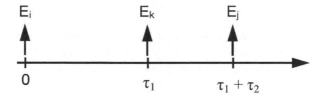

Figure 5.1. *Occurrences of states*

However:

$$prob(X(\tau_1 + \tau_2) = j \text{ and } X(\tau_1) = k \mid X(0) = i)$$

$= prob(X(\tau_1) = k \mid X(0) = i).prob(X(\tau_1 + \tau_2) = j \mid X(\tau_1) = k \text{ and } X(0) = i)$ using conditional probabilities

$= p_{ik}(\tau_1). \; prob(X(\tau_1 + \tau_2) = j \mid X(\tau_1) = k \text{ and } X(0) = i)$ according to assumption 5.2(1)

$= p_{ik}(\tau_1).prob(X(\tau_1 + \tau_2) = j \mid X(\tau_1) = k)$ according to assumption 5.1(1) (memoryless)

$= p_{ik}(\tau_1).prob(X(\tau_2) = j \mid X(0) = k)$ according to assumption 5.2(1) again

$= p_{ik}(\tau_1).p_{kj}(\tau_2)$

Figure 5.2. *Andreï Kolmogorov (1903–1987)*[1]

COMMENT ON FIGURE 5.2.– *Kolmogorov was a Russian mathematician who published a book on axiomatic systems of probability theory. His work is often compared to Euclid's on the topic of geometry. He also worked on information theory, supplementing Shannon's contributions. He also solved Hilbert's thirteenth problem, the solution of which can be summarized by saying that a function of three variables can be expressed as a sum of the functions of two variables.*

5.2. Poisson process

We often face event-counting situations between date 0 and date t, i.e. $N(t)$, the number of events occurring in the interval $[0, t]$.

For example, number of births in a population, number of radioactivity decays, number of arrivals at a counter, number of telephone calls to a call center, number of IP packets reaching a router, number of fish caught by an angler, number of vehicles passing through a particular area, etc.

What all of these situations have in common are events which occur randomly over time (Figure 5.3).

0   t

Figure 5.3. *Occurrences of random events*

---

1 The photograph of Andreï Kolmogorov comes from the online bibmath library: http://www.bibmath.net/bios/images/kolmogorov.jpg.

It should be noted that:

– t is a continuous variable (and not discrete as in Markov chains);

– $N(t)$ is an integer, and therefore a discrete variable.

$N(t)$ varies as a function of t in the form of a stepped curve. Assuming that only one event can occur at a given moment, there will be a representation of $N(t)$ as shown in Figure 5.4.

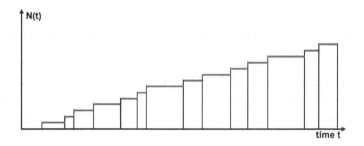

Figure 5.4. *Variation in the number of events over time*

Of all these processes giving rise to counting, there is one that merits deeper study: the Poisson process. We know the Poisson probability distribution and we will see that the Poisson process is linked to this distribution (hence the name!).

A Poisson process is a homogeneous Markov process, so it verifies the previous assumptions that can be recalled here in the context of event counting.

ASSUMPTION 5.1(2).– The process is memoryless.

The occurrence of events before date t does not influence the occurrence of events after date t.

For two disjoint time intervals $[t_1, t_2]$ and $[t_2, t_3]$, the random variables $N(t_2) - N(t_1)$ and $N(t_3) - N(t_2)$ are independent, such that the number of events in $[t_2, t_3]$ has a probability that is not dependent on that of the number of events in $[t_1, t_2]$.

ASSUMPTION 5.2(2).– The probability of having n events in a given interval does not depend on the date.

This means that the variables $N(t + \tau) - N(t)$ and $N(\tau) - N(0)$ have the same probability law, therefore:

$$\mathrm{prob}(N(t + \tau) - N(t) = n) = \mathrm{prob}(N(\tau) - N(0) = n) = \mathrm{prob}(N(\tau) = n) = P_n(\tau)$$

because we use the assumption $N(0) = 0$ (the count is zero at the initial time 0).

$P_n(\tau)$ represents the probability of n events occurring between $t = 0$ and $t = \tau$ (here we use the notation P_i, not to be confused with the transition probability p_{ij}).

We add a third assumption 5.3(1), which is the specific feature of the Poisson process.

ASSUMPTION 5.3(1).– In an interval of length h, with h being small, the probability of having more than one event is small compared to h, which is expressed by:

$$P_n(h) = o(h) \text{ for } n \geq 2$$

In other words, for h, which can be as small as we like, $P_2(h)$ is zero (as well as $P_3(h)$, $P_4(h)$...). In the interval h, we can only have 0 or 1 event. It is sometimes said that $N(t)$ corresponds to a "rare event" process. The notation $o(h)$ means that when $h \rightarrow 0$, $o(h) \rightarrow 0$ as well, but quicker than h.

The real situations envisaged above are more or less in agreement with these conditions. If they are (and only in this case), we can apply the results relating to the Poisson process that we are going to get now.

Consider two successive intervals $[0, t]$, then $[t, t + h]$, with h as small as we like to respect assumption 5.3(1), and suppose that we have 0 events in the interval $[0, t + h]$. This can only happen if there are 0 events in $[0, t]$ and 0 events in $[t, t + h]$. In terms of probabilities:

$$\mathrm{Prob}\{N(t + h) - N(0) = 0\} = \mathrm{Prob}\{N(t) - N(0) = 0\}.\ \mathrm{Prob}\{N(t + h) - N(t) = 0\}$$

However, as $N(0) = 0$:

$$\mathrm{Prob}\{N(t + h) = 0\} = P_0(t + h)$$

$$\mathrm{Prob}\{N(t) = 0\}. = P_0(t)$$

$$\mathrm{Prob}\{N(t + h) = 0\} = \mathrm{Prob}\{N(h) = 0\} = P_0(h)$$

We therefore have the equation:

$$P_0(t + h) = P_0(t).P_0(h)$$

The unique solution of this equation is well known: $P_0(t) = e^{-\lambda t}$ with $\lambda > 0$. The parameter λ is called "process intensity". We will see its practical significance later on.

For h, with h being small, the limited development of $P_0(h)$ is $P_0(h) = 1 - \lambda h + o(h)$. As in a very small interval h (according to assumption 5.3(1)) we can only have 0 or 1 event, we have:

$$P_1(h) = 1 - P_0(h) = \lambda h + o(h)$$

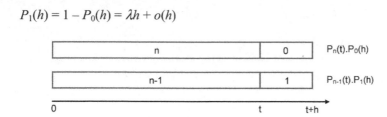

Figure 5.5. *The two possible cases*

Now consider the occurrence of n events in the interval $[0, t + h]$. Considering this interval as composed of $[0, t]$ followed by $[t, t + h]$, we can only have the two cases shown in Figure 5.5: either we have n events from 0 to t and no event from t to $t + h$, or we have $n - 1$ events from 0 to t and 1 event from t to $t + h$.

The total probability is:

$$P_n(t + h) = P_n(t).P_0(h) + P_{n-1}(t).P_1(h)$$

With the help of previous results for $P_0(h)$ and $P_1(h)$ and a small h, we obtain:

$$P_n(t + h) = P_n(t).(1 - \lambda h + o(h)) + P_{n-1}(t).(\lambda h + o(h))$$

where:

$$P_n(t + h) - P_n(t) = \lambda h[P_{n-1}(t). - P_n(t)] + o(h)$$

or:

$$\frac{P_n(t + h) - P_n(t)}{h} = \lambda[P_{n-1}(t) - P_n(t)] + \frac{o(h)}{h}$$

When $h \to 0$, the first term approaches the derivative of the function $P_n(t)$ and $o(h)/h$ approaches 0 because $o(h)$ approaches 0 "faster" than h:

$$P_n{}'(t) = \lambda[P_{n-1}(t) - P_n(t)]$$

As $e^{-\lambda t}$ is between 0 and 1, we can always write $P_n(t) = e^{-\lambda t}Q_n(t)$ by using an auxiliary function $Q_n(t)$, which leads to:

$$Q'_n(t) = \lambda Q_{n-1}(t)$$

We then successively have:

$$Q'_1(t) = \lambda Q_0(t) = \lambda \qquad \rightarrow \qquad Q_1(t) = \lambda t$$

$$Q'_2(t) = \lambda Q_1(t) = \lambda^2 t \qquad \rightarrow \qquad Q_2(t) = (\lambda t)^2/2$$

$$Q'_3(t) = \lambda Q_2(t) = \lambda^3 t^2/2 \qquad \rightarrow \qquad Q_3(t) = (\lambda t)^3/3\ !$$

etc.

By recurrence, we obtain $Q_n(t) = \dfrac{(\lambda t)^n}{n!}$ and consequently:

$$P_n(t) = e^{-\lambda t}\frac{(\lambda t)^n}{n!}$$

and we are back to the good old *Poisson distribution* ($n = 0, 1, 2,...$ and $\lambda > 0$).

We can now interpret the parameter λ. We know that the mean of the random variable following this Poisson distribution is $m = \lambda t$. So, we can deduce that λ is the *mean of the number of events per unit of time*.

We can show the Poisson process on a graph (Figure 5.6). States will be characterized by the number n. Considering that h is small, so that λh is less than 1, λh represents the transition probability from state n to state $n + 1$ (remember that $P_1(t) = \lambda h + o(h)$). The number of events can only increase and the probability of staying in the same state is $1 - \lambda h + o(h)$.

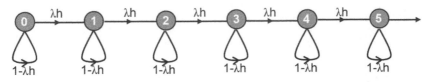

Figure 5.6. *Graph of the Poisson process*

5.3. Poisson distribution and exponential distribution

Exponential distribution is a common law of probability that has not been introduced yet.

DEFINITION.– A random variable X follows an *exponential distribution* of parameter λ when the probability density of this distribution is given by:

$f(x) = \lambda e^{-\lambda x}$ for $x \geq 0$

$f(x) = 0$ for $x < 0$

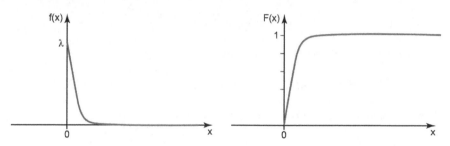

Figure 5.7. *Probability density and distribution function of exponential distribution*

The corresponding distribution function $F(x)$ is given by $\int_{-\infty}^{x} \lambda e^{-\lambda t}\, dt$, i.e.

$F(x) = 1 - e^{-\lambda x}$ for $x \geq 0$

$F(x) = 0$ for $x < 0$

The density $f(x)$ and the distribution function $F(x)$ are expressed in Figure 5.7.

The mean of the random variable x is:

$$m = \int_{-\infty}^{+\infty} \lambda x e^{-\lambda x}\, dx = \frac{1}{\lambda}$$

The variance is:

$$v = \int_{-\infty}^{+\infty} (x - m)^2 \lambda e^{-\lambda x}\, dx = \frac{1}{\lambda^2}$$

so the standard deviation is:

$$\sigma = \sqrt{v} = \frac{1}{\lambda}$$

What is the purpose of exponential distribution?

1) Exponential distribution is characteristic of "memoryless" phenomena. It is sometimes called the law of amnesia!

DEFINITION.– A random variable X is said to be *memoryless* if its probability satisfies the following condition:

$$Prob(X > t + h \mid X > t) = Prob(X > h) \ \forall t, h \geq 0$$

The previous condition can still be written:

$$Prob(X > t + h) = Prob(X > t)Prob(X > h)$$

The exponential distribution verifies this equality:

$$Prob(X > t).Prob(X > h) = \left[\int_{t}^{+\infty} \lambda e^{-\lambda x}\, dx\right]\left[\int_{h}^{+\infty} \lambda e^{-\lambda x}\right] = e^{-\lambda(t+h)}$$

Therefore:

$$Prob(X > t + h) = \int_{t+h}^{+\infty} \lambda e^{-\lambda x}\, dx = e^{-\lambda(t+h)}$$

We prove (accepted result) the opposite: a memoryless random variable follows the exponential distribution.

2) In the previous section, the parameter λ of the Poisson process was interpreted as the average rate of arrivals or births of events. Let us now look at the time interval between two consecutive events (arrivals or births).

First, in a Poisson process, if λ is the average rate of the occurrence of events, $1/\lambda$ clearly represents the average of the durations separating two consecutive events. Thus, if we have an average of 10 arrivals per second at a counter, there is an average of 0.1 seconds between two consecutive arrivals at this counter.

3) Let us go further. Let θ be the interval of time separating two consecutive events: one at date t_0 and the other at date $t_0 + \theta$. Let date $t = t_0 + h$ (subsequent to $t_0 + \theta$; see Figure 5.8).

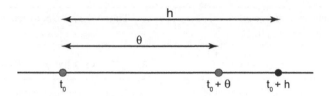

Figure 5.8. *Relationships between h, θ and t₀*

Consider the probability Prob($\theta \leq h$). If $f(t)$ is the density of the probability law of θ, we have:

$$Prob(\theta \leq h) = \int_{-\infty}^{h} f(t)dt = F(h)$$

where F is the distribution function of the probability law of θ (unknown for the moment) of density $f(t)$.

On the other hand, if $\theta \leq h$, this means that an event occurred between t_0 and $t_0 + h$, so:

$$Prob(\theta \leq h) = Prob(1 \text{ event between } t_0 \text{ and } t_0 + h)$$

$$= 1 - Prob(0 \text{ events between } t_0 \text{ and } t_0 + h)$$

$$= 1 - Prob(0 \text{ events between } 0 \text{ and } h)$$

$$= 1 - P_0(h)$$

$$= 1 - e^{-\lambda h}$$

So $F(h) = 1 - e^{-\lambda h}$.

Now $F(h)$ is the expression of the distribution function of the exponential distribution. So θ follows the exponential distribution of parameter λ.

As a result, the average interval between two consecutive events is $m = 1/\lambda$.

In conclusion, there is a connection in Table 5.1 (for the same parameter λ) between the Poisson distribution and the exponential distribution.

Occurrence of n events in the interval $[0, t]$	Time interval θ between two consecutive events
Poisson distribution $P_n(t) = e^{-\lambda t} \dfrac{(\lambda t)^n}{n!}$	Exponential distribution $P(\theta) = \lambda e^{-\lambda \theta}$
Law for a discrete random variable	Law for a continuous random variable
λ is the average rate of occurrences of events	$1/\lambda$ is the average of the inter-event times
Standard deviation: λ	Standard deviation: $1/\lambda$

Table 5.1. *Comparison between Poisson distribution and exponential distribution*

5.4. Birth process and death process

The Poisson process is a special case of a class of processes called *birth processes*. They concern the random arrival of elements. These arrivals are called births compared to the evolution of a population. We will agree, as before, that at date $t = 0$, there are no elements and therefore $N(0) = 0$.

Specifically, a birth process is a homogeneous Markov process (thus verifying the previous assumptions 5.1 and 5.2) and verifying assumption 5.3(2) similar in spirit to assumption 5.3(1), formulated for the Poisson process.

ASSUMPTION 5.3(2).– The process is a "rare events" process, since on an interval h, which is as small as we like, we can only have 0 births or 1 birth.

The probability of having 1 birth is clearly an increasing function of h (the longer the interval of time, the more likely there is to be a birth) and when h approaches 0, it assumes the form:

$$\rho_{n, n+1}(h) = \lambda_n h + o(h)$$

λ_n is characteristic of the transition $n \to n + 1$. It is called birth rate from state n. We could write it $\lambda_{n, n+1}$, but this is redundant because we can only progress in the interval h by 1 element (when h is very small). We see here that the birth process is more general than the Poisson process, which is a special case ($\lambda_0 = \lambda_1 = \dots = \lambda_n = \dots = \lambda$ in the case of the Poisson process).

As from state n we can only go to a state $n + 1$ or stay in state n, we essentially have $\rho_{n, n+1}(h) + \rho_{n, n}(h) = 1$, hence:

$$\rho_{n, n}(h) = 1 - \lambda_n h + o(h)$$

The process can be represented symbolically by the graph in Figure 5.9 with the transition probabilities for an infinitesimal time interval h.

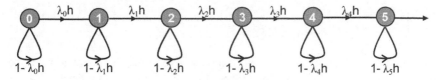

Figure 5.9. *Birth process*

Let $P_n(t)$ be the probability of having n elements at time t.

$$P_n(t) = \text{Prob}(N(t) - N(0) = n) = \text{Prob}(N(t) = n) \text{ as } N(0) = 0$$

Suppose that at time $t + h$ (h is very small), we have n elements. This means that:

– either there were n elements at time t and there were no births;

– or there were $n - 1$ elements at time t and there was 1 birth.

So, by applying the compound probabilities for $n > 0$:

$$P_n(t + h) = P_n(t)\rho_{n,\,n}(h) + P_{n-1}(t)\rho_{n-1,\,n}(h) = P_n(t)(1 - \lambda_n h) + P_{n-1}(t)\lambda_{n-1}h + o(h)$$

or:

$$\frac{P_n(t+h) - P_n(t)}{h} = \lambda_{n-1}P_{n-1}(t) - \lambda_n P_n(t)$$

and going to the limit $h \to 0$, the first member becomes the derivative of $P_n(t)$:

$$P'_n(t) = \lambda_{n-1}P_{n-1}(t) - \lambda_n P_n(t)$$

For the special case $n = 0$, we have:

$$P_0(t + h) = P_0(t)(1 - \lambda_0 h)$$

hence:

$$P'_0(t) = - \lambda_0 P_0(t)$$

Ultimately, the following differential system characterizes the evolution of the birth process:

$$\begin{cases} P'_n(t) = \lambda_{n-1}P_{n-1}(t) - \lambda_n P_n(t) \\ \quad\quad P'_0(t) = -\lambda_0 P_0(t) \end{cases}$$

The number of elements can only increase over time. So there is no hope of getting a limit (unless you force the process to stop for a given number).

The opposite process is a *death process*: the number of elements will decrease randomly over time to become zero. So here we have a very clear limit: 0.

However, the process of death is treated analogously to the birth process (it follows the same assumptions 5.1(2), 5.2(2) and 5.3(2) – replacing birth by death in the latter assumption).

It can be represented by the symbolic graph in Figure 5.10.

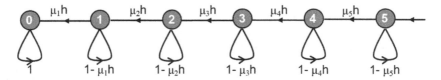

Figure 5.10. *Death process*

The parameters μ_i represent the mortality rates.

The differential system for a death process, obtained by a calculation analogous to that of the birth process, is:

$$\begin{cases} P'_n(t) = \mu_{n+1}P_{n+1}(t) - \mu_n P_n(t) \\ \quad\quad P'_0(t) = \mu_1 P_1(t) \end{cases}$$

5.5. Combination of the two processes, birth and death

We will now combine two homogeneous Markov processes: a birth process disturbed by a death process. The action of these two processes can be represented by the graph in Figure 5.11.

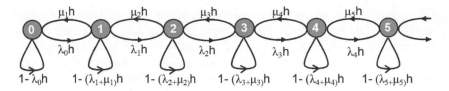

Figure 5.11. *Birth and death processes*

The parameters λ_i are the birth rates and the parameters μ_i are the mortality rates, i.e. the average number of births and deaths per unit of time.

Between time t and time $t + h$ (where h is very small), what are the possibilities of evolution? There are three as follows:

– n elements at t and 0 between t and $t + h$;

– $n + 1$ elements at t and 1 death between t and $t + h$;

– $n - 1$ elements at t and 1 birth between t and $t + h$.

As a result, the probability of having n elements at $t + h$ is, for $n > 0$:

$$P_n(t + h) = P_n(t).\rho_{n,\,n}(h) + P_{n+1}(t).\,\rho_{n+1,\,n}(h) + P_{n-1}(t).\,\rho_{n-1,\,n}(h)$$

$$= P_n(t)(1 - \lambda_n - \mu_n)h + P_{n+1}(t)\mu_{n+1}h + P_{n-1}(t).\lambda_{n-1}h + o(h)$$

We can deduce:

$$\frac{P_n(t + h) - P_n(t)}{h} = \lambda_{n-1}P_{n-1}(t) - (\lambda_n + \mu_n)P_n(t) + \mu_{n+1}P_{n+1}(t)$$

and going to the limit $h \to 0$, the first member becomes the derivative:

$$P'_n(t) = \lambda_{n-1}P_{n-1}(t) - (\lambda_n + \mu_n)P_n(t) + \mu_{n+1}P_{n+1}(t) \qquad [5.1]$$

For $n = 0$, in a similar way, we obtain:

$$P'_0(t) = -\lambda_0 P_0(t) + \mu_1 P_1(t) \qquad [5.2]$$

Over time, the system can evolve in a variety of ways. In particular, it can lead to an indefinitely increasing population or a continuously decreasing number of people. What interests us is when the system is in equilibrium, what we call the "*steady*" or *permanent state*. In this case (the word "steady" is telling), the probabilities $P_n(t)$ no longer depend on time. The equations [5.1] and [5.2] thus become ($P_n(t) = P_n$):

$$\lambda_{n-1}P_{n-1} - (\lambda_n + \mu_n)P_n + \mu_{n+1}P_{n+1} = 0 \qquad [5.3]$$

$$-\lambda_0 P_0 + \mu_1 P_1 = 0 \qquad [5.4]$$

[5.4] is used to obtain P_1:

$$P_1 = \frac{\lambda_0}{\mu_1}P_0$$

By recurrence, we have, using [5.3]:

$$P_2 = \frac{\lambda_0 \lambda_1}{\mu_1 \mu_2}P_0$$

and so on:

$$P_n = \frac{\lambda_0 \lambda_1 \cdots \lambda_{n-1}}{\mu_1 \mu_2 \cdots \mu_n}P_0$$

We still need to determine P_0, which can be done by using the sum of all the probabilities, which must be equal to 1:

$$\sum_i P_i = 1 \quad \Rightarrow \quad 1 + \frac{\lambda_0}{\mu_1} + \frac{\lambda_0 \lambda_1}{\mu_1 \mu_2} + \cdots = \frac{1}{P_0}$$

which is:

$$P_0 = \frac{1}{1 + \dfrac{\lambda_0}{\mu_1} + \dfrac{\lambda_0 \lambda_1}{\mu_1 \mu_2} + \cdots}$$

The problem of the steady state is thus solved. Let us move on to a few special cases.

The number of states is finite $n_{max} = N$.

We have in this case very simply:

$$P_n = \frac{\lambda_0 \lambda_1 \ldots \lambda_{n-1}}{\mu_1 \mu_2 \ldots \mu_n} P_0$$

$$P_0 = \frac{1}{1 + \dfrac{\lambda_0}{\mu_1} + \dfrac{\lambda_0 \lambda_1}{\mu_1 \mu_2} + \ldots \dfrac{\lambda_0 \lambda_1 \ldots \lambda_{N-1}}{\mu_1 \mu_2 \ldots \mu_N}}$$

If, in addition, $\lambda_i = \lambda$ and $\mu_i = \mu \ \forall i$, then:

$$P_0 = \frac{1 - \dfrac{\lambda}{\mu}}{1 - (\dfrac{\lambda}{\mu})^{N+1}}$$

and if $\lambda = \mu$:

$$P_0 = \frac{1}{N + 1}$$

The number of states is infinite. For there to be equilibrium, the series $\sum_i P_i$ must converge towards 1. The d'Alembert criterion guarantees it if $\dfrac{P_n}{P_{n-1}} < 1$, i.e. $\dfrac{\lambda_{n-1}}{\mu_n} <$ 1. If this condition is not fulfilled, there will be a continuous increase and we will leave the steady state.

The birth and death rates are constant:

$$\lambda_i = \lambda \text{ and } \mu_i = \mu \ \forall i$$

By putting $\Psi = \dfrac{\lambda}{\mu}$, we obtain:

$$P_n = \Psi^n P_0 \quad \text{and} \quad P_0 = \frac{1}{1 + \Psi + \Psi^2 + \cdots}$$

and $\quad P_0 = \frac{1}{1 + \Psi + \Psi^2 + \cdots}$

For a "closed" process: the maximum value of n is N:

$$P_0 = \frac{1 - \Psi}{1 - \Psi^{N+1}}$$

$$P_n = \Psi^n \frac{1 - \Psi}{1 - \Psi^{N+1}}$$

For an open process (no limit on n), provided that $\Psi = \frac{\lambda}{\mu} < 1$:

$$P_0 = 1 - \Psi$$

$$P_n = \Psi^n (1 - \Psi)$$

Queueing Systems

CONCEPTS DISCUSSED IN THIS CHAPTER.– This chapter directly applies a lot of what was covered in the previous chapter, especially the Poisson process.

After some definitions relating to queueing systems, we study the M/M/1 queue.

We then look at the more complex M/M/S queue.

The lengthy calculations are given in the appendix.

Recommended reading: [FAU 79, PHE 77, RUE 89].

6.1. Introduction

The phenomenon of queueing is common: waiting at a counter, the build-up of traffic jams and congestion, etc. To control these phenomena, we need to model them.

A *queueing system* is composed of *queues* and several *stations*. In what follows, we will only consider the case of a single queue. Figure 6.1 shows a queueing system with a single queue and a single station.

Individuals (as the elements are often called by analogy with a human queue) arrive in the queue from a *source* that can be infinite (*open* systems) or finite (*closed* systems). They advance in the queue following a particular *priority*, then are "served" individually at a station. They then leave the system.

All figures and tables are available in color online at www.iste.co.uk/cochard/stochastic.zip.

queueing system

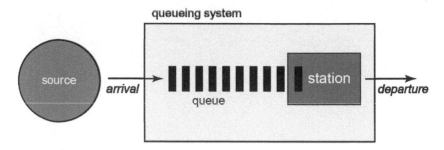

Figure 6.1. *Queueing system*

Two important parameters, usually stochastic, determine the behavior of the system over time:

- the frequency of arrival of individuals;

- the duration of service at the station.

Historically, the phenomenon of queueing has been studied since the beginning of the 20th Century, often during the implementation of telecommunication systems (Erlang's work on telephone exchanges). Numerous mathematicians have contributed to this problem: Engset, Borel, Khintchine, Pollarczek, Feller, etc.

Figure 6.2. *Agner Krarup Erlang (1878–1929), a Danish mathematician and statistician, studied queues as part of setting up telephone networks. He relied on Poisson's work to model data transmission networks and, as part of this, queues. He left his name to the unit of measurement of telephone traffic*[1]

---

1 The photograph of A.K. Erlang is from: https://en.wikipedia.org/wiki/Agner_Krarup_Erlang.

Kendall's notation is often used to describe the type of queueing system. Indeed, there are several categories of queueing systems. They are noted with six indicators: $a/s/C/K/m/Z$, where:

– a indicates the law of probability of the arrival times, i.e. the time which separates two consecutive arrivals. For the exponential distribution, $a = M$;

– s indicates the law of probability of service times. For the exponential distribution, $s = M$;

– C indicates the number of service stations: 1 to S;

– K indicates the *capacity* of the queueing system, which is the sum of the number of stations and the number of elements in the queue. By default $K = \infty$;

– m measures the population to *serve*. By default $m = \infty$;

– Z indicates the priority of the elements in the queue: FIFO (*first in, first out*) is the default; LIFO (*last in, first out*) and NN (*nearest neighbor*) are other priority systems.

Thus, M/M/1 indicates a queueing system in which the arrival and departure laws are the exponential distribution and where there is only one station. M/M/S indicates a system with exponential probability laws and S stations.

In what follows, we will consider only simple problems M/M/1 and M/M/S which means:

– it is about open systems, the capacity and the population concerned being considered as infinite. Note that closed systems lead to significant mathematical complexities;

– the priority rule is FIFO: the elements are placed in the queue in the order of their arrival.

We will consider a mathematical modeling of the M/M/1 and M/M/S queues. For this, we will apply the results obtained in Chapter 5.

Indeed, exponential distribution is taken as the probability law of the moments separating two consecutive arrivals. It is therefore a Poisson process.

In the same way, exponential distribution governs the service durations: departures from the stations also correspond to a Poisson process.

These two processes are concurrent; we thus recall the birth and death processes.

6.2. M/M/1 queue with 1 station

We put ourselves in the situation shown in Figures 6.2 or 6.3 which describe the same situation. One must beware of the fact that λ and μ express themselves in quantities relative to a time, while their opposites are times.

We must also keep the same unit of time throughout the whole context of the problem. We can choose seconds, minutes, hours, years and so on to handle reasonable numbers.

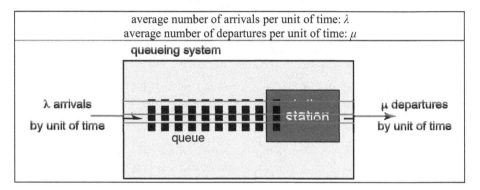

Figure 6.3. *Diagram with λ and μ*

Or in the same way:

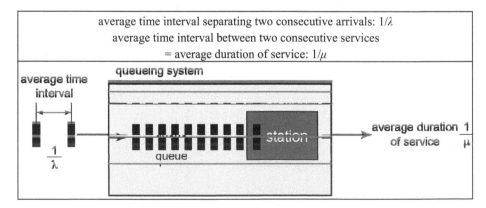

Figure 6.4. *Diagram with $1/\lambda$ and $1/\mu$*

The evolution of the queueing system can be represented with the graph in Figure 6.5.

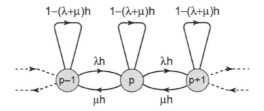

Figure 6.5. *Queueing system graph*

h is as small as we like, λh and μh respectively represent the transition probabilities from one state to the next or to the previous one. The states are defined by the number of elements in the queue.

The results obtained in the previous chapter in the section on birth and death processes apply directly: the probability that in a stationary state the queueing system comprises n elements is:

$$P_n = \Psi^n (1 - \Psi) \text{ with } \Psi = \frac{\lambda}{\mu}$$

Note that this result was obtained with the constraint $\lambda < \mu$, i.e. $\Psi < 1$. If λ is greater than μ, the previous result is no longer valid and corresponds to an indefinite extension of the queue, which is normal since the average arrival rate would be higher than the average departure rate.

From the previous result, we can draw some conclusions using Little's formula.

Let us find the average number of elements in the queueing system. By definition of the average, we have:

$$n_S = \sum_{n=0}^{\infty} n p_n = (1 - \Psi) \sum_{n=0}^{\infty} n \Psi^n = (1 - \Psi)[\Psi + 2\Psi^2 + 3\Psi^3 + \cdots]$$

$$= (1 - \Psi)\Psi[1 + 2\Psi + 3\Psi^2 + \cdots] = (1 - \Psi)\Psi \frac{d}{d\Psi}[\Psi + \Psi^2 + \Psi^3 + \cdots]$$

And (see the appendix at the end of the chapter):

$$1 + \Psi + \Psi^2 + \Psi^3 + \cdots = \frac{1}{1 - \Psi} \qquad (\Psi < 1)$$

hence:

$$\Psi + \Psi^2 + \Psi^3 + \cdots = \frac{\Psi}{1 - \Psi}$$

We can deduce:

$$n_S = (1 - \Psi)\Psi \frac{1}{(1 - \Psi)^2} = \frac{\Psi}{1 - \Psi}$$

If an element arrives at the system, it must wait for all elements to be served. Since there are on average n_s elements in the system and the average service time is $1/\mu$, it must wait in the queue for time $n_s.(1/\mu)$, hence the average waiting time in the queue:

$$t_f = \frac{n_S}{\mu} = \frac{\Psi}{(1 - \Psi)\mu} = \frac{\lambda}{(\mu - \lambda)\mu} = \frac{\Psi}{\mu - \lambda}$$

From the previous result, we can obtain the average time spent in the system. It is the sum of the average waiting time in the queue and the average service time: $t_s = t_f + 1/\mu$, that is:

$$t_S = t_f + \frac{1}{\mu} = \frac{1}{\mu(1 - \Psi)} = \frac{1}{\mu - \lambda}$$

Only the average number of elements in the queue remains to be evaluated. If there are n elements in the system, there are $n - 1$ elements in the queue. So just calculate the average of $n - 1$:

$$n_f = \sum_{n=2}^{\infty} (n - 1)p_n = (1 - \Psi) \sum_{n=2}^{\infty} (n - 1)\Psi^n$$

$$= (1 - \Psi)[\Psi^2 + 2\Psi^3 + 3\Psi^4 + \cdots] = (1 - \Psi)\Psi^2[1 + 2\Psi + 3\Psi^2 \ldots]$$

And (see the appendix at the end of the chapter):

$$[1 + 2\Psi + 3\Psi^2 + \cdots] = \frac{d}{d\Psi}[\Psi + \Psi^2 + \Psi^3 + \cdots] = \frac{d}{d\Psi}\left[\frac{1}{1-\Psi}\right]$$

$$= \frac{1}{(1-\Psi)^2}$$

We can deduce:

$$n_f = \frac{\Psi^2}{1-\Psi} = \frac{\lambda^2}{\mu(\mu-\lambda)}$$

Ultimately, the following results were obtained:

– average number of elements in the queue: $n_f = \frac{\Psi^2}{1-\Psi}$;

– average number of elements in the queueing system: $n_S = \frac{\Psi}{1-\Psi}$;

– average time spent in the queue: $t_f = \frac{\Psi}{\mu-\lambda}$;

– time spent in the queueing system: $t_S = \frac{1}{\mu-\lambda}$.

Note that $n_s = \lambda t_s$ and $n_f = \lambda t_f$. These much more general results are called "Little's laws".

EXAMPLE 6.1.– A local bank branch has a single counter. A statistical study shows there is an average of 54 customers per day for a daily opening of 6 hours. The average service time is 5 minutes per customer. It is assumed that the arrival and departure processes are Poisson processes.

1) Determine the parameters λ and μ.

The arrival rate is $\lambda = 54/6 = 9$ customers per hour, i.e. $\lambda = 0.15$ arrivals per minute.

The departure rate is $\mu = 1/5 = 0.2$ departures per minute.

$\Psi = 0.15/0.2 = 0.75$

2) Determine the values n_f, n_s, t_f, t_s.

$n_f = \Psi^2/(1-\Psi) = 2.25$ customers

$ns = \Psi/(1-\Psi) = 3$ customers

$tf = \Psi/(\mu - \lambda) = 15$ minutes

$ts = 1/(\mu - \lambda) = 20$ minutes

Note that $t_s - t_f = 5$ minutes, the average service time.

3) In summer, the number of customers increases and doubles: 108 customers during the day.

The new parameter λ is $\lambda = 0.30$ and $\Psi = 3/2 > 1$. The preceding formulas no longer apply. The queue will increase continuously (until the branch closes: not all customers will be served). There should be other counters.

This case is discussed in section 6.3.

6.3. M/M/S queue with S stations

We now consider the case where there is only one queue, but there are S stations ($S > 1$), which are identical in terms of service duration (Figure 6.6).

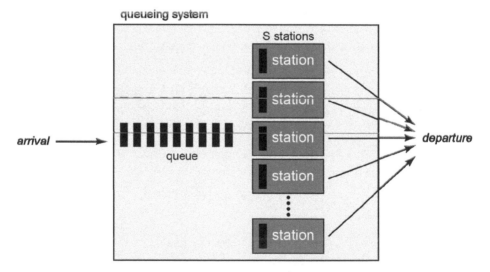

Figure 6.6. *Queueing system with S stations and one queue*

Using the previous notations: λ (average number of arrivals per time unit), μ (average number of services per time unit and per station) and $\Psi = \lambda/\mu$, n (number of individuals in the system at time t), there are three cases to consider (Table 6.1).

$n = 0$	$1 \leq n < S$ (no queue)	$n \geq S$ (queue)
No station is busy: no queue	n stations of S are busy: no queue	All S stations are busy: queue

Table 6.1. *Three possible cases*

Clearly, the condition for not having congestion is $\lambda < S\mu$, i.e. $\Psi/S < 1$.

Repeat the reasoning of the birth and death processes in the previous section before using the stationary assumption.

– **Case $n = 0$.**

At time $t + h$, there are 0 elements in the system. This can come from two states preceding the time t:

- 1 element at time t (essentially at one station) and 1 departure between t and $t + h$: probability $P_1(t).\mu h$;

- 0 elements at time t and 0 arrivals, 0 departures between t and $t + h$: probability $P_0(t)(1 - \lambda h - \mu h)$.

Therefore, $P_0(t + h) = P_1(t).\mu h + P_0(t)(1 - \lambda h - \mu h)$, hence $P_0(t + h) - P_0(t) = \mu h P_1(t) - \lambda h P_0(t)$ and so $P'_0(t) = \mu P_1(t) - \lambda P_0(t)$.

In a stationary state, $P'_0(t) = 0$ and $\lambda P_0 = \mu P_1$ or $P_1 = \Psi P_0$.

– **Case $1 \leq n < S$.**

At time $t + h$, there are n elements in the system, essentially all at n stations. This can come from the three states preceding the time t:

- $n - 1$ elements at time t (all at $n - 1$ stations) and 1 arrival between t and $t + h$: probability $P_{n-1}(t).\lambda h$;

- $n + 1$ elements at time t (all at $n + 1$ stations) and 1 departure between t and $t + h$: probability $P_{n+1}(t)(n + 1)\mu h$;

- n elements at time t (all at n stations) and 0 arrivals, 0 departures between t and $t + h$: probability $P_n(t)(1 - \lambda h - n\mu h)$.

So:

$$P_n(t + h) = P_{n-1}(t)\lambda h + P_{n+1}(t)(n + 1)\mu h + P_n(t)(1 - \lambda h - n\mu h)$$

hence:

$$P_n(t + h) - P_n(t) = P_{n-1}(t)\lambda h + P_{n+1}(t)(n + 1)\mu h - P_n(t)(\lambda + n\mu)h$$

or:

$$P'_n(t) = \lambda P_{n-1}(t) - (\lambda + n\mu)P_n(t) + (n + 1)\mu P_{n+1}(t)$$

In a stationary state: $0 = \lambda P_{n-1} - (\lambda + n\mu)P_n + (n + 1)\mu P_{n+1}$.

This equation allows us to find P_n by recurrence:

$$P_n = \frac{\psi^n}{n!} P_0$$

By taking $n = S$, we also obtain the P_S expression:

$$P_S = \frac{\psi^S}{S!} P_0$$

– Case $n \geq S$.

At time $t + h$, there are n elements in the system (at stations or in the queue). This can come from the following three cases:

   - $n - 1$ elements at time t and 1 arrival between t and $t + h$: probability $P_{n-1}(t)\lambda h$;

   - $n + 1$ elements at time t and 1 departure between t and $t + h$: probability $P_{n+1}(t)S\mu h$;

   - n elements at time t and 0 arrivals, 0 departures between t and $t + h$: probability $P_n(t)(1 - \lambda h - S\mu h)$.

So:

$$P_n(t + h) = P_{n-1}(t)\lambda h + P_{n+1}(t)S\mu h + P_n(t)(1 - \lambda h - S\mu h)$$

hence:

$$P_n(t + h) - P_n(t) = P_{n-1}(t)\lambda h + P_{n+1}(t)S\mu h - P_n(t)(\lambda + S\mu)h$$

or:

$$P'_n(t) = \lambda P_{n-1}(t) - (\lambda + S\mu)P_n(t) + S\mu P_{n+1}(t)$$

In a stationary state: $0 = \lambda P_{n-1} - (\lambda + S\mu)P_n + S\mu P_{n+1}$.

The resolution is also made by recurrence. By taking $n = S$, we obtain P_{S+1} as a function of P_S and P_{S-1} obtained previously, then with $n = S + 1$, we will have P_{S+2} as a function of P_{S+1} and P_S and so on. We obtain the following result:

$$P_n = \frac{\psi^n}{S^{n-S}S!} P_0$$

Finally, all the P_n probabilities are expressed as a function of P_0. To determine P_0, it is sufficient to write that the sum of the P_n probabilities is equal to 1, which leads to (see the appendix at the end of the chapter for the calculation):

$$P_0 = \frac{1}{\sum_{n=0}^{S-1} \frac{\psi^n}{n!} + \frac{\psi^S}{S!\left(1 - \frac{\psi}{S}\right)}}$$

From this result, we deduce the following properties (see the appendix at the end of the chapter for the calculations):

– average number of elements in the queue: $n_f = \dfrac{\psi^{S+1}}{S.S!\left(1-\frac{\psi}{S}\right)^2} P_0$;

– average number of elements in the system: $n_s = n_f + \Psi$;

– average queueing time in the queue: $t_f = \dfrac{\psi^S}{S.S!\mu(1-\frac{\psi}{S})^2} P_0$;

– average queueing time in the system: $t_s = \dfrac{n_s}{\lambda}$;

– average number of unoccupied stations: $n_i = S - \Psi$.

EXAMPLE 6.2 (based on R. Faure [FAU 79]).– In a car repair garage, there is a counter from which spare parts are given to the workers. The boss wants to know, for the sake of economic optimization, if there should be one or more counters (and therefore, in this case, several servers). Currently, there is only one counter and one server. He or she analyzes the phenomenon by performing statistics.

Law of arrivals: over 100 5-minute intervals, the boss counts the number of workers arriving at each interval (Table 6.2).

Number of workers	0	1	2	3	N
Number of intervals	36	38	18	8	100
Frequency	0.36	0.38	0.18	0.08	
Poisson distribution	0.37	0.37	0.18	0.06	

Table 6.2. *Law of arrivals*

The average number of workers per interval is 0.98, rounded to 1, which means that there is an average of $\lambda = 0.2$ arrivals per minute. Poisson distribution with parameter 5λ is shown on the bottom line of the table. There is a certain similarity, hence the intention to assimilate the law of probability of arrivals to that of Poisson. To be sure, we apply the χ^2 test. The method will be explained in Chapter 8 and confirm the assumption of the Poisson distribution, so for now let us accept this result.

Law of service duration: 100 observations are made on service duration; the result of these observations is shown in Table 6.3. The average service duration is $1/\mu = 2.9$ minutes, rounded to 3 minutes. There is a similarity with the exponential distribution of parameter $\mu = 1/3$.

Service duration	[0,1[	[1,2[	[2,3[	[3,4[	[4,5[	[5,6[	[6,7[	[7,8[	[8,9[	[9,10[	[10,11[	[11,12[
Number of occurrences	26	20	15	12	8	6	6	3	2	1	1	0
Frequency	0.26	0.20	0.15	0.12	0.08	0.06	0.06	0.03	0.02	0.01	0.01	0.00
Exponential distribution	0.283	0.203	0.146	0.104	0.075	0.054	0.038	0.027	0.020	0.014	0.010	0.070

Table 6.3. *Law of services*

To be sure of "assimilating" the law of service duration with exponential distribution, we use the χ^2 test (see Chapter 8). We will accept, for the moment, that this assumption is verified and therefore that the law of service duration is an exponential distribution (or that the number of services per minute follows a Poisson distribution).

In short, the results of the M/M/1 and M/M/S queues can be applied.

ASSUMPTION 6.1.– One counter to provide spare parts.

$\Psi = \lambda/\mu = 0.6$. The formulas for a single-station queue result in the following results.

The number of workers in the system is $n_s = \Psi/(1 - \Psi) = 1.5$. The average queueing time in the queue is $t_f = n_s/\mu = 4.5$ minutes.

The time lost by the workers is: 8 h/day x 0.2 worker/min x t_f = 7.2 h.

The effective activity time of the server of spare parts is 8 h/day. 0.2 workers/min. $(1/\mu)$ = 4.8 h.

Let us say that a worker's inactivity is estimated at €20 /h and a server's inactivity at €10 /h (including hourly wages).

Under this assumption, the daily cost of inactivity is: $C_A = 7.2 \times 20 + (8 - 4.8) \times 10 = €176$.

ASSUMPTION 6.2.– Two counters (so two servers).

The relations of the M/M/S queue give: $p_0 = 0.539$, t_f = 0.3 min.

The calculation for the expense C_B is based on the previous estimations.

Total time lost by workers over a day: (8 h) $\times$ (0.2 workers/min) $\times t_f$ = 0.48 h.

Activity time of servers: (8 h) $\times$ (0.2 workers/min) $\times 1/\mu$ = 4.8 h.

Inactivity time of servers: (16 h – 4.8 h) = 11.2 h.

The daily cost of inactivity is: $C_B = 0.48 \times 20 + 11.2 \times 10 = €121.6$.

ASSUMPTION 6.3.– Three counters (so three servers).

$P_0 = 0.548$, t_f = 0.057 min

Total time lost by workers over a day: (8 h) $\times$ (0.2 workers/min) $\times t_f$ = 0.09 h.

Total activity time of servers over a day: 4.8 h (as previously, because there are as many workers to serve).

Total time lost by servers: 24 – 4.8 = 19.2 h.

The daily cost of inactivity is: $C_C = 0.09 \times 20 + 19.2 \times 10 = €193.80$.

The conclusion, under the previous assumptions, is that the use of two servers providing spare parts is optimal (in terms of cost!).

6.4. Appendix: calculations for M/M/S

To start, let us note the following results are valid when $|x| < 1$:

$$\sum_{n=0}^{\infty} x^n = 1 + x + x^2 + x^3 + \cdots . = \frac{1}{1-x}$$

$$\sum_{n=0}^{\infty} (n+1)x^n = 1 + 2x + 3x^2 + \cdots = \frac{1}{(1-x)^2}$$

and for every x:

$$\sum_{n=0}^{N} x^n = \frac{1 - x^{N+1}}{1-x}$$

6.4.1. *Calculation of P_0*

The P_n sum of the probabilities is 1:

$$\sum_{n=0}^{\infty} P_n = 1$$

with:

$$\begin{cases} P_n = \dfrac{\psi^n}{n!} P_0 & for\ 1 \leq n < S \\ P_n = \dfrac{\psi^n}{S!\ S^{n-S}} P_0 & for\ n \geq S \end{cases}$$

The condition for not having congestion is $\frac{\psi}{S} < 1$. So we have:

$$1 = P_0 + \sum_{n=1}^{S-1} P_n + \sum_{n=S}^{\infty} P_n = \sum_{n=0}^{S-1} P_n + \sum_{n=S}^{\infty} P_n = P_0 \sum_{n=0}^{S-1} \frac{\psi^n}{n!} + P_0 \sum_{n=S}^{\infty} \frac{\psi^n}{S!\ S^{n-S}}$$

But:

$$\sum_{n=S}^{\infty} \left(\frac{\Psi}{S}\right)^n = \sum_{n=0}^{\infty} \left(\frac{\Psi}{S}\right)^n - \sum_{n=0}^{S-1} \left(\frac{\Psi}{S}\right)^n = \frac{1}{1-\frac{\Psi}{S}} - \frac{1-\left(\frac{\Psi}{S}\right)^S}{1-\frac{\Psi}{S}} = \frac{\left(\frac{\Psi}{S}\right)^S}{1-\frac{\Psi}{S}}$$

So:

$$1 = P_0 \left[\sum_{n=0}^{S-1} \frac{\Psi^n}{n!} + \frac{\Psi^S}{S!\left(1-\frac{\Psi}{S}\right)} \right] \quad and \quad P_0 = \frac{1}{\sum_{n=0}^{S-1} \frac{\Psi^n}{n!} + \frac{\Psi^S}{S!\left(1-\frac{\Psi}{S}\right)}}$$

6.4.2. *Calculation of n_s*

The average number of elements in the queueing system is:

$$n_s = \sum_{n=0}^{\infty} nP_n = \sum_{n=1}^{S-1} nP_n + \sum_{n=S}^{\infty} nP_n = P_0 \sum_{n=1}^{S-1} \frac{n\Psi^n}{n!} + P_0 \frac{S^S}{S!} \sum_{n=S}^{\infty} \frac{n\Psi^n}{S^n}$$

$$= P_0 X + P_0 \frac{S^S}{S!} Y$$

$$X = \sum_{n=1}^{S-1} \frac{n\Psi^n}{n!} = \Psi + \Psi^2 + \frac{\Psi^3}{2!} + \frac{\Psi^4}{3!} + \cdots + \frac{\Psi^{S-1}}{(S-2)!}$$

$$= \Psi \left[1 + \Psi + \frac{\Psi^2}{2!} + \cdots + \frac{\Psi^{S-2}}{(S-2)!} + \frac{\Psi^{S-1}}{(S-1)!} - \frac{\Psi^{S-1}}{(S-1)!} \right]$$

$$= \Psi \left[\sum_{n=0}^{S-1} \frac{\Psi^n}{n!} - \frac{\Psi^{S-1}}{(S-1)!} \right]$$

And by using the relationship that gives P_0:

$$X = \Psi \left[\frac{1}{P_0} - \frac{\Psi^S}{S!\left(1-\frac{\Psi}{S}\right)} - \frac{\Psi^{S-1}}{(S-1)!} \right] = \Psi \left[\frac{1}{P_0} - \frac{\Psi^{S-1}}{(s-1)!\left(1-\frac{\Psi}{S}\right)} \right]$$

$$Y = \sum_{n=S}^{\infty} \frac{n\psi^n}{S^n} = S\frac{\psi^S}{S^S} + (S+1)\frac{\psi^{S+1}}{S^{S+1}} + (S+2)\frac{\psi^{S+2}}{S^{S+2}} + \cdots$$

$$= \frac{\psi^S}{S^S}\left[S + (S+1)\frac{\psi}{S} + (S+2)\frac{\psi^2}{S^2} + \cdots\right]$$

$$= \frac{\psi^S}{S^S}\left[S\left(1 + \frac{\psi}{S} + \frac{\psi^2}{S^2} + \cdots\right) + \frac{\psi}{S}\left(1 + 2\frac{\psi}{S} + 3\frac{\psi^2}{S^2} + \cdots\right)\right]$$

$$= \frac{\psi^S}{S^S}\left[\frac{S}{1 - \frac{\psi}{S}} + \frac{\frac{\psi}{S}}{\left(1 - \frac{\psi}{S}\right)^2}\right] = \frac{\psi^S}{S^S\left(1 - \frac{\psi}{S}\right)^2}\left(S - \psi + \frac{\psi}{S}\right)$$

So:

$$n_s = \psi - P_0\frac{\psi^S}{(S-1)!\left(1 - \frac{\psi}{S}\right)} + P_0\frac{\psi^S}{S!\left(1 - \frac{\psi}{S}\right)^2}\left(S - \psi + \frac{\psi}{S}\right)$$

$$= \psi + P_0\frac{\psi^{S+1}}{S.S!\left(1 - \frac{\psi}{S}\right)^2}$$

6.4.3. Calculation of n_f

For there to be elements in the queue, it is necessary that $n > S$. S elements are at stations, $n - S$ remains in the queue. So we have, on average:

$$n_f = \sum_{n=S+1}^{\infty}(n-S)P_n = \sum_{n=S+1}^{\infty}nP_n - S\sum_{n=S+1}^{\infty}P_n$$

$$= P_0\frac{S^S}{S!}\sum_{n=S+1}^{\infty}\frac{n\psi^n}{S^n} - P_0\frac{S^{S+1}}{S!}\sum_{n=S+1}^{\infty}\left(\frac{\psi}{S}\right)^n$$

$$= P_0\frac{S^S}{S!}\left(Y - \frac{S\psi^S}{S^S}\right) - P_0\frac{\psi^{S+1}}{S!}\sum_{n=0}^{\infty}\left(\frac{\psi}{S}\right)^n$$

$$= P_0\frac{S^S}{S!}\left(Y - \frac{S\psi^S}{S^S}\right) - P_0\frac{\psi^{S+1}}{S!\left(1 - \frac{\psi}{S}\right)}$$

$$= P_0\frac{\psi^S}{S!\left(1 - \frac{\psi}{S}\right)^2}\left[S - \psi + \frac{\psi}{S}\right] - P_0\frac{S\psi^S}{S!} - P_0\frac{\psi^{S+1}}{S!\left(1 - \frac{\psi}{S}\right)}$$

$$= P_0\frac{\psi^{S+1}}{S.S!\left(1 - \frac{\psi}{S}\right)^2}$$

We note that $n_s = \psi + n_f$.

6.4.4. *Calculation of t_s and t_f*

Little's formula is applied:

$t_f = n_f/\lambda$ et $t_s = n_s/\lambda = t_f + 1/\mu$

So we have:

$$t_f = P_0 \frac{\psi^S}{S\mu . S! \left(1 - \frac{\psi}{S}\right)^2}$$

$$t_s = \frac{1}{\mu} + p_0 \frac{\psi^S}{S\mu . S! \left(1 - \frac{\psi}{S}\right)^2}$$

6.4.5. *Calculation of n_i*

There are unoccupied stations if $n < S$. Their number is $S - n$. So:

$$n_i = \sum_{n=0}^{S}(S - n)P_n = P_0 S \sum_{n=0}^{S} \frac{\psi^n}{n!} - P_0 \sum_{n=0}^{S} \frac{n\psi^n}{n!}$$

$$\sum_{n=0}^{S} \frac{\psi^n}{n!} = \sum_{n=0}^{S-1} \frac{\psi^n}{n!} + \frac{\psi^S}{S!} = Z + \frac{\psi^S}{S!}$$

$$\sum_{n=0}^{S} \frac{n\psi^n}{n!} = \sum_{n=1}^{S} \frac{\psi^n}{(n-1)!} = \Psi \sum_{n=0}^{S-1} \frac{\psi^n}{n!} = \Psi Z$$

So:

$$n_i = P_0 S \left(Z + \frac{\psi^S}{S!}\right) - P_0 \Psi Z = P_0(S - \Psi)Z + P_0 \frac{\psi^S}{(S - 1)!}$$

Z is replaced by its expression taken from that of P_0:

$$Z = \frac{1}{P_0} - \frac{\psi^S}{S!\left(1 - \frac{\psi}{S}\right)} = \frac{1}{P_0} - \frac{\psi^S}{(S-1)!\,(S-\psi)}$$

hence:

$$n_i = P_0(S - \psi)\left[\frac{1}{P_0} - \frac{\psi^S}{(S-1)!\,(S-\psi)}\right] + P_0\frac{\psi^S}{(S-1)!} = S - \psi$$

Various Applications

CONCEPTS DISCUSSED IN THIS CHAPTER.– This section discusses various applications of random processes.

First, we look at a classic application: reliability and availability of equipment.

Then, we focus on the large research field of genetics.

This is followed by population dynamics, with the predator–prey model.

Finally, the chapter analyzes Brownian motion, which takes us from physics to finance.

Recommended reading: [DUP 05, FAU 14, LEB 12, LES 14, PEL 97, RUE 89].

7.1. Reliability and availability of equipment

7.1.1. *Reliability and instantaneous failure rate*

In many processes, a technical device is expected to perform a required operation for a given time period. This quality is called "reliability". Knowing that the device operates at time $t = 0$, the *reliability* $R(t)$ is the probability that it still operates at a later time t. The operating time T of the device is a random variable, because generally we cannot predict failures that may occur. T is a continuous variable that takes positive values. Therefore, we put:

$$R(t) = \mathrm{prob}(T > t)$$

All figures and tables are available in color online at www.iste.co.uk/cochard/stochastic.zip.

Since $R(t)$ is a probability, it is between 0 and 1. It is assumed that at moment 0, the device operates, so $R(0) = 1$. Subsequently, the device may fail and therefore $R(t) < 1$ for $t \in]0, +\infty[$. The more time passes, the higher the probability of failure and the reliability decreases.

T is the lifetime or service time of the device. If it is measured from a moment of origin, T is also the moment when a failure occurs.

The distribution function of the random variable T is by definition $F(t) = \text{prob}(T \le t)$. Given the definition of $R(t)$, we have:

$$F(t) = 1 - R(t)$$

The probability distribution of T is expressed by the density of probability $f(t)$, as T is a continuous random variable and thus, by definition also:

$$f(t) = F'(t) = \frac{dF}{dt} = -\frac{dR}{dt} = -R'(t)$$

Figure 7.1 shows the functions $f(t)$, $R(t)$, $F(t)$.

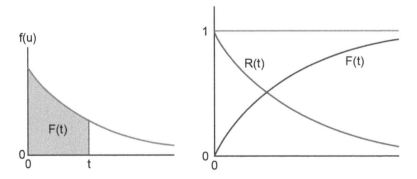

Figure 7.1. *Appearance of functions f(t), R(t), F(t)*

Now consider a time interval Δt as small as we like and specifically consider the reliability at time $t + \Delta t$, knowing that the device was in operation at moment t. Consider the following two events A and B:

  – A: the device is in operation at moment t: $p(A) = \text{prob}(T > t) = R(t)$;

  – B: a failure occurs in the interval $[0, t + \Delta t]$: $p(B) = \text{prob}(T \le t + \Delta t)$.

We have:

$$p(A \cap B) = \text{prob}(t < T < t + \Delta t) = F(t + \Delta t) - F(t) = R(t) - R(t + \Delta t).$$

The conditional probability that a failure arises between t and $t + \Delta t$, knowing that at moment t the device was working, is:

$$p(B|A) = \frac{p(A \cap B)}{p(A)} = \frac{R(t) - R(t + \Delta t)}{R(t)}$$

The derivative of $R(t)$ at point t is:

$$R'(t) = \frac{dR}{dt} = \lim_{\Delta t \to 0} \frac{R(t + \Delta t) - R(t)}{\Delta t}$$

The instantaneous failure rate $\lambda(t)$ is defined by:

$$\lambda(t) = \lim_{\Delta t \to 0} p(B|A) = \lim_{\Delta t \to 0} \left[\frac{1}{\Delta t} \frac{R(t) - R(t + \Delta t)}{R(t)} \right]$$
$$= - \lim_{\Delta t \to 0} \left[\frac{1}{R(t)} \frac{R(t + t) - R(t)}{\Delta t} \right] = - \frac{R'(t)}{R(t)}$$

which leads to the differential equation $R'(t) + \lambda(t)R(t) = 0$ whose well-known solution is:

$$R(t) = e^{- \int_0^t \lambda(u)du}$$

The function $\lambda(t)$ usually has a characteristic "bathtub" shape (Figure 7.2). This form has three parts corresponding to three periods of the device's life: a period of youth, a useful life period and an aging period.

Now, let us introduce MTTF (Mean Time To Failure), which is the average lifetime of the device:

$$MTTF = E(T) = \int_0^\infty tf(t)dt$$

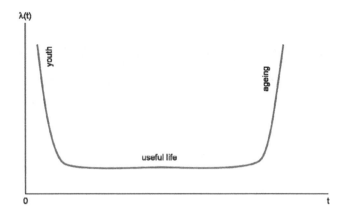

Figure 7.2. *Appearance of function λ(t)*

MTTF can be related to reliability. Indeed, we have seen that $R'(t) = -F'(t) = -f(t)$, so that we can integrate the previous integral in parts by putting $U = t$ and $dV = f(t)dt = -R'(t)dt$, hence:

$$MTTF = \int_0^\infty U dV = [UV]_0^\infty - \int_0^\infty V dU = [tR(t)]_0^\infty + \int_0^\infty R(t)dt$$

which is:

$$MTTF = \int_0^\infty R(t)dt$$

assuming that $tR(t)$ approaches 0 when t approaches infinity. This assumption is, in fact, obvious, because there is no ageless device.

	f(t)	F(t)	R(t)	λ(t)
f(t)		$\dfrac{dF(t)}{dt}$	$-\dfrac{dR(t)}{dt}$	$\lambda(t)e^{\int_0^t \lambda(u)du}$
F(t)	$\int_0^t f(u)du$			$1 - e^{-\int_0^t \lambda(u)du}$
R(t)	$\int_t^\infty f(u)du$	$1-F(t)$		$e^{-\int_0^t \lambda(u)du}$
λ(t)	$\dfrac{f(t)}{\int_t^\infty f(u)du}$	$\dfrac{1}{1-F(t)}\dfrac{dF(t)}{dt}$	$-\dfrac{R'(t)}{R(t)}$	

Table 7.1. *Summary table*

To conclude these generalities, Table 7.1 shows the relations between $f(t)$, $F(t)$, $R(t)$, $\lambda(t)$.

7.1.2. *Some probability distributions*

The exponential distribution is often used for the variable T. This is particularly the case for electronic components.

Therefore, according to the previous general results:

$$f(t) = \lambda e^{-\lambda t}$$

$$R(t) = 1 - F(t) = e^{-\lambda t}$$

$$MTTF = \frac{1}{\lambda}$$

$$\lambda(t) = -\frac{R'(t)}{R(t)} = \lambda$$

The instantaneous failure rate is here constant (which is not usually the case). Remember also that exponential distribution is characteristic of a memoryless system, which means that the probability that the device operates in the interval $[t_1, t_2]$ depends only on the length $t_2 - t_1$ of the interval and not on the date.

Another distribution is often used in reliability issues: the Weibull distribution (it is less mathematically friendly than the previous distribution). This distribution is an extension of the exponential distribution. We give the results without proving them:

$$f(t) = \alpha \beta t^{\beta-1} e^{-\alpha t^\beta}$$

$$R(t) = e^{-\alpha t^\beta}$$

$$MTTF = \Gamma\left(1 + \frac{1}{\beta}\right) \alpha^{-\frac{1}{\beta}}$$

$$\lambda(t) = \alpha \beta t^{\beta-1}$$

where the Euler function $\Gamma(u)$ is given by the expression:

$$\Gamma(u) = \int_0^\infty e^{-x} x^{u-1} dx$$

7.1.3. *Non-repairable systems*

A device can be composed of multiple elements. We will call this device a complex system. We will assume that the failure of an element is independent of the failure of the other elements.

Systems can be divided into two categories:

– Systems with redundancy: component failure does not cause system failure. The following two cases can be considered:

- Active redundancy: all component elements operate at the same time;

- Passive redundancy: there are component elements that are idle during the operation of the system;

– Systems without redundancy: the system only operates if all the elements work.

This section begins with systems for which, in the event of failure, no repair is planned. If the system fails, it remains like that indefinitely. We will examine cases with repairs in the next section.

Taking electrical circuits as an analogy, a complex system can be represented by a reliability diagram. Let us take a few illustrative cases.

7.1.3.1. *Systems in series*

The reliability diagram is in the form shown in Figure 7.3, assuming that n elements make up the system.

Figure 7.3. *Systems in series*

It is clear that the system should be classified as a system without redundancy: the failure of one element causes the system to fail.

If $T_1, T_2, \ldots, T_n$ are the lifetimes of the various elements $E_1, E_2, \ldots, E_n$, the lifetime of the system is, of course, the smallest of these lifetimes:

$$T = \min(T_1, T_2, \ldots, T_n)$$

As a result, the reliability of the system is:

$$R(t) = prob(T > t) = prob(T_1 > t).prob(T_2 > t)...prob(T_n > t)$$

$$= \prod_{i=1}^{n} prob(T_i > t) = \prod_{i=1}^{n} R_i(t)$$

where $R_i(t)$ represents the reliability of the component E_i. Since the probabilities are less than 1, it is evident that $R(t) < R_{i0}(t)$, where E_{i0} is the least reliable element.

If we consider the special case of the exponential distribution for the random variables T_i, T also obeys the exponential distribution of parameter $\lambda = \lambda_1 + \lambda_2 + ... + \lambda_n$ and:

$$MTTF = \cfrac{1}{\cfrac{1}{MTTF_1} + \cfrac{1}{MTTF_2} + \cdots + \cfrac{1}{MTTF_n}} = \frac{1}{\lambda_1 + \lambda_2 + \cdots . + \lambda_n} = \frac{1}{\lambda}$$

7.1.3.2. Systems in parallel

A reliability diagram for n elements in parallel is shown in Figure 7.4.

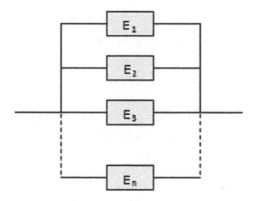

Figure 7.4. *Systems in parallel*

This is a system with redundancy. If T_1, T_2,..., T_n are the lifetimes of the various elements E_i, the lifetime of the system is, of course, the greatest of these lifetimes:

$$T = \max(T_1, T_2,..., T_n)$$

$$F(t) = prob(T \leq t) = prob(T_1 \leq t).prob(T_2 \leq t)\dots.prob(T_n \leq t)$$

$$= \prod_{i=1}^{n} F_i(t)$$

The reliability $R(t)$ of the system is therefore:

$$R(t) = 1 - F(t) = 1 - \prod_{i=1}^{n}(1 - R_i(t))$$

where $F_i(t)$ and $R_i(t)$ are relative to element E_i. Unlike the previous case, if E_{i0} is the most reliable element, $R(t) > R_{i0}(t)$.

If the probability distribution of T_i is exponential, the distribution of T is no longer exponential. If the components are identical with $\lambda = \lambda_1 = \lambda_2 = \dots = \lambda_n$, the reliability of the system becomes:

$$R(t) = 1 - \left(1 - e^{-\lambda t}\right)^n$$

The calculation of the MTTF is as follows:

$$MTTF = \int_0^{\infty} R(t)dt = \int_0^1 \frac{1 - u^n}{\lambda(1 - u)} du \quad \text{by putting } u = 1 - e^{-\lambda t}$$

Hence:

$$MTTF = \frac{1}{\lambda}\int_0^1 [1 + u + u^2 + \dots + u^{n-1}]\, du = \frac{1}{\lambda}(1 + \frac{1}{2} + \frac{1}{3} + \dots + \frac{1}{n})$$

7.1.3.3. *Systems with mixed structures*

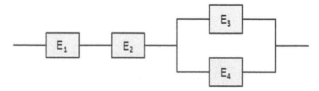

Figure 7.5. *Systems with mixed structures*

By combining components in series and components in parallel, reliability diagrams of the form given in Figure 7.6 are obtained.

Here, we have a system in series followed by a system in parallel. The components E_1 and E_2 can be reduced to a single reliability component $R_{12}(t) = R_1(t)R_2(t)$. Similarly, the system in parallel E_3, E_4 can be reduced to a single reliability component $R_{34}(t) = 1 - (1 - R_3(t))(1 - R_4(t))$. So for the system, we have:

$$R(t) = R_{12}(t)R_{34}(t) = R_1(t)R_2(t)[R_3(t) + R_4(t) - R_3(t)R_4(t)]$$

The case studied is simple. However, there may be more complicated reliability diagrams, as shown in Figure 7.6.

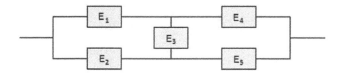

Figure 7.6. *More complicated case*

To find the reliability of this system, we can consider the following two cases: the one where E_3 operates and the one where E_3 does not operate.

Using conditional probabilities, we have:

$$R(t) = \text{prob}(T > t) = \text{prob}(T > t \,|T_3 \geq t).\text{prob}(T_3 \geq t) + \text{prob}(T > t \mid T_3 < t).\text{prob}(T_3 < t)$$

The first term corresponds to Figure 7.7 and the second term corresponds to Figure 7.8.

Applying the previous results, we obtain for the first term:

$$R_{\text{I}}(t) = [1 - (1 - R_1(t))(1 - R_2(t))][1 - (1 - R_4(t))(1 - R_5(t))]R_3(t)$$

and for the second:

$$R_{\text{II}}(t) = [1 - (1 - R_1(t)R_4(t))(1 - R_2(t)R_5(t))](1 - R_3(t))$$

hence:

$$R(t) = [R_1(t) + R_2(t) - R_1(t)\ R_2(t)][R_4(t) + R_5(t) - R_4(t)R_5(t)]R_3(t) + [R_1(t)R_4(t) + R_2(t)R_5(t) - R_1(t)R_2(t)R_4(t)R_5(t)](1 - R_3(t))$$

If all the components were identical, we would have $R(t) = 2r^5(t) - 5r^4(t) + 2r^3(t) + 2r^2(t)$ where $r(t)$ is the reliability of each component.

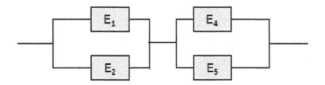

Figure 7.7. *First term*

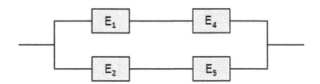

Figure 7.8. *Second term*

7.1.4. *Reparable systems*

It is now assumed that if the system fails, it can be repaired, and then resume service. The repair time can be (and usually is) random. A failing element is not necessarily repaired immediately; it depends on the repair capacity, i.e. the number of elements that can be simultaneously repaired; if this capacity is exceeded, a failing element will have to wait to be repaired. An element in a system can therefore be in three possible states:

– in operation;

– under repair;

– waiting to be repaired.

A repairable system evolves in the following way: initially in operation, it fails and waits to be returned to service; back in operation, it then fails and waits to be returned to service, etc., as shown in Figure 7.9, in which we show new definitions.

MTBF (Mean Time Between Failures) is the average time between two consecutive failures. MDT (Mean Down Time) is the average down time of the system. MUT (Mean Up Time) is the average service time of the system. Of course, $MTBF = MDT + MUT$. MTTR (Mean Time To Repair) is the average repair time.

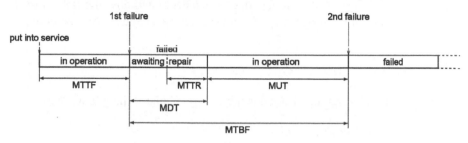

Figure 7.9. *MTBF, MDT, MUT and MTTR*

The concept of reliability $R(t)$ studied in the preceding sections is here extended to the concept of **availability** $A(t)$: $A(t)$ is the probability that the system is operating at time t, knowing that it is operating at time 0.

For a non-repairable system, $A(t) = R(t)$, but for a repairable system, $A(t) \geq R(t)$. The definition of $R(t) = \text{Prob}(T > t)$ implies that the system operates continuously between 0 and t.

To illustrate the concept of availability, consider two situations.

– Case of a system with only one element with a repair capacity of 1. If the system fails, it will be repaired without waiting. The system can only be in two states (Figure 7.10): state 0 corresponding to the operation of the system and state 1 corresponding to the system under repair.

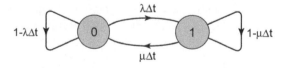

Figure 7.10. *One element system*

If λ designates the failure rate and μ the repair rate, we can consider that if we are in the case of the exponential distribution (which is assumed for the following):

$$MTBF = \frac{1}{\lambda} \quad \text{and} \quad MTTR = \frac{1}{\mu}$$

Let $P_0(t)$ be the probability of being in state 0 at moment t. Therefore, we have $A(t) = P_0(t)$. Moreover, $P_1(t) = 1 - P_0(t)$.

Now consider $P_0(t + \Delta t)$ where Δt is a small time interval. For the system to operate at moment $t + \Delta t$, it either operates at moment t and does not fail between t and $t + \Delta t$, or fails at moment t, but it is repaired between t and $t + \Delta t$. Therefore, we have:

$$P_0(t + \Delta t) = P_0(t)[1 - \lambda \Delta t] + [1 - P_0(t)]\,\mu\,\Delta t$$

Using the usual technique, from this relation by Δt approaching 0, we draw:

$$P'_0(t) = -(\lambda + \mu)P_0(t) + \mu$$

We know how to solve this differential equation, but our intention is to consider the stationary state for which $P_0(t) = P_0$ and $P'_0(t) = 0$ (and $A(t) = A$), which leads to:

$$P_0 = \frac{\mu}{\lambda + \mu}$$

By transforming this expression, we obtain the average availability:

$$A = \frac{\dfrac{1}{MTTR}}{\dfrac{1}{MTBF} + \dfrac{1}{MTTR}} = \frac{MTBF}{MTBF + MTTR}$$

We can also use the transition matrix:

$$T = \begin{bmatrix} 1 - \lambda \Delta t & \lambda \Delta t \\ \mu \Delta t & 1 - \mu \Delta t \end{bmatrix}$$

that can be considered as ergodic ($\lambda \Delta t < 1$ and $\mu \Delta t < 1$). It thus allows a fixed point $Q_0 = [x\ y]$ with $x + y = 1$. Here, x represents the probability P_0 and y represents the probability $P_1 = 1 - P_0$.

By solving the system $Q_0 T = Q_0$, we obtain without difficulty the same value as previously for P_0.

– Case of a system comprising two elements in parallel so that if one of the two elements fails, the system still functions. Let us always assume that the repair capacity is 1 (only one item is repaired at a time). The system can be in three states:

- state 0: both elements work, so the system works;

- state 1: one of the two elements fails, but the system works;

- state 2: both elements fail and the system does not work.

These three states are shown in Figure 7.11.

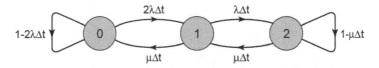

Figure 7.11. *System with two elements in parallel*

It is assumed that the exponential distribution governs the lifetime as well as the repair time of each component and that each of them has the same parameters λ and μ. Let $P_0(t)$, $P_1(t)$, $P_2(t)$ be the probabilities for the system to be in states 0, 1, 2 respectively. Here, availability is $A(t) = P_0(t) + P_1(t)$.

Proceeding as in the previous case, calculating the probabilities at $t + \Delta t$, we obtain the following equations:

$$P_0(t + \Delta t) = P_0(t)(1 - 2\lambda\Delta t) + P_1(t)\mu\Delta t$$

$$P_1(t + \Delta t) = P_1(t)(1 - (\lambda + \mu)\Delta t) + P_0(t)2\lambda\Delta t + P_2(t)\mu\Delta t$$

$$P_2(t + \Delta t) = P_2(t)(1 - \mu\Delta t) + P_1(t)\lambda\Delta t$$

From which we take, while Δt approaches 0:

$$P'_0(t) = -2\lambda P_0(t) + \mu P_1(t)$$

$$P'_1(t) = -(\lambda+\mu)P_1(t) + 2\lambda P_0(t) + \mu P_2(t)$$

$$P'_2(t) = -\mu P_2(t) + \lambda P_1(t)$$

In a stationary state, P_0, P_1, P_2 no longer depend on time and:

$$0 = -2\lambda P_0 + \mu P_1$$

$$0 = -(\lambda + \mu)P_1 + 2\lambda P_0 + \mu P_2$$

$$0 = -\mu P_2 + \lambda P_1$$

This system is easily solved and we obtain as results:

$$P_0 = \frac{\mu^2}{\mu^2 + 2\lambda\mu + 2\lambda^2}, \quad P_1 = \frac{2\lambda\mu}{\mu^2 + 2\lambda\mu + 2\lambda^2}, \quad P_2 = \frac{2\lambda^2}{\mu^2 + 2\lambda\mu + 2\lambda^2}$$

so the average availability is:

$$= P_0 + P_1 = 1 - P_2 = \frac{\mu^2 + 2\lambda\mu}{\mu^2 + 2\lambda\mu + 2\lambda^2}$$

For each component:

$$MTBF = \frac{1}{\lambda}, \quad MTTR = \frac{1}{\mu}, \quad \eta = \frac{MTBF}{MTTR} \quad \text{such that } A = \frac{\eta + 2}{\eta + 2 + \frac{2}{\eta}}$$

The same result can be obtained with the transition matrix:

$$T = \begin{bmatrix} 1 - 2\lambda\Delta t & 2\lambda\Delta t & 0 \\ \mu\Delta t & 1 - (\lambda + \mu)\Delta t & \lambda\Delta t \\ 0 & \mu\Delta t & 1 - \mu\Delta t \end{bmatrix}$$

T has zeros, but T^2 no longer has them, so the matrix T can be considered as ergodic. Its fixed point $Q_0 = [x\ y\ z]$ with $x + y + z = 1$ (x, y, z correspond to P_0, P_1, P_2) satisfies $Q_0 T = Q_0$ which leads to the system of equations:

$$(1 - 2\lambda\Delta t)x + \mu\Delta t y = x$$

$$2\lambda\Delta t x + (1 - (\lambda + \mu)\Delta t)y + \mu\Delta t z = y$$

$$\lambda\Delta t y + (1 - \mu\Delta t)z = z$$

whose solution for P_0, P_1, P_2 is the same as above.

7.2. Applications in genetics

7.2.1. Mendel's laws

The monk Mendel conducted experiments on the hybridization of plants, especially peas. From these, he drew conclusions (which we here call "laws"), which only became really well-known after his death.

Figure 7.12. *Johann Mendel, known as Gregor (1822–1884)*

COMMENT ON FIGURE 7.12.– *Mendel performed botany experiments in his monastery in Brno. He was a monk and teacher who studied the hybridization of plants, from which he deduced his famous laws, presented in his paper* "Experiments on Plant Hybridization". *His works were only explored 35 years after his death. Note that he was a contemporary of Charles Darwin*[1].

Without redoing Mendel's experiments, let us imagine the forced hybridization of purple flowering plants with white flowering plants. It is assumed that these plants have a pure strain, i.e. the self-fertilization of plants with purple flowers will always give plants with purple flowers, and the same goes for plants with white flowers. The result leads to plants with pink flowers (mixture of purple and white). All the plants obtained are identical in color, which is the only discriminating character. This is Mendel's first law.

MENDEL'S FIRST LAW.– All hybrids from pure lines differing in a single trait are similar and combine parental traits.

This can be explained by assuming that each plant has two color genes. The state of the color is an allele. In the cited experiment, purple flowering plants have two genes in the VV state (V is purple). Similarly, white flowering plants have two genes in the BB state (B is white). In hybridization, each type of plant gives a gene to the offspring. These will therefore have two genes in the VB or BV state. These two states are indistinguishable, so all offspring will have genes in the VB state. The mix of V and B gives the pink color, and all offspring will have this pink color.

---

1 The photograph of Johann (Gregor) Mendel is from Wikimedia Commons: https://commons. wikimedia.org/wiki/Category:Gregor_Mendel.

Now imagine a second generation obtained, this time, by self-fertilization of plants with pink flowers (thus possessing the genes in the *VB* state). As each offspring takes a parent gene, the possibilities of the gene states of the descendants will be *VV* or *BB* or *VB* or *BV*, this being random, all cases being equiprobable. As *VB* and *BV* are indistinguishable, there will be ¼ of plants in *VV*, ¼ of plants in *BB* and ½ of plants in *VB*.

Note that there is also a return to the type of the grandparents' line (*VV* or *BB*).

mother

	YY/SS	YY/WW	GG/SS	GG/WW
YY/SS	YY/SS	YY/SW	YG/SS	YG/SW
YY/WW	YY/SW	GG/WW	YG/SW	YG/WW
GG/SS	YG/SS	YG/SW	GG/SS	GG/SW
GG/WW	YG/SW	YG/WW	GG/SW	GG/WW

(leftmost column label: father)

Table 7.2. *Parentage of peas*

Let us now take the case of two genes of different types. To take a famous example, we can consider the case of peas characterized by color (yellow *J* or green *V*) and by shape (smooth *L* or wrinkled *R*). For each plant, there are two color genes and two shape genes. So there can be, for the parents, the combinations *JJ/LL* for smooth yellow peas, or *JJ/RR* for wrinkled yellow peas, or *VV/LL* for smooth green peas or *VV/RR* for wrinkled green peas. By taking the principle of transmitting a father's color gene and a mother's color gene, a father's shape gene and a mother's shape gene, we have 16 possible combinations which are summarized in Table 7.3.

The combinations *JV* and *VJ* or *LR* and *RL* are indistinguishable. All the cases being equiprobable, by this hybridization we obtain:

– 1/16 smooth yellow peas (*JJ/LL*);

– 1/16 smooth green peas (*VV/LL*);

– 1/16 yellow wrinkled peas (*JJ/RR*);

– 1/16 green wrinkled peas (*VV/RR*);

– 1/8 yellow half-smooth half-wrinkled peas (*JJ/LR*);

– 1/8 green half-smooth half-wrinkled peas (*VV/LR*);

– 1/8 smooth yellow–green peas (*JV/LL*);

– 1/8 wrinkled yellow–green peas (*JV/RR*);

– 1/4 yellow–green half-smooth and half-wrinkled peas (*JV/LR*).

This example illustrates Mendel's third law (the second will come later).

MENDEL'S THIRD LAW.– The transmission of gene pairs (one from the father, one from the mother) is independent.

Indeed, for our example, the transmission of color genes is independent of the transmission of shape genes.

However, it is not that simple because some gene states are dominant over others. For example, assume that state J of the color gene is dominant over state V (written as v, a "recessive" state). A cross between two pure lines differ in the color state JJ and vv. We have Jv as the theoretical result, but it would appear as JJ if state v is recessive, i.e. it does not appear.

This property of dominance of a gene state makes it possible to differentiate between the genotype and the phenotype. The genotype is the composition of genes with their states as shown in the previous table. The phenotype takes into account more than dominance. Here, we have Jv as a genotype, but the phenotype behaves like JJ. In fact, everything occurs as if we had crossed JJ with JJ.

MENDEL'S SECOND LAW.– If the offspring of a cross between two pure lines that differ in a single trait all have the same phenotype, this phenotype (character) is called "dominant" (the other trait is called "recessive").

Similarly, in the case of two genes of different types, suppose that state J of the color gene is dominant over state V (recessive and still written as v) and state L of the shape gene is dominant over state R (recessive and now written as r). Thus, with the dominance of J over v and L over r, we obtain for the genotype of Table 7.2 the phenotype of Table 7.3 where, for simplicity, we have kept the state of the dominant gene.

mother

		YY/SS	GG/ww	gg/YY	gg/ww
father	YY/SS	Y/S	Y/S	Y/S	Y/S
	YY/ww	Y/S	Y/w	Y/S	Y/w
	gg/SS	Y/S	Y/S	g/S	g/S
	gg/ww	Y/S	Y/w	g/S	g/w

Table 7.3. *Influence of dominance*

In our example, if we have dominant genes (J and L) and recessive genes (v and r), we obtain in reality:

– 9/16 smooth yellow peas;

– 3/16 wrinkled yellow peas;

– 3/16 smooth green peas;

– 1/16 wrinkled green peas.

7.2.2. *Heredity and genetic evolution*

Let us move away from plants and look at humans. The cells of the human body have 23 pairs of chromosomes, which contain genes, which can take several states (alleles) as shown schematically in Figure 7.13.

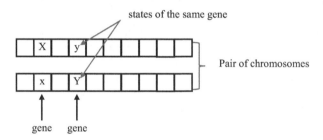

Figure 7.13. *Chromosomes, genes and alleles*

In each pair, one of the chromosomes comes from the father while the other comes from the mother. Of the 23 pairs of chromosomes, 22 are identical, but the 23rd pair behaves differently. In women, the two chromosomes of this pair are identical: X and X; in men, the two chromosomes are different: X and Y.

7.2.2.1. *Boys/girls*

In reproduction, XX is crossed with XY, which leads to XX or XY, i.e. a boy or a girl. Both cases are equiprobable, which explains why we have as many boys as girls (disregarding other factors, of course).

7.2.2.2. *Albinism, color blindness, hemophilia*

The X chromosome has genes responsible for albinism (white pigmentation), color blindness (non-recognition of certain colors) or hemophilia (blood coagulation disorder). Take the case of the gene responsible for albinism. It has two alleles A and a. The state A (frequent) is dominant over a (rare).

The possible states for a woman are AA, Aa and aa. The possible states for a man are AY and aY. In reproduction, the possibilities shown in Table 7.4 are obtained.

woman

		A/A	A/a	a/a
man	A/Y	A/Y, A/Y, A/A, A/A	A/Y, a/Y, A/A, A/a	a/Y, a/Y, A/a, A/a
	a/Y	A/Y, A/Y, a/A, a/A	A/Y. a/Y, a/A, a/a	a/Y, a/Y, a/a, a/a

Table 7.4. *Influence of dominance*

The dominance of the A character implies that the A/Y, A/A, A/a individuals will not be affected by albinism. This is also the case for a/Y, since before the character a there is no dominant character. Only the case a/a corresponds to the case of albinism.

If we count the possibilities, we find that (knowing that a/A and A/a are indistinguishable): A/Y represents 1/4 of the cases, as well as a/Y and A/a. A/A and a/a each represent 1/8 of the cases. The case of albinism therefore corresponds to a probability of 0.125.

7.2.2.3. *Blood groups*

The blood group is defined by a gene that can take three states: A, B, O. For an individual, a pair of genes can therefore be in states AA, AB, AO, BB, BO, OO, i.e. six genotypes. However, the A and B alleles are dominant relative to O, so that for an individual, we can only have four phenotypes A, AB, B, O, keeping only the dominant alleles.

Under these assumptions, we can predict the possible blood groups for children (Table 7.5).

	mother					
	A /A	A/B	A/O	B/B	B/O	O/O
A/A	A/A	A/A, A/B	A/A, A/O	A/B	A/B, A/O	A/O
A/B	A/A, A/B	A/A, A/B, B/B	A/A, A/O, B/O	A/B, B/B	A/B, A/O, B/B, B/O	A/O, B/O
A/O	A/A, A/O	A/A, A/B, A/O, B/O	A/A, A/O, O/O	A/B, B/O	A/B, A/O, B/O, O/O	A/O, O/O
B/B	A/B	A/B, B/B	A/B, B/O	B/B	B/B, B/O	B/O
B/O	A/B, A/O	A/B, B/B, A/O, B/O	A/B, B/O, A/O, O/O	B/B, B/O	B/B, B/O, O/O	B/O, O/O
O/O	A/O	A/O, B/O	A/O, O/O	B/O	B/O, O/O	O/O

(father labels the rows)

Table of genotypes

	mother			
	A	AB	B	O
A	A, O	A, B, AB	AB, A, B, O	A, O
AB	A, AB, B	A, AB, B	AB, A, B	A, B
B	AB, A, B, O	AB, A, B	B, O	B, O
O	A, O	A, B	B, O	O

(father labels the rows)

Table of phenotypes

Table 7.5. *Possible blood groups*

7.2.2.4. *Hardy–Weinberg's principle and genetic evolution*

Assume that a population, at generation n, is made up of genotypes AA, Aa, aa with frequencies u_n, v_n, w_n ($u_n + v_n + w_n = 1$). In the mechanism of reproduction, each individual transmits a gene. The gene of allele A can be transmitted by AA or Aa with the probability $p_n = u_n + v_n/2$ as A is certainly transmitted by AA while A is transmitted by Aa every other time.

Similarly, the gene of allele a can be transmitted by aa or Aa with the probability $q_n = w_n + v_n/2$ for the same reasons as above. We clearly have $p_n + q_n = 1$.

generation n + 1 :

		mother		
		AA	Aa	aa
father	AA	AA (u_n^2)	AA ($u_n v_n/2$) Aa ($u_n v_n/2$)	Aa ($u_n w_n$)
	Aa	AA ($u_n v_n/2$) Aa ($u_n v_n/2$)	AA ($v_n^2/4$) Aa ($v_n^2/2$) aa ($v_n^2/4$)	Aa ($v_n w_n/2$) aa ($v_n w_n/2$)
	aa	Aa ($u_n w_n$)	Aa ($v_n w_n/2$) aa ($v_n w_n/2$)	aa (w_n^2)

Table 7.6. *Possible results of random marriages*

The next generation, $n + 1$, will result from marriages between individuals of generation n. If we assume that marriages are random, Table 7.6 gives the possible results (with frequencies in brackets).

From this table, we take the frequencies of appearance of genotypes *AA*, *Aa*, *aa*:

$$u_{n+1} = u_n^2 + \frac{1}{2}u_n v_n + \frac{1}{2}u_n v_n + \frac{1}{4}v_n^2 = u_n^2 + u_n v_n + \frac{1}{4}v_n^2 = \left(u_n + \frac{v_n}{2}\right)^2$$
$$= p_n^2$$

$$v_{n+1} = \frac{1}{2}u_n v_n + u_n w_n + \frac{1}{2}u_n v_n + \frac{1}{2}v_n^2 + \frac{1}{2}v_n w_n + u_n w_n + \frac{1}{2}v_n w_n$$
$$= u_n v_n + v_n w_n + 2u_n w_n + \frac{1}{2}v_n^2$$
$$= 2\left(u_n + \frac{v_n}{2}\right)\left(w_n + \frac{v_n}{2}\right) = 2p_n q_n$$

$$w_{n+1} = \frac{1}{4}v_n^2 + \frac{1}{2}v_n w_n + \frac{1}{2}v_n w_n + w_n^2 = w_n^2 + v_n w_n + \frac{1}{4}v_n^2 = \left(w_n + \frac{v_n}{2}\right)^2$$
$$= q_n^2$$

We deduce:

$$p_{n+1} = u_{n+1} + \frac{v_{n+1}}{2} = p_n^2 + p_n q_n = p_n(p_n + q_n) = p_n$$

$$q_{n+1} = w_{n+1} + \frac{v_{n+1}}{2} = q_n^2 + p_n q_n = q_n(q_n + p_n) = q_n$$

which shows that from one generation to the next, the transmitted proportions of alleles *A* and *a* are constant. We can then put $p_n = p$ and $q_n = q$ ($p + q = 1$). It is also deduced that the proportions of genotypes *AA*, *Aa*, *aa* remain constant. These two results constitute the Hardy–Weinberg principle.

7.2.2.5. *Natural selection*

The Hardy–Weinberg principle appears to state that the population does not evolve in its genetic makeup. However, we know this is not true. The previous result is based on restrictive assumptions:

– there is no mutation: an allele of a gene does not transform into another allele, just as a gene does not multiply;

– marriages occur at random without preference factors;

– the population remains in a vacuum: there are no new individuals who arrive or individuals who disappear;

– the population is considered infinite or at least very significant in number;

– there is no natural selection: all alleles have the same ability to survive in their environment (fitness).

Figure 7.14. *Charles Darwin (1809–1882)*

COMMENT ON FIGURE 7.14.– *Darwin made a major contribution to biology by studying the evolution of species. As a young student, he traveled on the HMS* Beagle*, a ship responsible for mapping the coasts of South America. He took the opportunity to study the local flora and fauna and send his observations to England. Working at the Royal Geographical Society, he continued his research and published* "On the Origin of Species"*, without applying his theory to humans so as not to offend religious beliefs. This did not prevent criticism of the idea that humans are descended from monkeys*[2].

Natural selection is a concept introduced by Charles Darwin. It involves factors that select the offspring. A very simple example is provided by a population of rabbits, some brown, others white. A predator like a hawk will spot a white rabbit more easily than a brown rabbit and will reduce the population of white rabbits, so that the proportions of brown rabbits and white rabbits will vary, since there will be fewer white rabbits than brown rabbits for breeding. We can also consider that the fecundity rate of *aa* individuals is low compared to that of other genotypes. This is another cause of natural selection.

The rabbit's color is due to a gene that takes the value *A* (dominant) for a brown rabbit and *a* for a white rabbit. It follows that the composition of alleles *A* and *a* will vary over successive generations.

Suppose we have a population of individuals (rabbits, for example) of genotypes *AA* (brown rabbit), *Aa* (brown rabbit as *a* is recessive) and *aa* (white rabbit). We can predict that the number of *aa* rabbits will diminish (because of the hawk) unlike the number of brown rabbits (the hawk does not distinguish between *AA* and *Aa*).

2 The photograph of Charles Darwin (by Elliott & Fry) is from Wikimedia Commons: https://commons.wikimedia.org/wiki/Category:Charles_Darwin.

Introduce the factors k_1, k_2, k_3 of *fitness* for AA, Aa, aa. These are coefficients that change a population during growth.

Let p_n be the frequency of alleles A and q_n the frequency of alleles a of the population of generation n at its birth ($p_n + q_n = 1$). Then, the frequencies of the genotypes AA, Aa, aa are p_n^2, $2p_n q_n$, q_n^2.

Now, during the growth of the n generation, the *fitness* coefficients change the proportions. At maturity, the proportions become $k_1 p_n^2$, $2k_2 p_n q_n$, $k_3 q_n^2$ (the hawk has been around!).

The sum of these three quantities is no longer 1. Normalize by dividing by the sum:

$$s = k_1 p_n^2 + 2k_2 p_n q_n + k_3 q_n^2$$

Therefore, the frequencies are:

$$\frac{k_1 p_n^2}{s} \qquad 2\frac{k_2 p_n q_n}{s} \qquad \frac{k_3 q_n}{s}$$

According to the calculations of the preceding paragraph, at generation $n + 1$, we will have, for the alleles A and a, the frequencies:

$$p_{n+1} = \frac{k_1 p_n^2 + k_2 p_n q_n}{s}$$

$$q_{n+1} = \frac{k_3 q_n^2 + k_2 p_n q_n}{s}$$

$$p_{n+1} + q_{n+1} = 1$$

Suppose then that the genotype aa is disadvantaged by nature (the white rabbits are about to be devoured by hawks) and take $k_1 = k_2$ and $k_3 = 0$. The frequencies become:

$$p_{n+1} = \frac{p_n^2 + p_n q_n}{p_n^2 + 2p_n q_n} = \frac{1}{p_n + 2q_n} = \frac{1}{1 + q_n}$$

$$q_{n+1} = \frac{p_n q_n}{p_n^2 + 2p_n q_n} = \frac{q_n}{p_n + 2q_n} = \frac{q_n}{1 + q_n}$$

The process iterates from generation to generation. If q_0 is the initial probability of a (generation 0), we will successively have:

$$q_1 = \frac{q_0}{1 + q_0}$$

$$q_2 = \frac{q_1}{1 + q_1} = \frac{q_0}{1 + 2q_0}$$

$$q_3 = \frac{q_2}{1 + q_2} = \frac{q_0}{1 + 3q_0}$$

And so:

$$q_n = \frac{q_0}{1 + nq_0}$$

To see how many generations it will take for the frequency of a to halve, we can just solve the equation $q_n = q_0/2$, which leads to $n = 1/q_0$. The values of q_0 may be low, for example $q_0 = 0.01$, which leads to $n = 100$ generations. It is conceivable that the process of natural selection may be slow.

7.3. Population dynamics, predator–prey model

It was by studying the problem of the evolution of sardine populations in the Mediterranean that Vito Volterra defined an explanatory model. The same problem was studied almost simultaneously by Alfred J. Lotka.

Hence, the resulting model is called the "Lotka–Volterra model" so they both share the credit.

Figure 7.15. *Vito Volterra (1860–1940)*

COMMENT ON FIGURE 7.15.– *Italian mathematician and physicist, Volterra taught in Pisa, then Turin and Rome. He studied the integro-differential equations and, more importantly, for what we are interested in, population dynamics. An antifascist, he went abroad to flee the Mussolini regime. He only returned to Italy at the end of his life. A recognized and honored scientist (he received the French Legion of Honor), he is behind the predator–prey model.*

Figure 7.16. *Alfred James Lotka (1880–1949)*

COMMENT ON FIGURE 7.16.– *American mathematician of Austro-Hungarian origin, Lotka studied population dynamics. His publication in this area* ("Elements of Physical Biology") *proposes a prey–predator model, independently of Vito Volterra. However, after their publications on this model, the two researchers got in touch. Also a statistician, Lotka was interested in the age pyramid and the application of physical laws, particularly thermodynamic laws, in the field of biology[3].*

Since Volterra's starting point was sardines, let us take the case of two populations, sardines and their predators, for example sharks.

Sardines may increase indefinitely in numbers (in theory, because they have to find edible resources), but are limited by the sharks who love to eat them. Moreover, sharks can also increase indefinitely, but must eat to live and so will die if there are no sardines.

7.3.1. *Deterministic model*

Let $X(t)$ and $Y(t)$ denote the sardine population and the shark population at moment t, knowing that at moment 0 the populations are $X(0) = X_0$ and $Y(0) = Y_0$.

---

3 The photograph of Vito Volterra (photographer unknown) is from https://commons.wikimedia. org/wiki/Category:Vito_Volterra; the photograph of Alfred James Lotka is from https://en. wikipedia.org/wiki/Alfred_J._Lotka.

We assume as a hypothesis:

– the growth rate of prey-sardines is the composition of a constant birth rate a ($a > 0$) and a mortality rate $bY(t)$ ($b > 0$) proportional to the number of predators-sharks;

– the growth rate of predators-sharks is the composition of a birth rate $cX(t)$ ($c > 0$) proportional to the number of prey-sardines and a constant death rate d ($d > 0$).

As a result, increases in sardines and sharks during the interval Δt are:

$$X(t + \Delta t) - X(t) = [a - bY(t)]\Delta t X(t)$$

$$Y(t + \Delta t) - Y(t) = [cX(t) - d]\Delta t Y(t)$$

We therefore have to solve a system of two equations with two unknowns:

$$\begin{cases} \dfrac{X(t + \Delta t) - X(t)}{\Delta t} = [a - bY(t)]X(t) \\ \dfrac{Y(t + \Delta t) - Y(t)}{\Delta t} = [cX(t) - d]Y(t) \end{cases}$$

By Δt approaching 0, we obtain a differential system:

$$\begin{cases} \dfrac{dX}{dt} = [a - bY(t)]X(t) \\ \dfrac{dY}{dt} = [cX(t) - d]Y(t) \end{cases}$$

with the initial conditions specified above. This differential system constitutes a rudimentary model that can be improved (and thus made much more complex!) by no longer considering the coefficients a, b, c, d as constants. We will stay with this simple model, however, in what follows.

In the absence of sharks, the differential equation of sardines ($Y(t) = 0$) is easily solved.

$X(t) = e^{at}$: the sardine population is growing exponentially. Similarly, in the absence of sardines ($X(t) = 0$), the differential equation of sharks is solved in the same way: $Y(t) = e^{-dt}$: the shark population goes extinct exponentially.

We can first look at the case where the populations are balanced (stationary state). In this case, the derivatives are null and we are brought back to a classical system:

$[a - bY]S = 0$

$[cX - d]R = 0$

which has the solutions $(X, Y) = (0, 0)$ and $(X, Y) = (d/c, a/b)$.

The resolution of the non-stationary system has been studied by mathematicians. Their conclusions are as follows:

– there are solutions and they are positive (thankfully!);

– the system has two equilibrium states that are those previously determined for the stationary state;

– the solutions are periodic;

– over a period, the average prey population is d/c and the average predator population is a/b.

Let us give some justifications for these results.

First, consider the function:

$H(X, Y) = cX - d\text{Ln}X + bY - a\text{Ln}Y$

defined for $X, Y \in [0, \infty[$ where X and Y are the functions of time t and a, b, c, d are the coefficients of the Lotka–Volterra differential system. It is easy to show that $H(X, Y)$ is constant with respect to time.

Indeed:

$$\frac{dH}{dt} = c\frac{dX}{dt} - \frac{d}{X}\frac{dX}{dt} + b\frac{dY}{dt} - \frac{a}{Y}\frac{dY}{dt} = \frac{1}{X}(cX - d)\frac{dX}{dt} + \frac{1}{Y}(bY - a)\frac{dY}{dt}$$
$$= \frac{1}{XY}\frac{dX}{dt}\frac{dY}{dt} - \frac{1}{XY}\frac{dX}{dt}\frac{dY}{dt} = 0$$

Therefore, $H(X, Y) = K$ if X and Y satisfy the Lotka–Volterra differential system. This equation defines a family of closed curves in the X, Y plane, each member of the family being identified by a value of the constant K. This constant is determined by the initial conditions X_0, Y_0.

In the X, Y plane, for non-zero X and Y, we can consider four regions P1, P2, P3, P4, as shown in Figure 7.17.

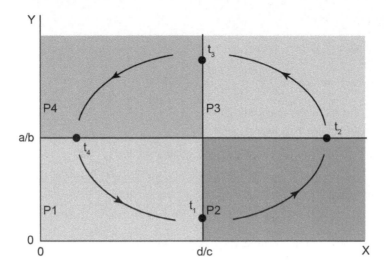

Figure 7.17. *Possible regions for X and Y*

These regions, delimited by the straight lines $X = d/c$ and $Y = a/b$, are characterized by the following facts:

$$\text{region P1}: X < \frac{d}{c} \text{ and } Y < \frac{a}{b} \implies \frac{dY}{dt} < 0 \text{ and } \frac{dX}{dt} > 0$$
$$\implies X \text{ is increasing and } Y \text{ is decreasing;}$$

$$\text{region P2}: X > \frac{d}{c} \text{ and } Y < \frac{a}{b} \implies \frac{dY}{dt} > 0 \text{ and } \frac{dX}{dt} > 0$$
$$\implies X \text{ and } Y \text{ are increasing;}$$

$$\text{region P3}: X > \frac{d}{c} \text{ and } Y > \frac{a}{b} \implies \frac{dY}{dt} > 0 \text{ and } \frac{dX}{dt} < 0$$
$$\implies X \text{ is decreasing and } Y \text{ is increasing;}$$

$$\text{region P4}: X < \frac{d}{c} \text{ and } Y > \frac{a}{b} \implies \frac{dY}{dt} < 0 \text{ and } \frac{dX}{dt} < 0$$
$$\implies X \text{ and } Y \text{ are decreasing.}$$

Therefore, in each region, the curve $H(X, Y) = K$ appears as shown in Figure 7.17. We can also deduce that there are times $t_1 < t_2 < t_3 < t_4 < \dots$ where the curve $H(X, Y) = K$ crosses the lines that delimit the four regions. However, if the curve passes, for example, through the point $X(t_1)$, $Y(t_1)$ at moment t_1 shows that it passes through the same point at the subsequent moment t_5 where the curve passes from region P1 to region P2.

We have $H(X(t_1), Y(t_1)) = H(X(t_5), Y(t_5)) = K$ and $X(t_1) = X(t_5) = a/b$. It must be shown that $Y(t_1) = Y(t_5)$. The previous equalities imply that:

$$bY(t_1) - aLnY(t_1) = bY(t_5) - aLnY(t_5) \qquad [7.1]$$

The function $h(Y) = bY - aLnY$, defined for $Y \in [0, a/b]$, is a decreasing monotonic function since:

$$\frac{dh}{dY} = b - \frac{a}{Y} < 0 \ in \ regions \ P1 \ and \ P2 \ since \ Y < \frac{a}{b}$$

The equality [7.1] is simply written $h(Y(t_1)) = h(Y(t_5))$ and as the function h is monotonic, we can only have $Y(t_1) = Y(t_5)$. This result shows that the function $Y(t)$ is periodic. We show that the function $X(t)$ is also periodic.

Figure 7.18 gives a result obtained by a numerical method: the (periodic) numbers of prey and predators and the curve $H(X, Y) = K$. The chosen values are $a = 1; b = 10^{-4}; c = 10^{-4}; d = 2; X_0 = 26000; Y_0 = 4000$.

We can see a difference between the curves $X(t)$ and $Y(t)$, which is normal since there is inevitably a delay in the reaction. When the number of prey decreases, predators have less food and their number decreases some time later. Similarly, when the number of predators decreases, the number of prey will increase thereafter.

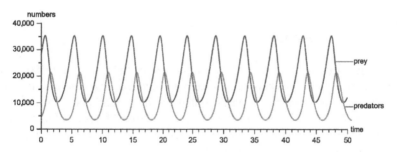

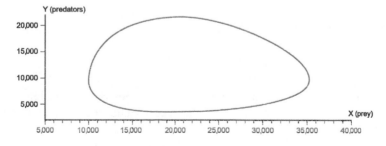

Figure 7.18. *Results of a numerical method*

7.3.2. *Solution near the equilibrium*

For values of X and Y close to the equilibrium (d/c, a/b), approximate analytic expressions can be obtained (see demonstration in the appendix at the end of this chapter):

$$X(t) \cong \frac{d}{c}[1 + \alpha \cos(t\sqrt{ad} + C))$$

$$Y(t) \cong \frac{a}{b}[1 + \alpha \sqrt{\frac{d}{a}} \sin(t\sqrt{ad} + C))$$

where C and α are constants satisfying the conditions:

$$C > 0 \ and \ \alpha < Min\left(1, \sqrt{\frac{d}{a}}\right)$$

The values X and Y oscillate around the equilibrium with a period:

$$T = \frac{2\pi}{\sqrt{ad}}$$

7.3.3. *External influence*

Let us now examine a more specific aspect, that of fishing, which challenges the preceding considerations. There is no denying that fishing amounts to taking a quantity of prey and predators proportional to their numbers. This amounts to modifying the differential system by subtracting eX from the second member of the first equation of the system and eY from the second member of the second equation of the system (e is a new positive coefficient):

$$\begin{cases} \dfrac{dX}{dt} = [a - e - bY(t)]X(t) \\ \dfrac{dY}{dt} = [cX(t) - d - e]Y(t) \end{cases}$$

To examine the impact of this fishing, we will not review the resolution of the differential system again, but calculate the mean values of prey and predator numbers over a period.

Let us first consider the case without fishing. T being the period, for predators we have the relation:

$$\int_0^T \frac{\frac{dY(t)}{dt}}{Y(t)} dt = Ln\frac{Y(T)}{Y(0)} = 0 \quad \text{because } Y(0)$$

$$= Y(T) \quad \text{because of the periodicity}$$

Therefore, for the second equation of the differential system, we have:

$$0 = \int_0^T \frac{\frac{dY(t)}{dt}}{Y(t)} dt = c \int_0^T X(t)\, dt - dT \quad \text{or} \quad \bar{X} = \frac{1}{T}\int_0^T X(t)dt = \frac{d}{c}$$

Similarly, we can show that:

$$\bar{Y} = \frac{1}{T}\int_0^T Y(t)dt = \frac{a}{b}$$

Now if we replace a by $a - e$ and d by $d + e$, we will obtain in the case of fishing:

$$\bar{X} = \frac{d + e}{c} \quad \text{and} \quad \bar{Y} = \frac{a - e}{b}$$

which shows that fishing favors prey at the expense of predators, which is not surprising.

7.3.4. Stochastic models

In all of the above, we used the Lotka–Volterra model which is, in essence, deterministic. What about if we place ourselves within the framework of a stochastic model, i.e. of two paired birth and death processes?

It is then considered that the process can be modeled by a Markov process (time is continuous). A state is represented at a moment t by the value pairs (x, y) which represent, for x, the number of prey and, for y, the number of predators at that moment. The x and y values are the random variables $X(t)$ and $Y(t)$.

For a small time interval h, it is assumed that at moment $t + h$, the following eventualities can occur:

– $(x, y) \rightarrow (x, y)$: no change;

– $(x, y) \rightarrow (x - 1, y)$: death of prey with a transition rate axh;

– $(x, y) \rightarrow (x + 1, y)$: birth of prey with a transition rate $bxyh$;

– $(x, y) \rightarrow (x, y + 1)$: birth of predator with a transition rate $cxyh$;

– $(x, y) \rightarrow (x, y - 1)$: death of predator with a transition rate dyh.

During interval h, it is assumed that only one of these cases can occur (Figure 7.19).

The probability for the transition $(x, y) \rightarrow (x, y)$ is $[1 - ax - bxy - cxy - dy]h$. The probability of having the state (x, y) at moment $t + h$ is then:

$$P_{x, y}(t + h) = [1 - ax - bxy - cxy - dy]hP_{x, y}(t) + a(x - 1)hP_{x - 1, y}(t)$$
$$+ b(x + 1)hP_{x+1, y}(t) + cx(y - 1)hP_{x, y-1}(t) + d(y + 1)hP_{x, y+1}(t)$$

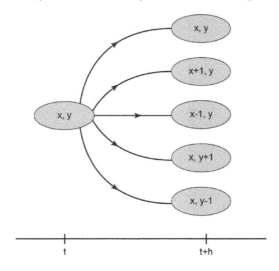

Figure 7.19. *Possible transitions*

By rearranging this expression and having interval h approaching 0, we obtain:

$$P'_{x, y}(t) = - (ax + bxy + cxy + dy)P_{x, y}(t) + a(x - 1)P_{x - 1, y}(t) + b(x + 1)yP_{x + 1, y}(t) + cx(y - 1)P_{x, y-1}(t) + d(y + 1)P_{x, y+1}(t)$$

This equation is difficult to solve analytically. It must be done by numerical methods. However, we demonstrate the following results, which we give without demonstration.

If the Markov process is homogeneous, the mathematical expectations $E(X)$ and $E(Y)$ satisfy the differential system:

$$\begin{cases} \dfrac{\partial E(X)}{\partial t} = aE(X) - bE(XY) \\ \dfrac{\partial E(Y)}{\partial t} = cE(XY) - dE(Y) \end{cases}$$

We find a similarity with the differential system of Lotka–Volterra, except that we cannot consider that $E(X) = x(t)$ nor that $E(Y) = y(t)$, because $E(XY) \neq E(X)E(Y)$, the variables X and Y not being independent.

If we model the process by two independent and non-homogeneous processes $X(t)$ and $Y(t)$, we obtain a better result, because in this case we can replace $E(XY)$ with $E(X)E(Y)$. We can then consider $E(X)$ and $E(Y)$ as solutions of the Lotka–Volterra differential system. In addition, it can be predicted that the extinction of prey and predators is certain, but at the end of an infinite time.

7.4. From physics to finance: Brownian motion

7.4.1. *Brownian motion in physics*

Brownian motion is originally, as observed by Robert Brown in 1827, the motion of particles in a fluid: grains of pollen jittering continuously while the fluid is still.

The explanation of the phenomenon, known as Brownian motion, comes from the kinetic theory of gases and the hypothesis of particulate matter.

Figure 7.21 shows the simulated erratic path of a pollen grain in a two-dimensional space (see also the very fine B. Duplantier article [DUP 05]).

Einstein offered an explanation in 1905, followed by Smoluchowski in 1906. Langevin resumed this work in 1908 by proposing another version. Finally, Jean Perrin confirmed all these theories through experiments and noted the fractal dimension of particle paths.

Albert Einstein   Marian Smoluchowski   Paul Langevin   Jean Perrin

Figure 7.20. *Albert Einstein (1879–1955), German-born physicist; Marian Smoluchowski (1872–1917), Polish physicist; Paul Langevin (1872–1946), French physicist; Jean Perrin (1870–1942), French physicist*[4]

Figure 7.21. *Simulation of Brownian motion*

Einstein's formula gives, for a one-dimensional problem, the relation between the mean value of the square of the distance traveled x after a time t and the absolute temperature T, knowing that at $t = 0$, $x = 0$:

$$E(x^2) = 2\frac{kT}{\mu}t$$

---

4 The photographs of Albert Einstein (author: Orren Jack Turner), Marian Smoluchowski (photographer unknown), Paul Langevin (author: Henri Manuel, 1874–1947, source: Wellcome Images, ICV28615, V0028151, licensed by Creative Commons) and Jean Perrin (author: Agence de presse Meurisse) are from Wikimedia Commons.

where k is the Boltzmann constant and μ is a coefficient related to the physical properties of the fluid and the particle. $k = R/N = 1.38,10^{-23}$ J/°K where $R = 8.32$ J/°K is the constant of perfect gases and $N = 6.10^{23}$ is Avogadro's number.

On the contrary, the density of particles $n(x, t)$ per unit length at a moment t obeys the diffusion equation:

$$\frac{\partial n(x,t)}{\partial t} = D\frac{\partial^2 n(x,t)}{\partial x^2}$$

with $D = kT/\mu$ where μ is a coefficient of friction. The solution of this equation is, for standard initial conditions:

$$n(x,t) = \frac{N}{\sqrt{4\pi Dt}}e^{-\frac{x^2}{4Dt}}$$

7.4.2. Standard model of Brownian motion

Consider first a discrete time process. It is assumed that from a constant N ($N \geq 1$), the time is discretized in intervals of width $1/N$. We imagine a process characterized by a random variable B which, starting from $B(0) = 0$, increases or decreases with each step of the quantity $1/\sqrt{N}$ with an equal probability $(1/2)$. Figure 7.22 shows this process, which is stochastic.

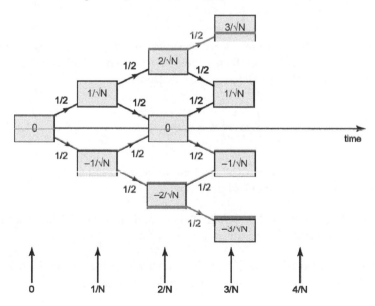

Figure 7.22. *Possible variations of B over time*

The value of B at moment k/N is:

$$B\left(\frac{k}{N}\right) = \sum_{i=1}^{k} B\left(\frac{i}{N}\right) = \frac{1}{\sqrt{N}} \sum_{i=1}^{k} e_i$$

In this expression, the e_i are independent random variables, taking the $+1$ or -1 values in an equiprobable manner. For each e_i, we have $E(e_i) = 0$ and $v(e_i) = 1$.

Therefore, we can put:

$$B\left(\frac{k}{N}\right) = \frac{1}{k} \frac{k}{\sqrt{N}} \sum_{i=1}^{k} e_i = \frac{1}{k} \sum_{i=1}^{k} Z_i$$

The independent random variables Z_i have as a mean $E(Z_i) = 0$ and as variance $v(Z_i) = k^2/N$, hence a standard deviation $\sigma(Z_i) = k/\sqrt{N}$.

For large values of k, we can then apply the central limit theorem which indicates that $B(k/N)$ follows a normal probability distribution of mean 0 and standard deviation $k/\sqrt{N}$, which is expressed by:

$$Prob\left(B\left(\frac{k}{N}\right) \le x\right) = \int_{-\infty}^{x} \frac{\sqrt{N}}{\sqrt{2k\pi}} e^{-\frac{u^2}{2\frac{k}{N}}} du$$

Let us now go from discrete time to continuous time by having N approach infinity. The time intervals $1/N$ then become smaller and smaller and for $t \in [k/N, (k+1)/N]$, the value k/N approaches t. We can deduce:

$$Prob\ (B(t) \le x) = \int_{-\infty}^{x} \frac{1}{\sqrt{2\pi t}} e^{-\frac{u^2}{2t}} du$$

where $B(t)$ represents a family of random variables, each following the normal distribution of mean 0 and standard deviation $\sqrt{t}$.

We have thus constructed a "standard" Brownian movement. The definition of a standard Brownian motion is as follows.

DEFINITION.– A standard Brownian motion $B(t)$ is a sequence of continuous random variables defined for $t \ge 0$ and satisfying the following properties:

$- B(0) = 0$;

– the increments over disjunct periods are independent. Therefore, $B(t + h) − B(t)$ is, for example, independent of $B(s) − B(0)$ for $t > s$ and $h > 0$;

– the increments follow a normal distribution of mean 0 and variance equal to the time interval. Therefore, $B(t + h) − B(t)$ follows a normal distribution of mean 0 and variance h. Note that given the first property, we have $B(t) = B(t) − B(0)$ and so $B(t)$ follows a normal distribution of mean 0 and variance t.

The previously constructed Brownian motion responds well to these conditions.

Note also that the standard Brownian motion is a Markov process since it satisfies the following assumptions:

ASSUMPTION 7.1.– The process is memoryless because of the independence of the increments.

ASSUMPTION 7.2.– The process is homogeneous, which means that increments are stationary. Their probabilities depend only on the time interval and not on the date.

Brownian motion is often characterized by the properties of continuity, independence and stationarity.

It is interesting to establish a property of the probability density:

$$f(x,t) = \frac{1}{\sqrt{2\pi t}} e^{-\frac{x^2}{2t}}$$

Calculate the first derivative in t and the second derivative in x of the density $f(x, t)$:

$$\frac{\partial f}{\partial t} = \frac{1}{2t\sqrt{2\pi t}} \left[-1 + \frac{x^2}{t}\right] e^{-\frac{x^2}{2t}}$$

$$\frac{\partial f}{\partial x} = -\frac{x}{t\sqrt{2\pi t}} e^{-\frac{x^2}{2t}}$$

$$\frac{\partial^2 f}{\partial x^2} = \frac{1}{t\sqrt{2\pi t}} \left[-1 + \frac{x^2}{t}\right] e^{-\frac{x^2}{2t}}$$

So that:

$$\frac{\partial f}{\partial t} = \frac{1}{2}\frac{\partial^2 f}{\partial x^2}$$

which is the well-known equation of diffusion. Here, we find similarities with physics.

7.4.3. *Brownian motion with drift*

We can generalize the standard model by assuming that the evolution probabilities are no longer equal. The mean will no longer be equal to 0 and we are talking about Brownian motion with drift. It is very simply defined by:

$$X(t) = \mu t + \sigma B(t)$$

where $B(t)$ is a standard Brownian motion. μ is called the drift of $X(t)$ and σ is called the volatility.

The mean and the variance of $X(t)$ are easily calculated:

$$E(X) = \mu t + \sigma E(B) = \mu t$$

$$v(X) = \sigma^2 v(B) = \sigma^2 t$$

It should be noted that the mean varies linearly with time t and that the standard deviation varies linearly with $\sqrt{t}$.

The reasoning of the preceding paragraph could be continued by considering a process that evolves in steps of $1/N$, the variable $X(k/N)$ increasing or decreasing according to the rule for each step i:

$$\text{increase of } e_i = \frac{\sigma}{\sqrt{N}} \qquad \text{with probability } \frac{1}{2}\left(1 + \frac{\mu}{\sigma\sqrt{N}}\right)$$

$$\text{decrease of } e_i = \frac{\sigma}{\sqrt{N}} \qquad \text{with probability } \frac{1}{2}\left(1 - \frac{\mu}{\sigma\sqrt{N}}\right)$$

In this case, the value of $X(k/N)$ is:

$$X\left(\frac{k}{N}\right) = \frac{\sigma}{\sqrt{N}}\sum_{i=1}^{k} e_i = \frac{1}{k}\frac{\sigma k}{\sqrt{N}}\sum_{i=1}^{k} e_i = \frac{1}{k}\sum_{i=1}^{k} z_i$$

The average value of e_i is:

$$E(e_i) = \frac{1}{2}\left(1 + \frac{\mu}{\sigma\sqrt{N}}\right) - \frac{1}{2}\left(1 - \frac{\mu}{\sigma\sqrt{N}}\right) = \frac{\mu}{\sigma\sqrt{N}}$$

And the variance of e_i is:

$$v(e_i) = E(e_i^2) - E^2(e_i) = \frac{1}{2}\left(1 + \frac{\mu}{\sigma\sqrt{N}}\right) + \frac{1}{2}\left(1 - \frac{\mu}{\sigma\sqrt{N}}\right) - \frac{\mu^2}{\sigma^2 N}$$

$$= 1 - \frac{\mu^2}{\sigma^2 N}$$

The random variable Z_i thus has a mean $E(Z_i)$, a variance $v(Z_i)$ and a standard deviation $\sigma(Z_i)$:

$$E(Z_i) = \frac{k\mu}{N} \quad v(Z_i) = \frac{\sigma^2 k^2}{N}\left(1 - \frac{\mu^2}{\sigma^2 N}\right) \quad \sigma(Z_i) = \sqrt{1 - \frac{\mu^2}{\sigma^2 N}}$$

For a large N, the central limit theorem indicates that $X(k/N)$ obeys a normal distribution of mean $E(Z_i)$ and standard deviation $\sigma(Z_i)/\sqrt{k}$.

When N approaches infinity, to join the continuous case, k/N approaches t and so $X(k/N)$ approaches $X(t)$ following a normal distribution of mean μt and standard deviation $\sigma\sqrt{t}$. Our results are therefore consistent.

7.4.4. Black–Scholes model

Fischer Black   Myron Scholes   Robert C. Merton

Figure 7.23. *Fischer Black (1938–1995), American mathematician and professor of finance, and Myron Scholes (1941), Canadian economist, are the fathers of the famous Black–Scholes model, which could also bear the name of Robert C. Merton (1944)*[5]

5 The photographs of Fischer Black (author: Dalmatine, source: English Wikipedia page), Myron Scholes (author: Nobel laureates photographer, source: English Wikipedia page, licensed by Creative Commons) and Robert C. Merton (author: Digarnick, source: Wikipedia page) are from Wikimedia Commons.

In market finance, the value of an asset is modeled by the random variable:

$$Y(t) = Y(0)e^{X(t)}$$

where $t \geq 0$, $X(t)$ is a Brownian motion.

If we consider the discrete case where time varies in steps of $1/N$, we have the expression:

$$Y\left(\frac{k}{N}\right) = Y(0)e^{\frac{1}{k}\sum_{i=1}^{k} Z_i} \quad \text{with} \quad X\left(\frac{k}{N}\right)$$

$$= \frac{1}{k}\sum_{i=1}^{k} Z_i \text{ according to the previous paragraph}$$

From the properties of the exponential, we deduce:

$$Y\left(\frac{k}{n}\right) = Y(0) \prod_{i=1}^{k} e^{\frac{1}{k}Z_i}$$

The return on an asset is the relative change in its value between two steps. Thus between $(k-1)/N$ and k/N, the return is:

$$\frac{Y\left(\frac{k}{N}\right) - Y\left(\frac{k-1}{N}\right)}{Y\left(\frac{k-1}{N}\right)} = e^{\frac{1}{k}Z_k} - 1 = e^{\frac{\sigma}{\sqrt{N}}e_k} - 1$$

For a large N, we can derive the approximation:

$$e^{\frac{\sigma}{\sqrt{N}}e_k} \cong 1 + \frac{\sigma}{\sqrt{N}}e_k + \frac{\sigma^2}{2N}e_k^2$$

We use this development to calculate the average return value:

$$E\left(e^{\frac{\sigma}{\sqrt{N}}e_k} - 1\right) = \frac{\sigma}{\sqrt{N}}E(e_k) + \frac{\sigma^2}{2N}E(e_k^2) = \frac{1}{N}\left(\mu + \frac{\sigma^2}{2}\right)$$

From this expression, we deduce the following conclusions:

– positive return, asset increase: $\mu + \sigma^2/2 > 0$;

– zero return, asset neutral: $\mu + \sigma^2/2 = 0$;

– negative return, asset decrease: $\mu + \sigma^2/2 < 0$.

Let us look at the particular case of options to buy an asset (e.g. an action). An asset purchase option is called a *call*. There are also options to sell assets; an asset sale option is called a *put*.

For a *call*, it is a commitment (contract) to pay $KY(0)$ an asset whose exact value will be known (but not predictable) at a later time T which is the expiry date (usually T varies from 1 day to 5 years). There are two types of purchase options:

– the "American" call, for which the call can be exercised at any time up to date T;

– the "European" call for which the call can be exercised only on date T. The gain is provided by the famous Black–Scholes formula that we will see later.

In the following, we will only focus on European calls.

EXAMPLE 7.1.– Let an action of value $Y(0) = 20$ € at the time of the *call* contract. The purchase amount is 40 € ($K = 2$) and $T = 6$ months.

Suppose that, 3 months later, the value of the action is 30 €. The holder of the European call must wait until the expiry date to execute his or her purchase contract.

If after 6 months the value of the action is 35 €, the holder of a European call could also buy, since the expiry date has occurred, but he or she is not obliged to. He or she is not interested in this case.

If after 6 months the value of the action is 45 €, the holder of the European call will exercise his or her right of purchase from which there is a gain of 45 - 40 = 5 €.

Note, however, that the signing of a call contract incurs a fee of x €, which must be deducted from the gain realized. In case of non-purchase on the expiry date for a European call, the holders of the call will therefore have a loss of x €.

Let there be an asset of initial value $Y(0)$ whose value at a later moment t evolves according to:

$$Y(t) = Y(0)e^{X(t)}$$

where $X(t)$ follows a normal distribution of mean μt and standard deviation $\sigma\sqrt{t}$. Let a European call have expiry T and purchase value $KY(0)$. $KY(0)$ is the price that will be paid on the date t. At time $t = 0$, this value must be discounted (downwards) taking the interest rate r into account, which leads to the value $K_0 Y(0)$ with $K_0 = Ke^{-rt}$. The expectation of $Y(t) - Y(0)K_0$ is $Y(0)E(e^{X(t)} - K_0)$. However, this mathematical expectation is not the one which interests us; the one we are interested in is where $e^{X(t)} - K_0$ is positive (i.e. for $X(t) > LnK_0$), which we denote $E([e^{X(t)} - K_0]^+)$ where $[e^{X(t)} - K_0]^+ = Max(e^{X(t)} - K_0; 0)$. Therefore, we have, using the normal distribution:

$$E\left([e^{X(t)} - K_0]^+\right) = \int_{LnK}^{+\infty} (e^x - K_0)\frac{1}{\sigma\sqrt{2\pi t}}e^{-\frac{(x-\mu t)^2}{2\sigma^2 t}}\,dx$$

The calculation of this integral, although uncomplicated, is long. It can be found in the appendix. We obtain as result:

$$C(t) = E([Y(t) - Y(0)K_0]^+)$$
$$= Y(0)\left[\Phi\left(\sigma\frac{\sqrt{t}}{2} - \frac{LnK_0}{\sigma\sqrt{t}}\right) - K_0\Phi\left(-\frac{\sigma\sqrt{t}}{2} - \frac{LnK_0}{\sigma\sqrt{t}}\right)\right]$$

on the condition that the average return is zero, i.e. as seen above, that $\mu + \sigma^2/2 = 0$.

It is the famous Black–Scholes formula that gives the correct price of the asset $C(t)$ which represents the expected gain. The function Φ is the Gaussian probability:

$$\Phi(v) = \int_{-\infty}^{v} \frac{1}{\sqrt{2\pi}}e^{-\frac{x^2}{2}}\,dx$$

EXAMPLE 7.2.– Let an action of value $Y(0) = 40\,€$ on date 0. Its volatility is estimated at 0.5. A European purchase option is entered into on date 0 with an expiry date of 1 year and a purchase value of $KY(0)$. It is assumed that the interest rate is 5% ($r = 0.05$). Applying the Black–Scholes formula, calculate the expected gain in the two following cases:

$K = 1.25$ which is $Y(t) = 50\,€$

$K = 0.75$ which is $Y(t) = 30\,€$

First case:

$$K_0 = 1.25e^{-0.05} = 1.19 \qquad \text{Ln}K_0 = 0.174$$

$$\sigma\frac{\sqrt{t}}{2} - \frac{\text{Ln}K_0}{\sigma\sqrt{t}} = \frac{0.5}{2} - \frac{0.174}{0.5} = -0.098$$

$$-\sigma\frac{\sqrt{t}}{2} - \frac{\text{Ln}K_0}{\sigma\sqrt{t}} = -\frac{0.5}{2} - \frac{0.174}{0.5} = -0.598$$

$C(1) = 40[\Phi(-0.098) - 1.19\Phi(-0.598)] = 40[1 - \Phi(0.098) - 1.19(1 - \Phi(0.598)] = 5.35$ € using the standard normal distribution tables.

Second case:

$$K_0 = 0.75e^{-0.05} = 0.713 \qquad \text{Ln}K_0 = -0.338$$

$$\sigma\frac{\sqrt{t}}{2} - \frac{\text{Ln}K_0}{\sigma\sqrt{t}} = \frac{0.5}{2} + \frac{0.338}{0.5} = 0.926$$

$$-\sigma\frac{\sqrt{t}}{2} - \frac{\text{Ln}K_0}{\sigma\sqrt{t}} = -\frac{0.5}{2} + \frac{0.338}{0.5} = 0.426$$

$$C(1) = 40[\Phi(0.726) - 0.713\Phi(0.226)] = 13.83 \text{ €}$$

If the premium of the option was 20 €, the holder of the call would lose in both cases. If it was 5 €, he or she would earn some money in the first case and a little more in the second.

It is conceivable that the use of predictive models like the Black–Scholes model is justified. However, the latter undergoes a lot of criticism. Improvements to the model have been suggested. However, we will leave it at that.

7.5. Appendix

7.5.1. *Solution to the predator–prey problem near the equilibrium*

The differential system to be solved is:

$$\begin{cases} \dfrac{dX}{dt} = [a - bY(t)]X(t) \\ \dfrac{dY}{dt} = [cX(t) - d]Y(t) \end{cases}$$

where $X(t)$ and $Y(t)$ represent the prey and predator numbers, respectively. We are interested in the solutions to this system near the equilibrium $(d/c, a/b)$.

Let us start by changing the origin of the X, Y coordinates by taking the equilibrium point as the new origin. Therefore, we have a change of variables:

$x(t) = X(t) - d/c$ and $y(t) = Y(t) - a/b$

The differential system with the new variables x, y is then written as:

$$\begin{cases} \dfrac{dx}{dt} = -byx - \dfrac{bd}{c}y \\ \dfrac{dy}{dt} = cxy + \dfrac{ac}{b}x \end{cases}$$

Near the equilibrium (x and y close to 0), we can neglect the expressions in xy, which considerably simplifies the differential system:

$$\begin{cases} \dfrac{dx}{dt} \cong -\dfrac{bd}{c}y \\ \dfrac{dy}{dt} \cong \dfrac{ac}{b}y \end{cases}$$

We can deduce:

$$\dfrac{\frac{dx}{dt}}{\frac{dy}{dt}} = -\dfrac{b^2 dy}{ac^2 x} \quad \text{or} \quad ac^2 x\dfrac{dx}{dt} + b^2 dy\dfrac{dy}{dt} = 0$$

This last expression easily integrates:

$$ac^2 x^2 + b^2 dy^2 = A$$

where A is an integration constant (positive). Note that this is the Cartesian equation for an ellipse, which specifies the shape of the curve $H(x, y) = C^{te}$.

We can draw y from this expression as a function of x:

$$y = \sqrt{\dfrac{A - ac^2 x^2}{b^2 d}}$$

We can introduce this expression in the first equation of the differential system:

$$\frac{dx}{dt} = -\sqrt{ad}\sqrt{\frac{A}{ac^2} - x^2} \qquad \text{or} \qquad \frac{dx}{\sqrt{\frac{A}{ac^2} - x^2}} = -\sqrt{ad}\,dt$$

Knowing that a primitive of $\frac{1}{\sqrt{k^2-x^2}}$ is $-$ arc cos(x/k), we obtain by integrating:

$$\text{arc cos}\frac{x}{\sqrt{\frac{A}{ac^2}}} = t\sqrt{ad} + C$$

where $C > 0$ is a new integration constant. By switching to inverse functions, we obtain:

$$x = \alpha\frac{d}{c}\cos(t\sqrt{ad} + C)$$

by putting $A = \alpha^2 d^2 a$ where α is a new constant.

Returning to the old coordinates, we have:

$$X(t) = \frac{d}{c}[1 + \alpha\cos(t\sqrt{ad} + C))$$

Similarly, we obtain:

$$Y(t) = \frac{a}{b}[1 + \alpha\sqrt{\frac{d}{a}}\sin(t\sqrt{ad} + C)$$

Since X and Y are positive, it follows that the constant α must verify the inequalities:

$$1 - \alpha > 0 \ \ (for\ X)\ \ and\ \ 1 - \alpha\sqrt{\frac{d}{a}} > 0 \ \ (for\ Y)\ \text{i.e. } \alpha < Min\left(1, \sqrt{\frac{d}{a}}\right)$$

7.5.2. *Root mean square path and diffusion equation*

The fundamental law of the dynamics for a particle of mass m moving on the x-axis is written in most cases knowing that $x = 0$ at moment $t = 0$:

$$m\frac{d^2x}{dt^2} = -\mu v + F$$

where $-\mu v$ is the viscosity force opposing the displacement of the particle (proportional to the velocity $v \equiv v_x$ with a constant coefficient μ) and F is a force responsible for the Brownian motion of zero mean value. By multiplying the two members of the equation by x, we obtain:

$$mx\frac{d^2x}{dt^2} = -\mu xv + xF$$

Using the appended calculations:

$$v = \frac{dx}{dt} \qquad xv = x\frac{dx}{dt} = \frac{1}{2}\frac{d(x^2)}{dt} \qquad x\frac{dv}{dt} = x\frac{d^2x}{dt^2} = \frac{1}{2}\frac{d^2(x^2)}{dt^2} - v^2$$

The previous equation becomes:

$$\frac{m}{2}\frac{d^2(x^2)}{dt^2} - mv^2 = -\frac{\mu}{2}\frac{d(x^2)}{dt} + xF$$

Moving to the average values:

$$\frac{m}{2}\frac{d^2E(x^2)}{dt^2} - mE(v^2) = -\frac{\mu}{2}\frac{dE(x^2)}{dt}|$$

The term in F has disappeared because of the nullity of the average value of F (or of x). If we put:

$$u = \frac{1}{2}\frac{dE(x^2)}{dt}$$

the previous equation is reduced to the differential equation:

$$m\frac{du}{dt} + \mu u = mE(v^2)$$

The solution to this equation is known:

$$u = \frac{mE(v^2)}{\mu} + Ce^{-\frac{\mu t}{m}}$$

The exponential term rapidly approaches 0, because μ/m is very large and so we obtain:

$$\frac{dE(x^2)}{dt} = 2\frac{m}{\mu}E(v^2)$$

By integrating a second time:

$$E(x^2) = 2\frac{m}{\mu}E(v^2)t$$

using the initial condition. To interpret the term $E(v^2)$, we use the kinetic theory that implies a quantum of energy $kT/2$ per degree of freedom (here only one) where k is the Boltzmann constant and T is the absolute temperature. Therefore, we have for the kinetic energy of the particle:

$$\frac{1}{2}mE(v^2) = \frac{kT}{2}$$

Ultimately:

$$E(x^2) = \frac{2kT}{\mu}t$$

Now consider the density of particles $n(x, t)$ per unit length at moment t. Over a length dx, we have $n(x, t)dx$ particles.

Consider a later moment $t + \tau$ during which the coordinate of a particle varies from Δ (positive or negative) with a density probability $\Phi(\Delta)$ symmetric in Δ. The number of particles in dx at moment $t + \tau$ is related to the number of particles in $x + \Delta$ at moment t by:

$$n(x, t + \tau)dx = dx \int_{-\infty}^{+\infty} n(x + \Delta, t)\Phi(\Delta)d\Delta \qquad [7.2]$$

For a small value of τ, we can make the following approximation:

$$n(x, t + \tau) = n(x, t) + \tau\frac{\partial n(x, t)}{\partial t}$$

Furthermore, we can develop in series $n(x + \Delta, t)$:

$$n(x + \Delta, t) = n(x, t) + \Delta \frac{\partial n(x, t)}{\partial x} + \frac{\Delta^2}{2} \frac{\partial^2 n(x, t)}{\partial x^2} + \cdots$$

So that the equation [7.2] is written, simplifying by dx:

$$n(x, t) + \tau \frac{\partial n(x, t)}{\partial t}$$

$$= n(x, t) \int_{-\infty}^{+\infty} \Phi(\Delta) d\Delta + \frac{\partial n(x, t)}{\partial x} \int_{-\infty}^{+\infty} \Delta \, \Phi(\Delta) d\Delta$$

$$+ \frac{1}{2} \frac{\partial^2 n(x, t)}{\partial x^2} \int_{-\infty}^{+\infty} \Delta^2 \, \Phi(\Delta) d\Delta + \cdots$$

In this equation:

$$\int_{-\infty}^{+\infty} \Phi(\Delta) d\Delta = 1 \qquad \int_{-\infty}^{+\infty} \Delta \, \Phi(\Delta) d\Delta = 0 \; (parity \; of \; \Phi)$$

All the terms with an odd power of Δ are zero and we retain only the term with Δ^2 (we neglect the following) for which we put:

$$D\tau = \frac{1}{2} \int_{-\infty}^{+\infty} \Delta^2 \, \Phi(\Delta) d\Delta = \frac{1}{2} E(\Delta^2) = \frac{kT}{\mu} \tau$$

by virtue of the result obtained above. In short:

$$\frac{\partial n(x, t)}{\partial t} = D \frac{\partial^2 n(x, t)}{\partial x^2} \tag{7.3}$$

which is the differential equation of diffusion, the diffusion coefficient D worth kT/μ. The Stokes relations define the coefficient $\mu = 6\pi\eta a$ where η is the viscosity of the fluid and a is the radius of the particle related to a sphere.

The number of particles is obtained by:

$$N = \int_{-\infty}^{+\infty} n(x, t) dt$$

The solution of [7.3] for the initial condition $f(x, 0) = 0$ is:

$$n(x,t) = \frac{N}{\sqrt{4\pi Dt}} e^{-\frac{x^2}{4Dt}}$$

as it is easy to check by derivation. The probability of finding a particle between x and $x + dx$ is:

$$g(x,t)dx = \frac{n(x,t)dx}{N} = \frac{dx}{\sqrt{4\pi Dt}} e^{-\frac{x^2}{4Dt}}$$

where $g(x, t)$ is a probability density whose expression is Gaussian:

$$g(x,t) = \frac{1}{\sqrt{4\pi Dt}} e^{-\frac{x^2}{4Dt}}$$

$g(x, t)$ is also the solution to the diffusion equation.

7.5.3. *Expression of the Black–Scholes formula*

The expression to calculate is:

$$E\left(\left[e^{X(t)} - K_0\right]^+\right) = \int_{LnK}^{+\infty} (e^x - K_0)\frac{1}{\sigma\sqrt{2\pi t}} e^{-\frac{(x-\mu t)^2}{2\sigma^2 t}} dx$$

Let us start by changing the variable:

$$z = \frac{x - \mu t}{\sigma\sqrt{t}} \quad dz = \frac{dx}{\sigma\sqrt{t}} \quad z_0 = \frac{LnK_0}{\sigma\sqrt{t}} + \frac{\sigma\sqrt{t}}{2}$$

The integral becomes:

$$E\left(\left[e^{X(t)} - K_0\right]^+\right) = \int_{z_0}^{+\infty} (e^{\mu t}e^{z\sigma\sqrt{t}} - K_0)\frac{1}{\sqrt{2\pi}} e^{-\frac{z^2}{2}} dz$$

$$= e^{\mu t} \int_{z_0}^{+\infty} e^{z\sigma\sqrt{t}}\frac{1}{\sqrt{2\pi}} e^{-\frac{z^2}{2}} dz$$

$$- K_0 \int_{z_0}^{+\infty} \frac{1}{\sqrt{2\pi}} e^{-\frac{z^2}{2}} dz = I_1 - K_0 I_2$$

To calculate I_1, we perform a simple change of variable:

$$u = z - \sigma\sqrt{t} \qquad du = dz \qquad z_0 = u_0 - \sigma\sqrt{t}$$

We can deduce:

$$I_1 = e^{\mu t} e^{\frac{\sigma^2 t}{2}} \int_{u_0}^{+\infty} \frac{1}{\sqrt{2\pi}} e^{-\frac{u^2}{2}} du$$

Therefore, we put:

$$\Phi(v) = \int_{-\infty}^{v} \frac{1}{\sqrt{2\pi}} e^{-\frac{x^2}{2}} dx$$

Hence:

$$I_1 = e^{\left(\mu+\frac{\sigma^2}{2}\right)} \int_{u_0}^{+\infty} \frac{1}{\sqrt{2\pi}} e^{-\frac{u^2}{2}} du$$

$$= \int_{u_0}^{+\infty} \frac{1}{\sqrt{2\pi}} e^{-\frac{u^2}{2}} du = \int_{-\infty}^{-u_0} \frac{1}{\sqrt{2\pi}} e^{-\frac{u^2}{2}} du = \Phi(-u_0)$$

where the relation $\mu + \sigma^2/2 = 0$ has been taken into account. Moreover:

$$I_2 = \int_{z_0}^{+\infty} \frac{1}{\sqrt{2\pi}} e^{-\frac{z^2}{2}} dz = \int_{-\infty}^{-z_0} \frac{1}{\sqrt{2\pi}} e^{-\frac{z^2}{2}} dz = \Phi(-z_0)$$

Ultimately:

$$E\left(\left[e^{X(t)} - K_0\right]^+\right) = \Phi\left(\frac{\sigma\sqrt{t}}{2} - \frac{LnK_0}{\sigma\sqrt{t}}\right) - K_0\Phi\left(-\frac{\sigma\sqrt{t}}{2} - \frac{LnK_0}{\sigma\sqrt{t}}\right)$$

Part 3

Simulation

8

Generator Programs

CONCEPTS DISCUSSED IN THIS CHAPTER.– The practice of simulation must generate random events, which results in the generation of random numbers. These random numbers can obey various laws, laws known as the usual distributions discussed in Chapter 2, or any laws.

This chapter is devoted first to the technique of generating random numbers for the usual distributions, then for any probability law.

The case where any law can be replaced by a usual distribution is the subject of the presentation of the χ^2 compliance test.

Recommended reading: [PHE 77].

8.1. Random and pseudo-random numbers

A number is random if it is chosen at random, but obeying a known or unknown law of probability. The simplest of these laws is the uniform distribution. We will begin by studying the problem of the generation of random numbers according to the uniform distribution. We will see that other laws can be simulated from this distribution.

But how are random numbers according to the uniform distribution generated? The first answers come from the observation of physical phenomena, the simplest being drawn from games called "games of chance", such as throwing a die (perfect) or the result of roulette (also perfect). What is more sophisticated is the generation of random numbers from electrical noise, which is impossible to predict from electronic circuits.

The use of roulette, simulated by an electronic mechanism, is at the origin of the RAND Corporation's famous table in the 1940s. This table produced lists of random numbers (1 million numbers in the 1947 version). It is interesting to note that this table had to be corrected because some numbers appeared more than others, which contradicts the equiprobability of the uniform distribution. Now we have computers, and this type of table is obsolete today.

Computers can produce random numbers using algorithms. These numbers are not really random, because the computer works deterministically. The numbers obtained are close to random numbers, but to distinguish them from random numbers, they are called "pseudo-random numbers". The quality of their randomness depends on the algorithm used. In the next section, we review some common algorithms that are supposed to produce uniformly distributed sequences of numbers.

8.2. Algorithms for the uniform distribution

Random number generation algorithms are programs that allow starting numbers (the seed) to provide a sequence of pseudo-random numbers. If we keep the same seed, we risk, because of the computer's finite memory resources, reverting to the same sequence after a while. In fact, the algorithm can be characterized by its period, which can be as long as we like. Another way to do this is to change the seed with each draw.

The choice of the seed is the only truly random element of the algorithm since the calculation that follows is entirely deterministic. An example of the choice of the seed is given by the last digits of the date, counted from a distant origin, of the computer's clock.

8.2.1. *Middle-square algorithm*

One of the first algorithms, proposed by von Neumann in 1951, is called the "middle-square method". Today there are more powerful generators, but it is still instructive to examine the method.

The seed is a number u_0 of $2m$ digits. It is squared, which gives a number of $4m$ digits (if necessary, zeros are added at the beginning), and we take as a result the number u_1 composed of $2m$ central digits. We repeat the process with u_1, which gives u_2, etc. We avoid cases where the central figures are all zero.

For example, $m = 2$ and $u_0 = 7367$:

$$u_0 = 7367 \qquad u_0^2 = 54272689$$

$$u_1 = 2726 \qquad u_1^2 = 07431076$$

$$u_2 = 4310 \qquad u_2^2 = 18576100$$

$$u_3 = 5761 \qquad u_3^2 = 33189121$$

$$u_4 = 1891 \qquad u_4^2 = 03575881$$

$$u_5 = 5758 \qquad \text{etc.}$$

which gives the sequence 73672726431057611891...

We can take them one by one to get a sequence of random digits (we omit the "pseudo" from now on) between 0 and 9. We can take them two by two to obtain a sequence of random numbers between 00 and 99, etc.

Figure 8.1. *John von Neumann (1903–1957), Hungarian-born American mathematician and physicist*

COMMENT ON FIGURE 8.1. *After working in mathematics (set theory), he focused on the new science of quantum physics and published* "The mathematical formulation of quantum mechanics" *in 1932, but he is best known for his contributions to computer science, especially computer architecture. The* "von Neumann machine" *remains the model of today's computers*[1].

8.2.2. *Fibonacci sequence*

The seed consists of three numbers u_0, u_1 and k, the latter being larger than the first two. We then generate a recurring sequence with the algorithm:

$$u_{n+2} = u_{n+1} + u_n + ak \text{ with } a = 0 \text{ if } u_{n+1} + u_n \leq k \text{ and } a = -1 \text{ if } u_{n+1} + u_n > k$$

For example, $u_0 = 05673$, $u_1 = 09251$, $k = 12654$:

$u_2 = 9251 + 567 - 12654 \qquad = 02270$

$u_3 = 2270 + 9251 \qquad = 11521$

$u_4 = 11521 + 2270 - 12654 \quad = 01137$

$u_5 = 1137 + 11521 - 12654 \quad = 00004$

$u_6 = 4 + 1137 \qquad = 01141$

$u_7 = 1141 + 4 \qquad = 01145$

$u_8 = 1145 + 1141 \qquad = 02286$

etc.

We then eliminate the first and the last digit of each number obtained, hence the result:

5679252271521130001141114228…

---

1 The photograph of John von Neumann (source: United States Department of Energy) is at https://en.wikipedia.org/wiki/John_von_Neumann.

Figure 8.2. *Leonardo Fibonacci (1175–1250), Italian mathematician in the Middle Ages, worked on the science of calculus, especially commercial arithmetic, and on numbers theory. He was little known, and introduced the Hindu-Arabic numeral system to Europe (he lived and traveled extensively in North Africa) replacing impractical Roman notation with calculations*[2]

8.2.3. *Congruences*

A generalization of the Fibonacci sequence can be given by the congruence formula:

$$u_n = (au_{n-1} + b) \bmod h$$

whose starting point is the seed u_0, a, b, h. Because of the modulo, the numbers u_n are between 0 and $h - 1$. The choice of the seed is crucial.

For example, $u_0 = 2357$, $a = 515$, $b = 0$, $h = 10000$:

$u_1 = 3855$

$u_2 = 5325$

$u_3 = 2375$

$u_4 = 3125$

$u_5 = 9375$

$u_6 = 8125$

etc.

2 The portrait of Leonardo Fibonacci is from the bibmath library: http://www.bibmath.net/bios/images/fibonacci.jpg.

Dividing by 10,000, we obtain random numbers between 0 and 1:

$x_1 = 0.3855$

$x_2 = 0.5325$

$x_3 = 0.2375$

$x_4 = 0.3125$

$x_5 = 0.9375$

$x_6 = 0.8125$

etc.

A satisfactory seed was given by Park and Miller: $a = 16{,}807 = 7^5$, $b = 0$, $u_0 = 1$, $h = 2{,}147{,}483{,}647 = 2^{32} - 1$. To obtain numbers x_n between 0 and 1, divide u_n by h.

There are many variations of this congruence method. Let us mention two examples:

– congruence with delay: $u_n = (au_{n-r} + b) \bmod h$. We first calculate the first terms $u_1, u_2, \ldots, u_{n-r}$ with the basic formula $u_n = (au_{n-1} + b) \bmod h$ and then use the formula with delay;

– congruence with inverse: $u_n = (au_{n-1}{}^* + b) \bmod h$ where $u_{n-1}{}^*$ is the inverse of u_{n-1} modulo h (i.e. $u_{n-1}u_{n-1}{}^* = 1 \bmod h$).

8.2.4. *Lehmer process*

We start from a seed composed of a number u_0 of m digits and a number k of n digits ($m > n$). We multiply them, which gives a number to $m + n$ digits (possibly adding zeros at the beginning). We separate the n digits on the left, which is a number d_0, and the m digits on the right, which is a number e_0. We calculate $e_0 - d_0$. We thus obtain u_1. The process is repeated with u_1, etc.

For example, $u_0 = 483215$ and $k = 678$:

$u_0 = 483215$ $u_0k = 327619770$ $d_0 = 327$ $e_0 = 619770$

$u_1 = 619443$ $u_1k = 419982354$ $d_1 = 419$ $e_1 = 982354$

$u_2 = 981935$ $u_2k = 665751930$ $d_2 = 665$ $e_2 = 751930$

$u_3 = 751265$ $u_3k = 509357670$ $d_3 = 509$ $e_3 = 357670$

$u_4 = 357161$ etc.

We get the sequence 4832156194439819357512653 57161...

8.2.5. *Decimals of Π*

This is a "natural" generator made up of decimals of π, a number that has aroused the curiosity of mathematicians since Antiquity. The irrationality of π means that the sequence of its decimals does not contain periodicity and the sequence of decimals is completely disordered.

It remains to be proven that the sequence of decimals is a sequence of random numbers. The calculation of frequencies of the digits from 0 to 9 gives similar results close to 0.1 for the 50,000,000,000 first decimals of π, which seems to indicate that these figures are distributed according to the uniform distribution. However, this question is still open.

8.3. Distribution function and random number generator

If we know the distribution function, which is the case for the normal probability distributions, we can theoretically determine the random number generator according to the probability distribution.

DEFINITION.– Given a probability distribution p of a random variable X, the distribution function is defined by:

$$F(X) = p(X \le x)$$

EXAMPLE 8.1.– A bag contains 10 red balls, 25 green balls and 15 blue balls; except for color, these balls are identical. The experiment consists of picking out a ball. There are three possible outcomes.

Picking out a red ball: $X = 1$ $p(X = 1) = 0.2$.

Picking out a green ball: $X = 2$ $p(X = 2) = 0.5$.

Picking out a blue ball: $X = 3$ $p(X = 3) = 0.3$.

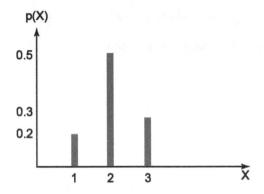

Figure 8.3. *The law of probability p(X)*

This probability law for the discrete variable X is represented by a bar graph (Figure 8.3).

Let us determine the distribution function $F(X)$.

For $x < 1$ $F(X) = 0.$

For $x \in [1, 2[$ $F(X) = 0.2.$

For $x \in [2, 3[$ $F(X) = 0.7.$

For $x \geq 3$ $F(X) = 1.$

The graphical representation of the function $F(X)$ is a stepped curve (Figure 8.4).

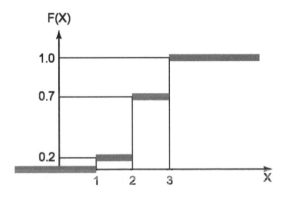

Figure 8.4. *Distribution function*

In general, $F(X)$ always looks like a growing curve, its value starting from 0 and going to 1. For a continuous random variable, the shape of $F(X)$ is given in Figure 8.5.

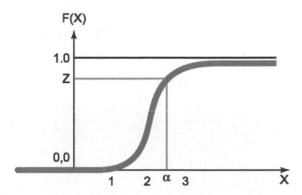

Figure 8.5. *Shape of the distribution function for a continuous variable*

Looking at this curve, we see that the solution to our problem consists of two steps:

– first step: draw at random (uniform distribution) a number z between 0 and 1;

– second step: using the inverse function of $F(x)$, determine a random number α according to the fixed probability distribution. $\alpha = F^{-1}(z)$.

We studied the first step in the previous section; we must focus on the second, more delicate step. It depends on the probability distribution considered, and the inverse function $F^{-1}(X)$ is not always easy to find. In the next section, we review the normal probability distributions to indicate how to solve this second step.

8.4. Generators for the normal distributions

8.4.1. *Uniform distribution*

Let us return to the uniform distribution. We have seen how to find (pseudo-) random numbers between 0 and 1.

Now, let us look at how to find random numbers between a and b ($b > a$). The calculation is very simple.

If z is a random number between 0 and 1, the numbers we are looking for are of the form:

$$\alpha = (b - a)z + a$$

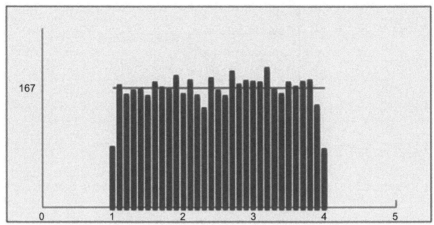

in blue: experimental values; in red: theoretical values

Figure 8.6. *Simulation of a uniform distribution*

Figure 8.6 shows the result of this generator for $a = 1$, $b = 4$ and 5,000 random numbers z between 0 and 1. The values of α were grouped in steps of 0.1. We therefore have 30 intervals. If the uniform distribution is respected, the height of the bars should be 166.66.

8.4.2. *Poisson distribution*

Since Poisson distribution is a discrete variable distribution, we must find an integer α such that:

$$\sum_{k=0}^{\alpha} e^{-m}\frac{m^k}{k!} \leq z \leq \sum_{k=0}^{\alpha+1} e^{-m}\frac{m^k}{k!}$$

where z is a random number between 0 and 1.

Figure 8.7 gives an example of the use of this generator for $m = 20$ and 5,000 random numbers z. The values of α were grouped in steps of 0.1.

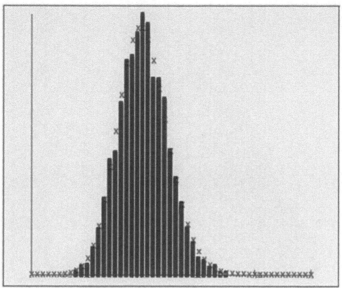

in blue: experimental values; in red: theoretical values

Figure 8.7. *Simulation of a Poisson distribution*

8.4.3. *Normal distribution*

For the normal distribution, the function $F(X)$ is difficult to reverse. So we use algorithms to approach it. The simplest of them is the following:

$$\alpha = \sigma \left[\sum_{i=1}^{12} z_i - 6 \right] + m$$

where z_i is a uniform number generated by the uniform distribution between 0 and 1, and m and σ are the parameters of the normal distribution (mean and standard deviation).

Figure 8.8 shows the use of this generator for $m = 20$, $\sigma = 10$ and 10,000 generator applications. The values of α were grouped in steps of 0.1. It can be observed that, despite its simplicity, this generator gives acceptable results.

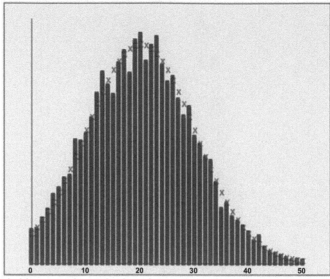

in blue: experimental values; in red: theoretical values

Figure 8.8. *Simulation of a normal distribution*

8.4.4. *Exponential distribution*

The exponential distribution has the function of distribution (Chapter 5) $F(x)$ such that:

$$F(x) = 1 - e^{-\lambda x} \text{ for } x \geq 0$$

$$F(x) = 0 \text{ for } x < 0$$

It is easy to reverse $F(x)$:

$$F^{-1}(z) = -\frac{1}{\lambda} Ln(1-z) \quad \text{for } 0 \leq y < 1$$

8.5. Generators for any law

How is a random number obeying any law generated? We will look at an example to explain the process.

Number of arrivals	0	1	2	3	4	5	6	7	8	9	10	11	12	>12
Number of occurrences	0	1	12	23	22	11	8	8	7	3	3	1	1	0

Table 8.1. *Law of arrivals*

Suppose customers are arriving to join a queue. Every 15 minutes we measure the number of customers who have arrived. We obtain a statistic (Table 8.1) of the arrival of customers on 100 measurements.

From this table, the statistical frequency can be calculated, which is the number of occurrences of events divided by 100. It is assumed that the statistical frequency gives an approximate value of the probability of occurrence of customer arrivals (second row of Table 8.2).

Number of arrivals	0	1	2	3	4	5	6	7	8	9	10	11	12	>12
Probability	0.00	0.01	0.12	0.23	0.22	0.11	0.08	0.08	0.07	0.03	0.03	0.01	0.01	0.00
Number of occurrences	0	1	12	23	22	11	8	8	7	3	3	1	1	0
Range of numbers	–	00	01 to 12	13 to 35	36 to 57	58 to 68	69 to 76	77 to 84	85 to 91	92 to 94	95 to 97	98	99	–

Table 8.2. *Distribution of 100 integers*

The probability is given to the nearest hundredth. We can multiply by 100 and consider that the number obtained measures a range whose size corresponds to a certain extent to the chances of seeing an event occur. Thus, for an arrival number of four customers, there is a range of 22 numbers which is larger than that of the arrival of nine customers which is only 3 (Figure 8.9).

Figure 8.9. *Range of numbers*

To this number of values measuring the importance of a range (row 3 of Table 8.2), we associate integers from 00 to 99. For the number of arrivals 1, we have a measurement range 1 and we will match the number 00. For the number of arrivals 2, the range is 12 and we will match the numbers from 01 to 12. For the number of arrivals 3, the range is 23 and we will match the numbers from 13 to 35, and so on. It is sufficient to apply the uniform distribution to draw a number from 00 to 99.

If, for example, this number is 48, it corresponds to the number of arrivals 4. We can thus generate random numbers according to the law of customer arrivals.

Let us check using an example of the process: Figure 8.10 gives the result for a draw of 2,000 random numbers between 0 and 99.

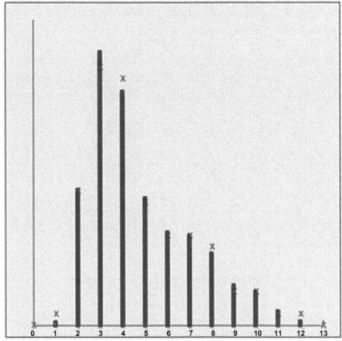

in blue: experimental values; in red: theoretical values

Figure 8.10. *Simulation of any law*

8.6. χ^2 test

As we saw previously, when the law of probability is known, it is simple to generate numbers according to this law. In the case of any law, we can use the method of the preceding section. However, this may not always be the case! Indeed, phenomena can follow a known (i.e. normal) probability distribution without this being obvious *a priori*.

The question then arises as to whether any law can be considered to be a usual law. The question can be formulated in another way: How do you make sure that a random variable follows a given probability law? An answer is given by a method called the "χ^2 test" (pronounced "chi–squared") that we will look at now.

The *probability distribution of χ^2* is a law for a continuous variable X of density of probability whose expression (which is not very nice!) is known. It is therefore a "usual" distribution whose probability density is for $x \geq 0$:

$$F(x) = \frac{2^{-\frac{v}{2}}}{\Gamma\left(\frac{v}{2}\right)} e^{-\frac{xv}{2x^2}-1}$$

where the parameter v is called "degree of freedom" and the function $\Gamma(p)$ is an extension of the factorial function for a continuous variable. It is defined by the integral:

$$\Gamma(p) = \int_0^\infty e^{-x}x^{p-1}dx$$

and has the following properties:

– $\Gamma(p) = (p-1)\Gamma(p-1)$ for $p > 0$;

– $\Gamma(p) = (p-1)!$ for p positive integer;

– $\Gamma(1/2) = \sqrt{\pi}$.

We prove that the mean of X is $E(X) = v$ and the variance is $v(X) = 2v$.

This distribution, which initially appears complex (because it is), has a very useful property.

FUNDAMENTAL THEOREM.– If X_1, X_2,..., X_n are independent normal random variables:

$$S = X_1^2 + X_2^2 + ... + X_n^2$$

follows a distribution from χ^2 to v degrees of freedom. We then have, in particular, $E(S) = v$ and $v(S) = 2v$.

The tables give the value of the probability $p(S \geq \chi_0^2) = \alpha$ according to the parameters α, called "risk threshold", ν the number of degrees of freedom (a concept that we will see later and which is related to the character of independence of the variables X_i).

Figure 8.11 expresses the variations of the probability density $f(x)$ and the representation of the probability p.

The $\chi 2$ test is widely used to compare an experimental distribution with a theoretical distribution (binomial distribution, Poisson distribution, normal distribution, etc.).

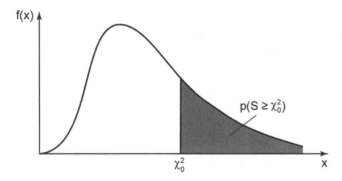

Figure 8.11. *Probability density of χ^2*

Suppose, after statistical study, we have the results of Table 8.3, where the theoretical number is relative to a normal probability distribution.

Character C	C_1	C_2	...	C_n
Experimental number	E_1	E_2	...	E_n
Theoretical number	T_1	T_2	...	T_n

Table 8.3. *Statistical diagram*

If we consider the experimental numbers as normal independent random variables E_i, we define a new random variable by:

$$S = \sum_{i=1}^{n} \frac{(E_i - T_i)^2}{T_i}$$

which expresses the relative quadratic difference between experiment and theory. The smallness of S indicates the match between experiment and theory. If S is 0, there is perfect convergence.

Based on the fundamental theorem of the χ^2 distribution, Pearson demonstrated that S follows a probability distribution of χ^2. The χ^2 test verifies the "null" hypothesis H_0: *the experiment conforms to the theory*. The χ^2 is then used as a conformity test:

– the value S is calculated;

– knowing α and ν, we determine the value of χ_0^2 such as $p(S \geq \chi_0^2) = \alpha$;

– if $S < \chi_0^2$, the hypothesis H_0 is accepted. There is a $\alpha \%$ chance that hypothesis H_0 will be rejected (Figure 8.12).

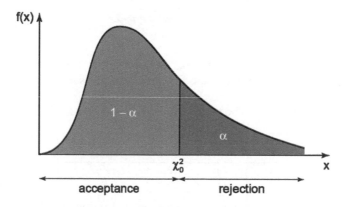

Figure 8.12. χ^2 *test*

The n values of the character represent classes that correspond to values or groups of values. In general, the parameters of the theoretical distribution are calculated from these experimental classes by means of p relations. These relations "break" the independence of the measurements and the difference $n - p$ represents the number ν of degrees of freedom.

If we want to study the adjustment of an experimental distribution to a theoretical distribution of probability, given the number of classes n, there is one less degree of freedom to be considered at first: the fact that the n values are linked by the relation "sum of values" $= N$. Indeed, the χ^2 test only applies to the numbers (not the frequencies). Now the theoretical model (usual law of probability) is expressed in terms of probabilities and to obtain the theoretical numbers, it is necessary to multiply the probabilities by N.

There are others, relative to the characteristic parameters of the theoretical distribution: for one parameter, the degree of freedom decreases by 1, for two parameters, it decreases by 2. Thus, if we want to compare an experimental distribution with a Poisson distribution, the number of degrees of freedom is $n - 2$ (there is only one parameter for Poisson distribution, the mean λ). For a normal distribution, the number of degrees of freedom is $n - 3$ (there are two parameters for the normal distribution: the mean m and the standard deviation σ).

EXAMPLE 8.2.– A large self-service store identified an establishment plan of customer arrivals at the checkouts at the store's exit (Table 8.4).

k: number of customer arrivals per minute	0	1	2	3	4	5	6	7	8	9	10	N
E_k: number observed	4	20	24	35	40	30	23	11	8	4	1	200

Table 8.4. *Law of arrivals*

It is assumed that customer arrivals are distributed according to a Poisson distribution $p(X = k) = e^{-m} \cdot m^k/k!$. What do we make of this supposition?

We will apply the χ^2 test. The table is filled in as shown in Table 8.5.

k	E_k	T_k	$(E_k - T_k)^2/T_k$
0	4	4	0.000
1	20	15	1.667
2	24	29	0.862
3	35	39	0.410
4	40	39	0.026
5	30	31	0.032
6	23	21	0.190
7	11	12	0.083
8	8	6	0.667
9	4	3	0.333
10	1	1	0.000
N	200	200	4.271

Table 8.5. *Calculation of χ^2*

The theoretical values are calculated as follows: first, we look for the mean k from the values k and E_k. We obtain $m = 4.04$, which we will approximate to 4 since the Poisson distribution is a distribution for a discrete variable. Then, we determine Poisson's probability $p(X = k)$ with this mean m. Next, we multiply by $N = 200$ to obtain the theoretical numbers (rounded to integers). Finally, we calculate the sum $S = 4.271$.

There are 10 classes, but we have calculated N and the mean m, which leads to 8 degrees of freedom.

Find in the table of χ^2 the value of χ_0^2 corresponding to the risk threshold $\alpha = 0.05$ for 8 degrees of freedom. We obtain $\chi_0^2 = 15.507$. As $S < \chi_0^2$, we can accept the hypothesis that the distribution of probability of arrivals is the Poisson distribution (with a 95% chance).

EXAMPLE 8.3.– Let us go back to Example 6.2 (Chapter 6). We had workers presenting themselves at a counter and we found, on the one hand, the similarity between the distribution of arrivals and the distribution of Poisson, and on the other, between the law of service duration and the exponential distribution, and recognized that it was indeed these laws. Let us check that this hypothesis can be used with the χ^2 test.

For the law of arrivals, let us return to the table of experimental data and fill it in Table 8.6.

k	E_k	P	T_k	$(E_k - T_k)^2/T_k$
0	36	0.368	37	0.0270
1	38	0.368	37	0.0270
2	18	0.184	18	0.0000
3	8	0.061	6	0.6667
N	100			0.7207

Table 8.6. *Calculation of χ^2 for arrivals*

k corresponds to the number of arrivals during an interval of 5 minutes, and E_k are the corresponding occurrences.

With these data, an average of 0.98 was calculated per 5-minute interval, i.e. $\lambda = 0.2$ arrival per minute by rounding. Column P indicates the probability of Poisson for an average of 5λ. Multiplying by N, we obtain the numbers T_k. We then calculate χ^2, whose value is 0.72. The tables give $\chi_0^2 = 0.72$ for a degree of freedom equal to $4 - 1 - 1 = 2$ and a risk threshold at 5%, or 5.99, well above the value of 0.72. The choice of the Poisson distribution is therefore justified.

Let us move on to the service duration that seems to follow the exponential distribution. Table 8.7 shows these calculations.

k	E_k	P	T_k	$(E_k - T_k)^2/T_k$
0.5	26	0.28	27.98	0.1402
1.5	20	0.201	20.12	0.0007
2.5	15	0.145	14.46	0.0200
3.5	12	0.104	10.4	0.2472
4.5	8	0.075	7.475	0.0369
5.5	6	0.054	5.374	0.0730
6.5	6	0.039	3.863	1.1818
7.5	3	0.028	2.777	0.0178
8.5	2	0.02	1.997	0.0000
9.5	1	0.014	1.435	0.1321
10.5	1	0.01	1.032	0.0010
11.5	0	0.007	0.742	0.7419
N	100			2.5927

Table 8.7. *Calculation of χ^2 for services*

In this table, k denotes the center of the classes and E_k the experimental numbers. We deduce the mean $1/\mu = 2.9$ or 3 approximately. Column P indicates the probabilities of the exponential distribution with a mean of $\mu = 1/3 = 0.33$. Multiplying these probabilities by $N = 100$ gives the theoretical numbers T_k. The calculation of S then gives $S = 2.59$.

In the tables, the value of χ_0^2 is 18.307 for $12 - 2 = 10$ degrees of freedom and $\alpha = 0.05$. This value is much greater than S. We deduce that we have a 95% chance that the distribution of probability is the exponential distribution. Our hypothesis is therefore justified.

9

Principles of Simulation

CONCEPTS DISCUSSED IN THIS CHAPTER.– In this chapter, we are interested in simulation in general. We will take characteristic examples to illustrate the concept.

We will begin by defining the word "simulation", mainly in relation to the content of this book.

Then, we will focus on stochastic simulation, which involves chance. Chance comes in the form of using random numbers. Nowadays, the computer is a valuable tool for performing simulations and generating random numbers.

To make numerical simulations on a computer, it is necessary to produce data that represent samples for the phenomena studied.

A modeling of manipulated random variables involves the normal probability distributions in general, although there is nothing to stop us defining our own probability laws from statistical observations. In the case of the normal distribution, we will show how a simulation constrained by these laws is carried out.

Recommended reading: [BAR 01, BER 07, DOD 08, FAU 14, VAL 07].

9.1. General information on simulation

What does the word "simulation" mean? To find out, we examine, like everyone else, the dictionary definitions. And here we have a fairly large choice.

All figures and tables are available in color online at www.iste.co.uk/cochard/stochastic.zip.

Larousse's definition of the word "simulation"[1]:

"Voluntary or semi-voluntary imitation of a mental or physical disorder.

Representation of the behavior of a physical, industrial, biological, economic or military process by means of a material model whose parameters and variables are the images of those of the studied process (simulation models usually take the form of computer programs that are sometimes associated with analog computing elements).

Concealment by the parties of a secret contract (counter letter) under cover of an apparent act".

Our study obviously corresponds to the second point, but since we will use the computer as a simulation tool, we can turn to Larousse for a more precise definition (please note that Larousse repeats part of the definition for "simulation"):

"Representation of the behavior of a physical, industrial, biological, economic or military process *by means of a material model whose parameters and variables are the images of those of the studied process.*

A numerical simulation is always based on a *model*, on the simplified representation of an object, a system or a physical, chemical or biological process. Scientists develop these models by taking into account laws and experiments: they can represent ocean currents, an airplane's trajectory and the study of migratory flows using numbers and mathematical equations. In a way, these models show reality in formulas.

These formulas enable computer programs. *We thus obtain a numerical simulation of reality that sometimes even replaces experimentation.* So, simulation can *reduce costs and delays.* Simulations are used for sizing and they provide information that is difficult to obtain by measurements. One can simulate a gas explosion in a building, or the effects of a nuclear weapon, without committing any damage at all. Simulations then make it possible to extrapolate while projecting in real size. Finally, a numerical simulation enables scientists to develop new physical models. It is impossible, for example, to write a theory that would account for climate movements on a global scale. But simulations, which integrate the effects of a

1 http://www.larousse.fr/dictionnaires/francais/simulation/72824.

large number of more or less simple phenomena, can get closer to this complex reality. There are too many variables for a single human being to analyze meteorological data. *Only a machine can predict the weather. For all these reasons, digital simulation has become indispensable for scientific research*".

We have highlighted the parts that seem to characterize the subject of our study (although we will not make anything explode in our simulations!).

Let us also give Futura Science's definition[2] on the concept of numerical (or computer) simulation:

"Computer simulation, or numerical simulation, is a series of calculations done on a computer which reproduce a physical phenomenon. It leads to the description of the result of this phenomenon, as if it had really happened. This representation can be a series of data, an image or even a film.

A simulator can react to parameter changes and modify its results accordingly. A flight simulator, for example, modifies the calculated trajectory of the aircraft according to the user's commands.

A numerical simulation can represent complex physical phenomena whose description is based on a mathematical model with partial differential equations. The computer then solves these equations numerically by using the finite element method. This is the case, for example, for modeling, relying on the mechanics of fluids, the flow of air or water around an aircraft or a ship".

Finally, let us look at Wikipedia's[3] definition of the word "simulation", which has several meanings:

"Simulation of real phenomena:

– Kriegsspiel, the wargame used in military schools;

– computer simulation or numerical simulation, using a computer (see also: Emulation);

– flight simulator;

– geostatistical simulation;

2 http://www.futura-sciences.com.
3 https://fr.wikipedia.org/wiki/Simulation – please note that this is a translation of the French Wikipedia's entry.

– simulation game, video games application.

Simulation: French nuclear defense program from 1996 to 2010.

Simulation in French private law.

Child simulation: the action of a person who pretends or registers that a child is their biological child (or someone else's) when the child is not.

Logical simulation, which consists of simulating the behavior of a digital circuit while it is still only described in the form of RTL or a netlist.

Preorder simulation (theoretical computing), a relationship between state transition systems.

Socio-fiscal microsimulation model, model for evaluating public policies".

As we can see, the word "simulation" can correspond to various situations of problems to be solved.

Similarly for "numerical simulation", Wikipedia[4] provides the following information:

"Computer or numerical simulation refers to the execution of a computer program on a computer or network in order to simulate a real and complex physical phenomenon (for example: a body falling on a soft support, an oil platform's resistance to swell, a material's fatigue under vibratory stress, a ball bearing's wear etc.). Scientific numerical simulations are based on the implementation of theoretical models that often use the finite element technique. They are thus an adaptation to the numerical means of mathematical modeling, and are used to study the functioning and properties of a modeled system and to predict its evolution. It also includes numerical computation. The graphical interfaces allow the visualization of the results of calculations by computer-generated images.

These computer simulations have quickly become essential for the modeling of natural systems in physics, chemistry and biology, as well as human systems in economics and the social sciences. They allow us

---

4 https://fr.wikipedia.org/Simulation-informatique. Please note that this quote is also a translation from French Wikipedia.

to limit the risk and avoid the cost of a series of real tests (example: vehicle testing). They can offer insights into the development of a system that is too complex to simulate with simple mathematical formulas (example: a hurricane).

Numerical simulation is used to:

– predict the final state of a system knowing its initial state (direct problem);

– determine the parameters of a system knowing one or more couples (initial state-final state) (inverse problem);

– prepare operators for rare conditions in their interaction with a complex system (training simulation)".

Faced with this avalanche of definitions, all that remains is to give ours, which is more restrictive, from the point of view of this presentation:

A simulation is a numerical method that allows us:

– either to represent the evolution of a real system by constraining it to a model;

– or to use numerical methods to calculate what is difficult to do analytically.

This definition is a casual shortcut that addresses two types of problems:

– the first type is stochastic processes that develop a system according to the laws of chance and initial constraints. In general, the goal is to predict the state of the system at a later time, which is defined at an initial time. In particular, two classic problems will be studied: stock management subject to the uncertainties of customer demand, and queues with random arrivals and departures;

– the second type is the estimation of a value by numerical methods. This type of problem is often called the "Monte Carlo method", making reference to casino games. Estimating the value of an integral or surface area falls into this category. In this case, it is more of a numerical method than a modeling of a real process. However, there is an important similarity with the first type: the use of random numbers.

Figure 9.1. *Georges-Louis Leclerc de Buffon (1707–1788) was a mathematician, biologist, naturalist and philosopher*

COMMENT ON FIGURE 9.1.– *He was a marquess, a viscount and then a count, successively. He worked on the* Encyclopedia *during the Age of Enlightenment. As a scientist, he was interested in various fields of science. He is best known for his work as a naturalist. He managed the Jardin des Plantes in Paris by transforming it into a research center and a museum*[5].

Below, we give examples of the first type and the second type (we will see others in the following sections).

9.2. Simulation by example

EXAMPLE 9.1. Buffon, his needle, the floor and the number π.

This experiment is famous because it is perhaps the first case ever of applying a method using chance to calculate quantities!

It involves throwing a needle of length L on a floor composed of parallel strips of the same width d. We count the number of times N we throw the needle and the number of times n where it lies across a line between two strips. Buffon has shown that the probability of the needle lying across a line upon landing (in the case where $d > L$): $2L/\pi d$.

---

5 The portrait of Georges-Louis Leclerc de Buffon (artist: François-Hubert Drouais, 1727–1775) is from Wikimedia Commons.

In other words, for a large N, the ratio n/N must tend towards this value, which makes it possible to deduce an approximate value of π:

$$\pi = \frac{2LN}{nd}$$

Where do Buffon's hypotheses come from?

Let us first examine the Buffon method and calculate the probability that the needle lies across a line between two strips. First, we can assume that the place of impact is indifferent (assuming that all the properties of the floor are equivalent). Therefore, we can address the problem with two random variables (choosing the horizontal strips and positioning one strip; Figure 9.2).

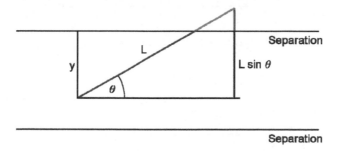

Figure 9.2. *Needles on the strips of a floor*

– The distance y of the lowest point of the needle relative to the separation of the top (which varies from 0 to d).

– The angle θ of the needle with the horizontal (which varies from 0 to π).

It is easy to see that the needle intersects the upper separation if $y < L\sin\theta$.

This relation can be drawn graphically: Figure 9.3 shows (in yellow) the different possible points when we randomly choose y and θ (assuming that there is uniform distribution).

First, we assume that $d > L$ (Figure 9.4). The curve $y = L\sin\theta$ is a sinusoid arc and the plane portion below (in green) corresponds to the situations where the needle intersects the separation. The desired probability is then the ratio of the areas of the green surface and the yellow rectangle (part of which is obscured by the green surface). The area of the yellow rectangle is πd; the area of the green portion is:

$$\int_0^\pi L\sin\theta d\theta = 2L$$

which leads to the probability:

$$p = \frac{2L}{\pi d}$$

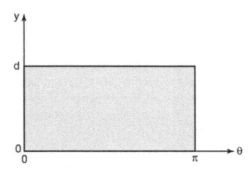

Figure 9.3. *Space for x and θ*

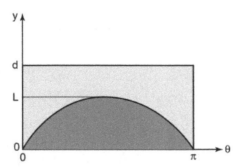

Figure 9.4. *Case where d > L*

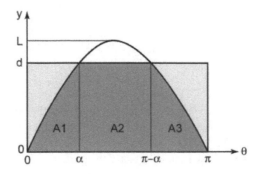

Figure 9.5. *Case where d < L*

When L > d, the calculation is a little longer (Figure 9.5). The green zone must be broken down into three parts of areas A1, A2, A3:

$$A1 = \int_0^\alpha L\sin\theta\,d\theta = L(1 - \cos\alpha) \qquad A2 = d(\pi - 2\alpha) \qquad A3 = A1$$

with $\alpha = \arcsin(d/L)$ which ultimately leads to the probability:

$$p = \frac{2L\left(1 - \sqrt{1 - \frac{d^2}{L^2}}\right) + d\left[\pi - 2\arcsin\left(\frac{d}{L}\right)\right]}{\pi d}$$

At the time, Buffon did not have a computer and had to perform the experiment "by hand". Today, you can simulate his experiment with a computer. It is sufficient to choose at random, according to the uniform distribution, a value of y between 0 and d and a value of θ between 0 and π, and then to check if $y < L\sin\theta$. If on N tests, n corresponds to this condition, we have:

$$\text{if } d \geq L \qquad \pi = \frac{2LN}{dn}$$

$$\text{if } d < L \qquad \pi = \frac{2\arcsin\left(\frac{d}{L}\right) - 2\frac{L}{d}\left(1 - \sqrt{1 - \frac{d^2}{L^2}}\right)}{1 - \frac{n}{N}}$$

EXAMPLE 9.2.– Monte Carlo method to calculate an estimate of π.

Now imagine calculating the number π by choosing random points in a square of side $2a$. In this square, the circle of radius a is written.

We count the total number N of points and the number n of points on the disk. If we assume that all the points of the square have the same probability (i.e. the corresponding distribution is the uniform distribution) to be chosen, the probability of choosing a point in the circle will be approximated by the ratio n/N.

Moreover, as the distribution of the points is assumed to be homogeneous, the number of points located in the square is proportional to the area of the square $4a^2$. In the same way, the number of points in the disk is proportional to the area of the disk πa^2. We can deduce:

$$\frac{n}{N} = \frac{\pi}{4} \qquad \text{i.e. } \pi = 4\frac{n}{N}$$

It is therefore sufficient to carry out a large number of experiments using, for convenience, a computer that will randomly draw the coordinates (x, y) of a point (the origin of the coordinates is in the center of the circle) following the uniform distribution and checking if $x^2 + y^2 \leq a^2$ (Figure 9.6).

This small example illustrates some features of a numerical simulation:

– we do not perform a real experiment (it would take a lot of time), but we use a computer to carry out the draws (random samples) and count favorable cases and possible cases. It is therefore a "virtual" experience;

– we quickly realize that if we want a significant result, we need a fairly high number of draws. This is also a good reason to use a computer.

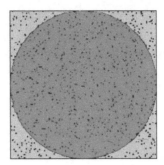

Figure 9.6. *Random point distribution*

EXAMPLE 9.3.– Calculation of integrals.

The previous method can be applied to surface area calculations. A special case is calculating complex integrals that the analytical calculus is not able to apply or has difficulty applying.

For example, the integral:

$$I = \int_0^1 x\mathrm{Ln}(1 + x)\mathrm{d}x$$

Its value, calculated with complex methods, is 1/4.

The integral is given by the area of the yellow surface in Figure 9.7. We proceed in the following way: random choice of N points (x, y) in the rectangle is defined by the intervals [0, 1] for x and [0, 0.8] for y. If the point is below the curve, we increment a counter n. The ratio n/N is equal to the yellow area/rectangle area ratio.

$I = $ (yellow area) = (rectangle area).n/N

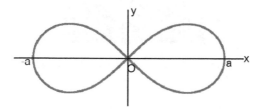

Figure 9.7. *Regions limited by the curve y = f(x)*

EXAMPLE 9.4.– Evaluation of an area.

Let us apply the Monte Carlo method to the calculation of any surface area.

Did you know that the "infinity" symbol is represented by a famous curve, called the "Lemniscate of Bernoulli" (Figure 9.8)? This curve has as a Cartesian equation:

$$(x^2 + y^2)^2 = a^2(x^2 - y^2)$$

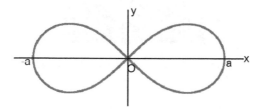

Figure 9.8. *Lemniscate of Bernoulli*

The analytical calculation of the surface area included in the loops of this curve is doable, though tedious. The result is surprisingly simple:

$$A = a^2$$

Let us try to find this value using a Monte Carlo simulation. Given the symmetry of the curve, it is sufficient to calculate the quarter-loop area in the first quadrant.

We will choose at random, according to the uniform distribution, N points in the square of side a, and count the number n of points which are in the quarter of the loop. These n points must satisfy the condition:

$$(x^2 + y^2)^2 < a^2(x^2 - y^2)$$

The result of a simulation (Figure 9.9) provides, for example, for $N = 1000$, the value $A = 0,968$ and for $N = 10000$, $A = 1.0084$.

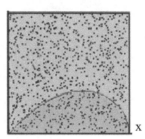

Figure 9.9. *First quadrant reduction*

Figure 9.10. *Francis Galton (1822–1911)*

COMMENT ON FIGURE 9.10.– *Francis Galton was, some may argue, the perfect scientist. He was interested in many scientific topics: meteorology, genetics, psychology, statistics, anthropology, etc. The bean machine in question (see Example 9.5) was used to experimentally justify two famous theorems of probability theory: the central limit theorem and the law of large numbers (see section 9.4). This bean machine was a real board with nails[6].*

6 The photograph of Francis Galton (author unknown) is from Wikimedia Commons, https://commons.wikimedia.org/wiki/Category:Francis_Galton.

EXAMPLE 9.5.– Galton's bean machine.

The device in Figure 9.11 consists of pegs separated by spaces. Balls are dropped from the top; this ball will go either to the right or to the left equiprobably and will bounce into lower pegs. The diagram gives an example of the path of a ball. Below the eight lower pegs, nine bins collect the balls.

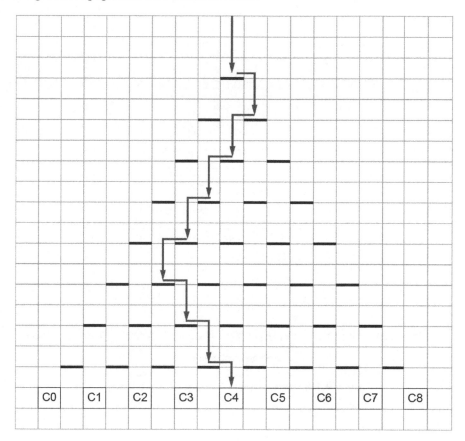

Figure 9.11. *Path of a ball*

To study the process and see the result, we will perform a simulation by dropping balls and, at each peg, we will "draw lots" as to whether the ball will go left or right. Figure 9.12 shows the result for 100 balls (which is a small number). We can compare the "experimental" probabilities to those of the binomial distribution.

We can, indeed, consider that the problem is that of tests repeated eight times where we have a probability 0.5 of going to the right. When the ball arrives at C0, it means that the "going right" event has never happened. At C1, it occurred only once; C2: twice, etc. We know that the phenomenon obeys the binomial distribution. Hence, we have given the corresponding probabilities in order to compare simulation and theory.

The path taken by the last ball is also shown in Figure 9.12.

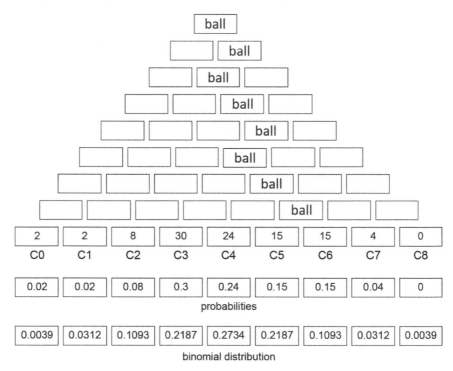

2	2	8	30	24	15	15	4	0
C0	C1	C2	C3	C4	C5	C6	C7	C8

0.02	0.02	0.08	0.3	0.24	0.15	0.15	0.04	0

probabilities

0.0039	0.0312	0.1093	0.2187	0.2734	0.2187	0.1093	0.0312	0.0039

binomial distribution

Figure 9.12. *Comparison of theory and experience*

EXAMPLE 9.6.– Random walk in a plane.

A plane is applied to an orthogonal coordinate system. A point originally at the origin ($x = 0$, $y = 0$) moves in four directions of 1 unit. The choice of direction is random in a uniform way. This means that we draw at random, according to the uniform distribution, an integer u between 0 and 3:

– if $u = 0$, the point moves to the right: $x = x + 1$;

– if $u = 1$, the point moves to the left: $x = x - 1$;
– if $u = 2$, the point moves to the top: $y = y + 1$;

– if $u = 3$, the point moves to the bottom: $y = y - 1$.

At each position, the process is repeated. After 10 steps, the point is in a square obtained by joining the points $(0, 10)$, $(10, 0)$, $(0, - 10)$, $(- 10, 0)$, but where?

The simulation program is quite simple to develop and the results can be expressed in a graph. We give two types of results in Figures 9.13 and 9.14.

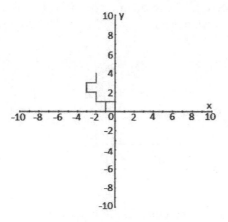

Figure 9.13. *Sample path*

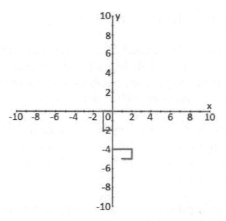

Figure 9.14. *Another sample path*

It is interesting to repeat the simulation many times and to superimpose the results to see how the final points are distributed. It can be seen that the 20×20 square is not uniformly filled, but that the distance between the end point and the origin O increases slowly. This is not surprising, because getting an end point like (0, 10) for a direct path is a very low probability: $(1/4)10 = 9.5,10^{-7}$.

However, let us calculate the average distance from an end point to the origin of the coordinates. This distance for a point in step i is given easily by its square $d_i^2 = x_i^2 + y_i^2$. The difference of the squares of the distances between two consecutive steps is $d_{i+1}^2 - d_i^2$. It is one of the four values $2x_i + 1, 2y_i + 1, -2x_i + 1, -2y_i + 1$, each with the probability 1/4. The mean of these four values is simply 1. We deduce that $E(d_{i+1}^2 - d_i^2) = 1$, which is $E(d_{i+1}^2) = E(d_i^2) + 1$. This recurrence formula, given that $E(d_1^2) = 1$, gives $E(d_i^2) = i$ or:

$$\sqrt{E(d_i^2)} = \sqrt{i}$$

Given the inequality:

$$\frac{d_1 + d_2 + \cdots + d_i}{i} \leq \sqrt{\frac{d_1^2 + d_2^2 + \cdots + d_i^2}{i}}$$

we deduce that $E(d_i) \leq \sqrt{i}$. Therefore, in our case, on average, the points are in the radius disc $\sqrt{10} = 3,16$.

9.3. Simulation according to a law of probability

It happens that we know the probability laws governing phenomena or, in the majority of cases, we assume a definite probabilistic model. In this case, it is possible, using the computer, to generate numbers whose distribution follows a law of probability. This problem has been studied in the previous chapter.

EXAMPLE 9.7.– Imagine a counter at which customers arrive. The number of customers who are arriving is measured every 15 minutes and the statistical results in Table 9.1 are obtained after 100 measurements. It is assumed that the customers who are not served form a queue.

Suppose this statistic approaches the supposedly unknown probability law of arrivals. The average is $\lambda = 4.77$ arrivals per quarter of an hour (taking as a unit the quarter of an hour).

In the same way, the number of customers served per quarter of an hour is also measured. 100 measurements provide the statistical Table 9.2.

Number of arrivals	0	1	2	3	4	5	6
Frequency	0.00	0.01	0.12	0.23	0.22	0.11	0.08

Number of arrivals	7	8	9	10	11	12	13
Frequency	0.08	0.07	0.03	0.03	0.01	0.01	0.00

Table 9.1. *Law of arrivals*

Number of services	0	1	2	3	4	5	6	7	8	9
Frequency	0.00	0.04	0.08	0.10	0.15	0.20	0.24	0.15	0.04	0.00

Table 9.2. *Law of services*

As before, we assume that this statistic approaches the law of probability of departures. We find that the average is $\mu = 4.91$ per quarter of an hour.

We want to study this queueing system and find the average length of the queue of customers waiting to be served by simulation.

We will begin by filling in the two preceding tables by matching each frequency to a range of two digit numbers (Table 9.3), following the method explained in Chapter 8.

Number of arrivals	0	1	2	3	4	5	6
Frequency	0.00	0.01	0.12	0.23	0.22	0.11	0.08
Numbers	...	00	01 to 12	13 to 35	36 to 57	58 to 68	69 to 76

Number of arrivals	7	8	9	10	11	12	13
Frequency	0.08	0.07	0.03	0.03	0.01	0.01	0.00
Numbers	77 to 84	85 to 91	92 to 94	95 to 97	98	99	...

Number of services	0	1	2	3	4	5	6	7	8	9
Frequency	0.00	0.04	0.08	0.10	0.15	0.20	0.24	0.15	0.04	0.00
Numbers	...	00 to 03	04 to 11	12 to 21	22 to 36	37 to 56	57 to 80	81 to 95	96 to 99	...

Table 9.3. *Preparation of draws*

Let us recall the method to obtain samples. Imagine that we have two random number sequences (or pseudo-random ones provided by a computer):

S1: 90 27 14 39 52 29 24 79...

S2: 72 71 67 53 43 97 30 98 60...

For the first quarter of an hour, we draw 90 for arrivals and 72 for departures; with the tables, this means that eight customers arrive and six customers are served during this quarter of an hour.

For the second quarter of an hour, we draw 27 for arrivals and 71 for services; these numbers correspond to four arrivals and six departures of customers.

This continues for an entire day of 6 hours (24 quarter-hour periods).

This translates into a computer program described in Figure 9.15, where N indicates the number of periods and L the length of the queue.

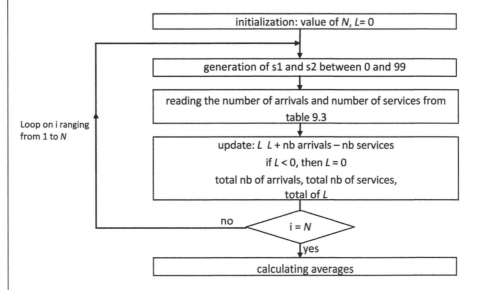

Figure 9.15. *Flowchart of the process*

The execution of the program leads to Table 9.4.

The simulation is repeated 10 times, which leads to the results in Table 9.5.

It may be noted that if the values of the number of arrivals and the number of services are fairly close according to the simulations (and close to the statistical averages), it is not the same for the length L of the queue that varies here from 3.36 to 16.04. The large values of L correspond, of course, to the case where the number of arrivals is lower than the number of services.

This shows that we must be careful (you can never be too careful!) and therefore, for more safety, whenever possible, perform more simulations. Perhaps it is also necessary to increase the number N of periods (and to repeat a more ambitious statistical study).

A simulation of this type can also lead to interesting results, such as calculating the server's rate of idleness. Taking, for example, the first simulation, we find that there were 442 customer arrivals and that the server could have made 504 services, resulting in a rate of idleness of 12.3%.

period	s1	s2	nb of arrivals	nb of services	L
1	29	75	3	6	0
2	85	98	8	8	0
3	68	43	5	5	0
4	12	14	2	3	0
5	87	62	8	6	2
6	68	59	5	6	1
7	20	77	3	6	0
8	63	56	5	5	0
9	52	85	4	7	0
94	23	58	3	6	3
95	51	63	4	6	1
96	74	71	6	6	1
97	72	94	6	7	0
98	35	70	3	6	0
99	38	29	4	4	0
100	16	76	3	6	0
average			4.42	5.04	3.36

Table 9.4. *Progress of a simulation*

simulation	nb of arrivals	nb of services	L
1	4.42	5.04	3.36
2	4.62	4.52	10.82
3	4.33	5.17	2.58
4	4.37	4.88	3.79
5	4.79	4.68	16.04
6	4.98	4.92	8.39
7	4.86	5.29	4.48
8	4.33	4.81	4.74
9	4.65	4.77	12.64
10	4.91	4.97	8.99
averages	**4.63**	**4.91**	**7.58**

Table 9.5. *Simulation results*

This study can be repeated, assuming that the arrivals and services statistics follow a normal distribution.

EXAMPLE 9.8.– Random walk on the edges of a cube.

We can walk from a vertex X to a vertex Y on the edges of the cube (Figure 9.16).

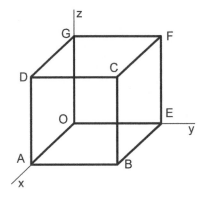

Figure 9.16. *The cube*

We define the following probability law; when we are on one of the vertices of the cube:

– the probability of moving parallel to the Ox axis is p_1;

– the probability of moving parallel to the Oy axis is p_2;

– the probability of moving parallel to the Oz axis is p_3.

Remember that since the sum of the probabilities is 1, it is sufficient to define the first two probabilities:

$$p_3 = 1 - p_1 - p_2$$

The term "step" denotes a displacement from a vertex to a neighboring vertex. What is the average number of steps it takes to go from a vertex A to a vertex B, knowing that at each vertex we apply the previous probability law?

To locate the vertices, we can assign them a binary number corresponding to their coordinates, assuming that the cube has an edge length of 1 unit in length.

In this case:

O: 0, 0, 0 → 000   D: 1, 0, 1 → 101

A: 1, 0, 0 → 100   E: 0, 1, 0 → 010

B: 1, 1, 0 → 110   F: 0, 1, 1 → 011

C: 1, 1, 1 → 111   G: 0, 0, 1 → 001

The transition from a vertex to a neighboring vertex is then done by modifying a single bit.

Carry out a simulation, following the probability law above, to obtain the average number of steps to go from A to B. We will make N attempts and we will calculate the average of the results. The graph shows the distribution of the number of steps. The initial conditions of the simulation consist of the definition of the probabilities p_1 and p_2 the choice of the starting point $A(x_A, y_A, z_A)$, the choice of the arrival point $B(x_B, y_B, z_B)$ and the number of attempts N.

The program to be carried out is described in Figure 9.17.

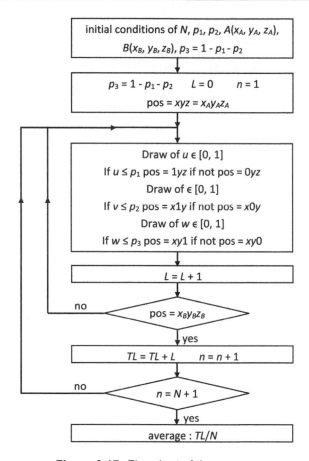

Figure 9.17. *Flowchart of the process*

For 100 attempts, $p_1 = 1/3$, $p_2 = 1/3$ (and so $p_3 = 1/3$), $A(0, 0, 0)$ and $B(1, 1, 1)$, we obtain, for example, the result 9.92 to compare with the exact result 10.

9.4. Mathematical foundations

A fundamental question arises as to the validity of a simulation. Indeed, how much can we trust the result of a simulation? The answer lies in the law of large numbers. This law has already been mentioned in Chapter 1. We will talk about it now in more detail and examine related mathematical results.

Intuitively, it is believed that a statistical result should join the concept of probability. It is also the foundation of statistics which, operating on samples of large numbers (in mathematics called "large numbers"), should approach the probability of occurrence of events. What does "large" mean in this case?

Two fundamental theorems known as the *laws of large numbers* justify the intuition. They are the *weak law of large numbers* (laid out by Jacob Bernoulli) and the *strong law of large numbers*. To understand these laws, we must define what we mean when we say that the statistical frequency "converges" towards probability.

In the case of a roll of a die, for example, we are convinced that if we count the number of times "1" must appear, we should, on average of all the results obtained by throwing the dice many times, get 1/6 which is the probability of "1" occurring. If n is the number of rolls of the die, we will put:

$$f_n = \frac{1}{n} \sum_{i=1}^{n} x_i$$

where x_i is the result of the ith throw, 1 if we get a "1", 0 if not. f_n is the statistical frequency that should, for a sufficiently large n, converge to the probability $p = 1/6$.

Before approaching the weak law of large numbers and the strong law of large numbers, let us first introduce a practical mathematical result, the Bienaymé–Chebyshev inequality.

9.4.1. *Bienaymé–Chebyshev inequality*

Let X be a random variable of mean μ and standard deviation σ, taking discrete values $x_1, x_2, \ldots, x_n$ with probabilities $p_1, p_2, \ldots, p_n$. Its variance is:

$$v(X) = \sigma^2 = \sum_i p_i (x_i - \mu)^2$$

Let us look at event A defined by $|X - \mu| \geq \varepsilon$ where ε is a positive real. In the sum of the variance, let $i(A)$ denote the indices i that correspond to this event. Therefore, we have:

$$\text{prob}(|X - \mu| \geq \varepsilon) = \sum_{i(A)} p_{i(A)}$$

and consequently:

$$v(X) = \sigma^2 \geq \sum_{i(A)} p_{i(A)}\left(x_{i(A)} - \mu\right)^2 \geq \sum_{i(A)} p_{i(A)}\varepsilon^2 = \varepsilon^2 \sum_{i(A)} p_{i(A)}$$

Hence:

$$\mathrm{prob}(|X - \mu| \geq \varepsilon) = \sum_{i(A)} p_{i(A)} \leq \frac{\sigma^2}{\varepsilon^2}$$

which gives the Bienaymé–Chebyshev inequality:

$$\mathrm{prob}(|X - \mu| \geq \varepsilon) \leq \frac{\sigma^2}{\varepsilon^2}$$

9.4.2. *Weak law of large numbers*

We will apply the Bienaymé–Chebyshev inequality to the case of the variable:

$$\overline{X}_n = \frac{1}{n} \sum_{i=1}^{n} X_i$$

defined as the mean of a sequence of n random variables X_i of the same probability distribution, of the same mean μ and of the same standard deviation σ.

For this variable, we have:

$$E\left(\overline{X}_n\right) = \frac{1}{n} \sum_{i=1}^{n} E(X_i) = \frac{n\mu}{n} = \mu \qquad v\left(\overline{X}_n\right) = \frac{1}{n^2} \sum_{i=1}^{n} v(X_i) = \frac{n\sigma^2}{n^2} = \frac{\sigma^2}{n}$$

The Bienaymé–Chebyshev inequality, applied to our variable, is written as:

$$\mathrm{prob}\left(|\overline{X}_n - \mu| \geq \varepsilon\right) \leq \frac{\sigma^2}{n\varepsilon^2}$$

Moving to the opposite event:

$$1 - \mathrm{prob}\left(|\overline{X}_n - \mu| < \varepsilon\right) \leq \frac{\sigma^2}{n\varepsilon^2}$$

and consequently:

$$\text{prob}\big(|\overline{X}_n - \mu| < \varepsilon\big) \geq 1 - \frac{\sigma^2}{n\varepsilon^2}$$

We see that if $\forall \varepsilon$, n tends towards infinity, the probability will tend towards 1. This result expresses the weak law of large numbers.

Given a sequence of random variables X_i which are independent and of the same probability law (mean μ, standard deviation σ), we put:

$$\overline{X}_n = \frac{1}{n}\sum_{i=1}^{n} X_i$$

$$\forall \varepsilon > 0 \quad prob\big(|\overline{X}_n - \mu| \geq \varepsilon\big) \longrightarrow 0 \text{ when } n \longrightarrow \infty$$

which means that it is highly unlikely that the difference $|\overline{X}_n - \mu|$ is greater than ε for a large value of n. It will be noted that, in this law, initially from Bernoulli, we are talking about the probability limit to 0 and not the limit of $\overline{X}_n$ to μ in the ordinary sense.

It is indeed a convergence in probability as we must specify:

$$\overline{X}_n \xrightarrow{\text{in probability}} \mu$$

EXAMPLE 9.9.– Let us simulate a game of dice. Suppose we want to check the odds of getting a "1" when throwing a die. We know that the corresponding probability is $1/6 = 0.6666...$

To do this, we produce a sample by randomly drawing 1000 integers between 1 and 6. We count the number of times we get a "1". We start again by making other samples, for example 100 tests in total. We thus obtain 100 values of the number of "successes". This gives a result similar to that in Table 9.6, which represents 100 tests. Each box represents the sum, for each test, of occurrences of "1" per 1000 draws.

The overall average obtained, 167.82, is close to the theoretical value, which is 166.66.

152	175	165	166	166	188	162	184	178	179
172	201	167	178	158	170	151	162	169	164
172	178	157	168	146	169	171	163	177	144
155	157	177	174	161	161	200	168	176	160
148	178	198	151	150	154	185	200	164	179
184	176	173	155	159	155	188	155	156	193
164	185	175	171	165	167	163	183	172	147
168	170	178	165	155	185	134	159	160	183
149	178	159	175	167	170	157	175	167	160
171	157	148	142	162	169	164	178	154	189

Table 9.6. *Results of 100 tests*

Now let us go back to the experiment for n draws. For each draw, we associate a random variable $X_i(i = 1$ to $n)$ which can take only two values: 1 if the "1" appears (probability 1/6) and 0 if not (probability 5/6). The draws are independent and the variables X_i follow the same law of probability whose parameters μ and σ^2 are:

$$\mu = 1 \times \frac{1}{6} + 0 \times \frac{5}{6} = \frac{1}{6}$$

$$\sigma^2 = \frac{1}{6} \times \left(1 - \frac{1}{6}\right)^2 + \frac{5}{6} \times \left(0 - \frac{1}{6}\right)^2 = \frac{5}{36}$$

Therefore, the standard deviation is $\sigma = 0{,}373$.

Let $\overline{X}_n$ denote the mean of the values obtained. Suppose we want to determine n so that the value of $\overline{X}_n$ approaches m unless 1%, i.e. $\varepsilon = 0.01$. According to the weak law of large numbers, we will have:

$$\text{prob}\left(\left|\overline{X}_n - \frac{1}{6}\right| < 0{,}01\right) \geq 1 - \frac{50000}{36n}$$

Suppose we want the previous probability to approach close to α, i.e. a value of the probability between $1 - \alpha$ and 1. It is then necessary that:

$$\alpha \geq \frac{50000}{36n} \quad \text{or} \quad n \geq \frac{50000}{36\alpha}$$

α is called the risk threshold. For a risk threshold of 5%, we obtain $n \geq 27778$.

In our experiment, $n = 100000$, therefore much higher than the value 27778. Therefore, we can be confident that the statistical average represents the average of the random variable. The term "large" is here correctly specified.

9.4.3. *Strong law of large numbers*

The first version of the strong law of large numbers comes from Émile Borel (1909). It is expressed as follows.

STRONG LAW OF LARGE NUMBERS.– Given a sequence of random variables X_i which are independent and of the same probability law (mean μ, standard deviation σ), we put:

$$\overline{X}_n = \frac{1}{n}\sum_{i=1}^{n} X_i$$

$$\forall \omega \in \Omega \quad prob\left(\overline{X}_n(\omega) \rightarrow \mu \quad \text{when} \quad n \rightarrow \infty\right) = 1$$

Although the beginning of the theorem resembles that of the weak law of large numbers, the conclusion is different. It means that it is "almost certain" that $\overline{X}_n$ tends towards μ when n becomes very large. Here, Ω represents the space of eventualities and ω an eventuality. The term "almost certain convergence" comes from the fact that there may be ω for which we do not have the desired convergence. However, these ω form a negligible series of zero probability. We will not look into this process further, as the weak law of large numbers already constitutes a very valuable tool.

Note, however, the difference between the two types of convergence: convergence "in probability" for the weak law and "almost certain" convergence for the strong law. For the weak law, the theorem rules on the limit of the probability, and for the strong law, the theorem rules on the probability of the limit.

We demonstrate and we will assume (thanking those who proved it!) that "almost certain" convergence implies convergence "in probability". The opposite is not true.

Figure 9.18. *Émile Borel (1871–1956)*

COMMENT ON FIGURE 9.18.– *Borel was a mathematician whose specialty was the study of functions and probabilities and, in particular, measure theory. His paradox of the monkey is famous: a monkey hitting keys at random on a typewriter indefinitely will end up writing Shakespeare's* Hamlet. *Émile Borel was also active in politics: he was a Minister in the cabinet of fellow mathematician Paul Painlevé[7].*

9.4.4. *Central limit theorem*

Let us now move on to another mathematical result well-known to statisticians: the central limit theorem. It is formulated as follows:

CENTRAL LIMIT THEOREM.– Let X_i be a sequence of random variables which are independent and with the same probability distribution (mean μ, standard deviation σ), i.e. the random variable:

$$\overline{X}_n = \frac{1}{n} \sum_{i=1}^{n} X_i$$

For a large enough n, the variable $\overline{X}_n$ follows a normal probability distribution (Laplace–Gauss) of mean m and standard deviation $\frac{\sigma}{\sqrt{n}}$.

We show that this is the case when n exceeds 30.

---

7 The photograph of Émile Borel (author: Agence de presse Mondial Photo-Press, source: National Library of France) is from Wikimedia Commons: https://commons.wikimedia.org/wiki/Category:Émile_Borel.

We should note that nothing is assumed about the nature of the law of probability of X_i. Yet their average follows a normal distribution. It is perhaps for this reason that Laplace–Gauss law is called "normal distribution" (who knows?).

EXAMPLE 9.10.– Let us give an experimental justification to the central limit theorem. We resume our roll of a die and look at the result "1". At each throw i of the die, we associate the random variable X_i, which only takes the values 1 if the "1" occurs and 0 if not. As seen in Example 9.9, X_i obeys the law of probability $p(1) = 1/6$ and $p(0) = 5/6$. The average is 1/6 and the variance is 5/36.

The simulation is performed on a computer that makes a draw for each throw of a random integer number between 1 and 6.

We thus perform n throws (with the computer) of the die, each throw corresponding to the value of a variable X_i, and we average the values of X_i, which leads to $\overline{X}_n$.

To study the distribution of $\overline{X}_n$, we perform N simulations, each of them reiterating the previous process.

According to the central limit theorem, for a large n, the mean of $\overline{X}_n$ must be 1/6 and its variance must be 5/36n.

Figure 9.19 gives the distribution of $\overline{X}_n$. (n = 100 repeated throws N = 1000 times).

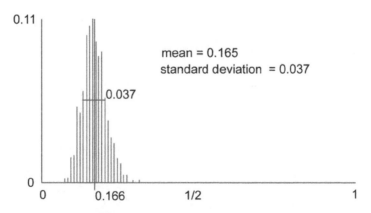

Figure 9.19. *Central limit theorem*

We can see that the shape of the distribution is close to Gaussian distribution, with results for the mean and the standard deviation close to what was expected.

10

Simulation of Inventory Management

CONCEPTS DISCUSSED IN THIS CHAPTER.– We start by defining what is needed to perform inventory management simulations, and in particular, a list of parameters to consider.

Then, we will consider a simple simulation example using a spreadsheet and then an *ad hoc* program.

Finally, we will look at a more general case, comparing several inventory management strategies.

Recommended reading: [PHE 77].

10.1. General provisions

To perform an inventory management simulation, many parameters must be defined:

1) **Economic parameters**. This is the replenishment cost, the unit cost of holding and the unit cost of shortage.

2) **Parameters related to how the company operates**. It must be determined whether the sale of items and deliveries takes place five, six or seven days a week. It is important to note that during non-working days, no orders, deliveries or customer requests can be made. However, the holding cost must cover seven days (refrigeration, security, etc.).

3) **Parameters for triggering replenishment**:

  – timing of replenishment trigger. It could be fixed day. It could be determined by the value of a danger level (the replenishment command is then launched), or, of course, other possibilities. Note that we also consider the time it takes for the supplier to receive the order (fixed or random);

– quantity to replenish. It can be fixed; it can correspond to the filling of the storage space; it can be equal to the quantity of items sold during the previous week; or, of course, there are other possibilities;

– delivery time of replenishment. Replenishment can be immediate (time = 0); the delivery time can be fixed (n days); the delivery time can be random and follow, in this case, a probability distribution which is given or yet to be determined; or, of course, there are other possibilities. It must also be determined when replenishment will be available for sale: when it has arrived or the next day.

4) **Parameters of customer demand**. Customer demand can be constant per day (simple, but not realistic). In general, it is random and therefore follows either a normal probability distribution or a probability distribution to be determined from the statistics.

5) **Initial conditions**. It is necessary to define the state of the stock at the beginning of the simulation.

6) **Parameters related to simulations**:

– determine the number of weeks to be considered in the simulation;

– determine the number of simulations to be performed. Then, we will take the average of the results.

Ultimately, there are many parameters to consider and many types of simulations to perform.

To perform a simulation, quite a few of the operations described in Figure 10.1 must be performed.

It is assumed here that the management is done day by day. Without going into too much detail (we will look at the specifics with examples of the different steps), the operations to be carried out consist of the following calculations:

– Calculation of the demand (to be done if it is a working day). If the demand is random, it will be necessary to determine it with its law of probability. Let γ be the demand of the day.

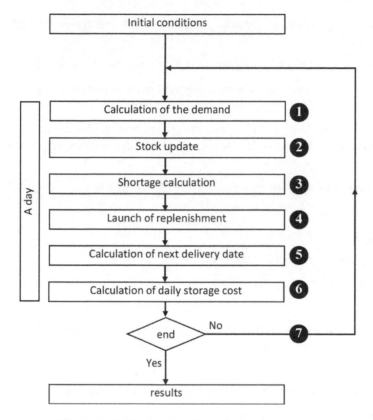

Figure 10.1. *Flowchart of inventory management*

– Stock update. The value of the stock in the morning, $S1$, is that of the previous evening:

- if the day is not a working day, the stock value is unchanged $S2 = S1$;

- if the day is a working day and if there was a replenishment delivery Q the day before, the quantity delivered to the stock must be added. The quantity γ sold to customers must then be subtracted. So, we have for the evening, $S' = S1 + Q - \gamma$.

– Shortage calculation:

- if there is no shortage on the previous working day, the evening stock is $S2 = S'$;

- if there was a shortage $P1$ on the previous working day, then $S'' = S' - P1$;

- if $S'' \geq 0$, then the value of the stock in the evening is $S2 = S''$ and the shortage is $P2 = 0$;

- if $S'' < 0$, the stock in the evening is $S2 = 0$ and the shortage is $P2 = - S''$;

– if it is the day on which the replenishment must be launched, the order must be sent to the supplier, specifying the quantity Q to be replenished.

– We also calculate the replenishment delivery time to identity the day when this replenishment will be available. This time depends on assumptions (fixed or random time).

– We summarize the costs:

- holding cost: $c_E(S1 + S2)/2$;

- shortage cost: $c_P.P2$;

- replenishment cost (if applicable): C_R.

– If the simulation is not completed, we prepare the next iteration: $S1 = S2$, $P1 = P2$.

In what follows, we will take two examples, a simple example and a more complex example.

10.2. Comparison of two inventory management policies

A stock is made up of identical objects. A statistical study (Table 10.1) makes it possible to get close to the probability of the daily demand for objects.

γ	0	1	2	3	4	5	6	7	8	9	10
$p(\gamma)$	0.03	0.04	0.12	0.18	0.30	0.10	0.10	0.04	0.04	0.03	0.02

Table 10.1. *Law of demand*

It is considered that beyond 10, the probability is zero.

The average demand is therefore $\bar{\gamma} = 4.19$.

Two different stock management policies are being considered.

Policy P1. Use of a danger level $S = 15$ defining the reorder points. The quantity ordered for replenishment is the cumulative demand from the previous week (five working days). The delivery time is not guaranteed and can range from two to seven days (excluding non-working days). A study makes it possible to obtain the following results (Table 10.2) for the delivery time in days.

d	2	3	4	5	6	7
p(d)	0.08	0.12	0.24	0.26	0.18	0.12

Table 10.2. *Law of delivery time*

Deliveries arrive in the evening (of course) and so the delivered items are only available to customers the next morning.

An order is only issued after the arrival of the current order.

Policy P2. The replenishment is cyclical and so is launched at regular intervals: the last working day of each week. The quantity requested for replenishment is the weekly average of the items requested over one week, i.e. 21 items.

Delivery is guaranteed on the last working day of the following week, and delivered items will be available the next day.

To perform the simulation, it is necessary to "draw" the demand and the delivery time (policy P1), which amounts to generating random numbers according to the preceding probability laws.

One can imagine using a simple spreadsheet Excel for the simulations, which provides the random function RANDBETWEEN(MIN;MAX), which returns an integer between MIN and MAX according to the uniform distribution. Be aware that the random number changes when writing on the spreadsheet.

For the daily demand, it will be necessary to draw numbers $N1$ between 0 and 99. It is the same for the delivery times (policy P1), which correspond to the numbers $N2$. Tables 10.3 and 10.4 give the connection between the demand and the delivery time.

γ	0	1	2	3	4	5	6	7	8	9	10
p(γ)	0.03	0.04	0.12	0.18	0.30	0.10	0.10	0.04	0.04	0.03	0.02
N1	00 to 02	03 to 06	07 to 18	19 to 36	37 to 66	67 to 76	77 to 86	87 to 90	91 to 94	95 to 97	98 to 99

Table 10.3. *Number ranges for demand*

d	2	3	4	5	6	7
p(d)	0.08	0.12	0.24	0.26	0.18	0.12
N2	00 to 07	08 to 19	20 to 43	44 to 69	70 to 87	88 to 99

Table 10.4. *Number ranges for delivery time*

Thus, the draw of a number equal to 38 corresponds to a request for four items and a delivery time of four days.

The simulation is carried out over 52 weeks to have a full year (seasonal phenomena can occur). It is initialized with a stock of 21 items and an order. Table 10.5 shows the start of the simulation (first three weeks). The "order" column indicates the quantity ordered in each replenishment. The "comment" column indicates whether a replenishment order is initiated.

Take as economic parameters the following values:

– replenishment cost (€20);

– unit holding cost (€0.4 per article and per day);

– unit shortage cost (€10 per article not sold).

The results of the simulation are shown in Table 10.6.

The P1 policy seems the best. We could vary the value of the danger level to see if we can improve the result. But this is difficult with an Excel spreadsheet (unless you use the relevant programming on spreadsheets).

Should we conclude that the P1 policy is better than the P2 policy? Certainly not, because it would be necessary to perform several simulations and average the results obtained, but it may be tedious with a spreadsheet. In this case, it is necessary to use a program (independent of a spreadsheet) with which one can more easily:

– vary the different parameters;

– perform several simulations to average the results.

	General data			Policy P1						
	Day	N1	γ	Stock at the start	Stock at the end	Order	N2	Delivery time	Shortage	Comment
	0	58	4	21	17					
Week 1	1	68	5	17	12	21	18	3	0	Order
	2	36	3	12	9				0	
	3	70	5	9	4				0	
	4	97	9	4	0				5	
	5	33	3	21	18				0	
Week 2	6	23	3	18	15				0	
	7	5	1	15	14	25	36	4	0	Order
	8	70	5	14	9				0	
	9	89	7	9	2				0	
	10	33	3	2	0				1	
Week 3	11	64	4	0	0				4	
	12	89	7	25	18				0	
	13	5	1	18	17				0	
	14	96	9	17	8	19	51	5	0	Order
	15	45	4	8	4				0	

	General data			Policy P2						
	Day	N1	γ	Stock at the start	Stock at the end	Order			Shortage	Comment
	0	58	4	21	17	21				Order
Week 1	1	68	5	17	12				0	
	2	36	3	12	9				0	
	3	70	5	9	4				0	
	4	97	9	4	0				5	
	5	33	3	0	0	21			3	Order
Week 2	6	23	3	21	18				0	
	7	5	1	18	17				0	
	8	70	5	17	12				0	
	9	89	7	12	5				0	
	10	33	3	5	2	21			0	
Week 3	11	64	4	23	19				0	
	12	89	7	19	12				0	
	13	5	1	12	11				0	
	14	96	9	11	2				0	
	15	45	4	2	0	21			2	Order

Table 10.5. *Progress of a simulation*

Policy P1	
no. of shortages:	265
average stock to hold:	2288
no. of replenishments:	39
replenishment cost:	€780.00
holding cost:	€915.20
shortage cost:	€2,650.00
total cost:	€4,345.20

Policy P2	
no. of shortages:	13
average stock to hold:	10902
no. of replenishments:	52
replenishment cost:	€1,040.00
holding cost:	€4,360.80
shortage cost:	€130.00
total cost:	€5,530.80

Table 10.6. *Comparing the two policies with a spreadsheet*

We used a computer program developed in PHP that allows us to get the results in a web page.

With the same basic data, 10 simulations were performed. The following results (Table 10.7) are obtained for the total cost of storage.

Simulation	Policy P1	Policy P2
1	€5 140.00	€3 801.60
2	€4 772.60	€4 961.00
3	€4 335.40	€5 299.00
4	€4 525.40	€2 934.60
5	€5 101.60	€2 953.80
6	€4 778.20	€3 720.20
7	€4 676.00	€4 293.80
8	€5 218.80	€3 278.60
9	€4 942.20	€3 469.00
10	€4 873.80	€3 859.80
Average	**€4 836.40**	**€3 857.14**

Table 10.7. *Comparison of the two policies by simulations*

We find that the result contradicts the simulation with the spreadsheet, which shows that we must be careful when making conclusions, and that a single simulation (or even 10!) is not enough. It is necessary to repeat the simulation many times to get as close to reality as possible.

10.3. Comparison of various stock policies

In this second example, we will be more ambitious in comparing various inventory management policies.

The parameters to consider are as follows, with several assumptions:

– Triggering replenishment. We will consider two cases (in both cases, we will assume that the supplier receives the order instantly):

 - triggering on a fixed day (e.g. an order is made every Wednesday);

 - triggering if the stock falls below a danger level.

– Quantity to be replenished. We will consider three cases:

 - replenishment of a fixed quantity;

 - replenishment to completely fill the storage space;

 - replenishment of an amount equal to the cumulative number of demands from the previous week.

– Delivery time of replenishment. We will consider three cases:

 - delivery in a fixed time;

 - delivery in a random time. We will choose a uniform distribution to generate the time;

 - fixed day delivery (e.g. Thursday). It was agreed that the delivery day is during the week after the order;

 - in all cases, it will be considered that a delivery time of d days means that the delivery will take place on the evening of the day after the order is made and that this delivery will be added to the stock the morning of $(d + 1)^e$ day.

– Customer demand. We will consider two cases:

 - constant daily demand;

 - random demand according to a law of probability. We will take three types of laws: uniform distribution, Poisson distribution and Gaussian distribution. In the first and third cases, we will generate integers.

We must also:

– define the number of working days in the week (five, six or seven days);

– determine the number of weeks for a simulation;

– determine the number of simulations to be performed (we will average the results);

– define the economic parameters (replenishment cost, unit cost of holding, unit cost of shortage);

– define the initial conditions of the simulation.

By mixing all the choices, we have $2 \times 3 \times 3 \times 4 = 72$ possibilities.

Finally, we must:

– define the number of working days in the week (five, six or seven days). It is important to note that during non-working days, no orders, deliveries or customer requests can be made. However, the holding cost must cover seven days (refrigeration, security, etc.);

– determine the number of weeks for a simulation;

– define the economic parameters (replenishment cost, unit cost of holding, unit cost of shortage);

– define the initial conditions of the simulation (the only condition to be determined is the initial stock that will be taken, such as the maximum storage capacity).

The simulation will start on a Monday.

We used a computer program developed in PHP that allows us to set the parameters and mix the assumptions with a web interface.

As an illustration, the following five stock policies are considered.

Policy P1:

– launch of replenishment on danger level (20 items);

– order a quantity equal to the sum of demands from the previous week;

– random delivery time according to the uniform distribution between one and seven days;

– estimated demand according to the Poisson distribution of average 5.

Policy P2:

– launch of replenishment on Friday;

– order a fixed quantity (20 items);

– random delivery time according to the uniform distribution between one and seven days;

– regular demand (five items per day).

Policy P3:

– launch of replenishment on danger level (20 items);

– order a fixed quantity (20 items);

– fixed delivery time (five days);

– regular demand (five items per day).

Policy P4:

– launch of replenishment on danger level (20 items);

– order to completely fill the stock;

– random delivery time according to the uniform distribution between one and seven days;

– estimated demand according to the Poisson distribution of average 5.

Policy P5:

– launch of replenishment on danger level (20 items);

– order a quantity equal to the sum of demands from the previous week;

– fixed delivery time (five days);

– estimated demand according to the Poisson distribution of average 5.

In the five policies, the number of working days in the week is considered to be five days. We are ignoring holidays. A 52-week simulation is carried out 10 times for each policy (except for the policy P3, where there is no risk), and we average the result by taking as a criterion of choice the total cost of storage, knowing that $C_R = €50$, $c_E = €0.4$, $c_P = €10$. Table 10.8 gives the results of the simulations.

Policy	P1	P2	P3	P4	P5
Total cost	€5,987.74	€7,091.20	€5,927.00	€6,534.50	€5,423.36

Table 10.8. *Results of comparing the policies*

Policy P5 seems to be the best.

11

Simulation of a Queueing Process

CONCEPTS DISCUSSED IN THIS CHAPTER.– We will begin by defining what is needed to perform simulations of a queueing process, in particular, a list of parameters to consider.

We will then describe the simulation method used for an M/M/1 queue and for an M/M/S queue. We will examine the results obtained by comparing them to the theoretical results.

Recommended reading [PHE 77].

11.1. General provisions

To simulate a queueing process, it is necessary to define the probability laws governing the arrivals of elements and the departures of elements, as well as the number of service stations. We will assume here and in the theoretical part that there is only one queue, regardless of the number of service stations.

The probability distributions are used to calculate the theoretical mean values of the arrival rate λ. For "departure rates" or inverse service times, it is assumed that they are identical for all stations (and also that the same probability distribution applies to stations).

We will then obtain, with the corresponding probability law, the average theoretical service time, $1/\mu$.

In addition, using a computer requires the use of discrete values for time, not continuous values. For time management, two attitudes are possible:

– varying the time with regular steps and examining the events that may occur between two consecutive instants;

– basing the time on the next event and therefore proceeding in stages based on the events.

In what follows, we will use the second method for the simulation of an M/M/1 queue and the first method for managing an M/M/S queue.

11.2. Simulation of an M/M/1 queue

The simulation assumes that a given number of elements N must be processed (arrivals and departures at the station). The elements will be recorded from 1 to N, the first element arriving at the station (there is no queue yet) at the date $t = 0$. Since the method of event processing is used in the chronological order of their occurrence date, we will obtain for each element considered: the arrival date at the station, the date of service (arrival date at the station), the departure date, the time spent in the queue and the time spent in the system.

At the end of the simulation, from the previous table, we can calculate the average of the time intervals between two consecutive arrivals (to be compared with the theoretical value $1/\lambda$), the average of the service times (to be compared with the theoretical value $1/\mu$) and the average of the time spent in the queue and in the system (which can be compared to the values of the theory).

For each element k ($k = 1,\dots, N$), the following quantities are defined:

– duration_interval[k] = – $(1/\lambda)$Ln$(1 - z)$, where z is a number between 0 and 1 generated by the uniform distribution. This quantity is thus generated according to the distribution of exponential probability (its inverse according to the probability of Poisson distribution). It represents the time elapsing between the arrival of the element $k - 1$ and the arrival of the element k;

– date_arrival[k] = date_arrival[$k - 1$] + duration_interval[k] predicting the arrival date of element k knowing the arrival date of element $k - 1$;

– date_service[k] = max(date_departure[$k - 1$], date_arrival[k]). Indeed, if element k waits to be served, the service date is the departure date of element $k - 1$; if, on the other hand, there is no queue, the service date will be the arrival date of the next element k in the system; this date being subsequent to that of the departure of element $k - 1$;

– duration_service[k] = – $(1/\mu)$Ln$(1 - z)$, where z is a number between 0 and 1 generated by the uniform distribution. This quantity is generated according to the exponential distribution assumed to be that of the duration of the services at the station;

– date_departure[k] = date_service[k] + duration_service[k];

– $t_f[k]$ = date_service[k] – date_arrival[k] which represents the time spent by element k in the queue;

– $t_s[k]$ = date_departure[k] – date_arrival[k] which represents the time spent by element k in the system.

The calculation is done by iteration of the elements with the following initial conditions for the first element:

– duration_interval[1] = 0;

– date_arrival[1] = 0;

– date_service[1] = 0;

– duration_service[1] = – $(1/\mu)$Ln$(1 - z)$;

– date_departure[1] = duration_service[1];

– $t_f[1]$ = 0;

– $t_s[1]$ = duration_service[1].

At the end of each iteration, we cumulate the values of duration_interval, duration_service, t_f and t_s in order to finally obtain the average (by dividing by N).

Figure 11.1 specifies the iteration.

Let us apply the method to a concrete case. Take the case of cars arriving at a highway toll. This toll has only one station. It can be seen from statistical studies that the time intervals separating the successive arrivals of two cars approximately follow an exponential distribution of average $1/\lambda$ and that the service times approximately follow an exponential distribution of average $1/\mu = 1$ minute. The highway and the toll station have varying levels of traffic throughout the year. We consider two cases:

– in busy periods, the average arrival rate of vehicles is 0.9 cars per minute (so, $1/\lambda \approx 1,111$ minutes);

– in quieter periods, the average arrival rate of vehicles is 0.5 cars per minute (i.e. $1/\lambda \approx 2$ minutes).

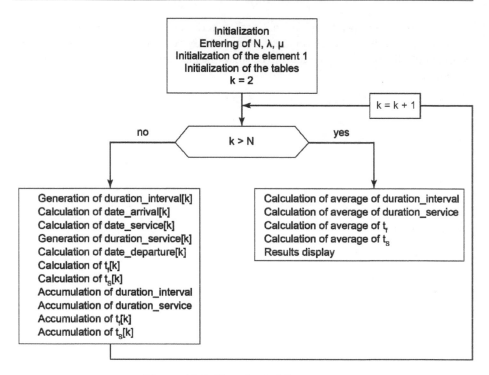

Figure 11.1. *Flowchart of the process*

For each case, 10 simulations are carried out with 500 vehicles. The synthetic results are reported in Tables 11.1 and 11.2.

It is interesting to calculate the dispersion of the results in terms of standard deviations. We thus have:

– for the first case: $\sigma_\lambda = 0.016$, $\sigma_\mu = 0.010$, $\sigma_{tf} = 1.199$, $\sigma_{ts} = 1.322$;

– for the second case: $\sigma_\lambda = 0.006$, $\sigma_\mu = 0.013$, $\sigma_{tf} = 0.069$, $\sigma_{ts} = 1.003$.

We note that $\lambda_{sim} - \sigma_\lambda \leq \lambda \leq \lambda_{sim} + \sigma_\lambda$ and $\mu_{sim} - \sigma_\mu \leq \mu \leq \mu_{sim} + \sigma_\mu$ in the first case. In the second case, the simulated values of λ and μ emerge from this range, only very slightly, at a standard deviation.

Theoretical results provide the values of t_f and t_s:

$$t_f = \frac{\lambda}{\mu(\mu - \lambda)} \qquad t_s = \frac{1}{\mu - \lambda}$$

Simulation	Theoretical value of λ	Simulated values of λ	Theoretical value of μ	Simulated values of μ	Theoretical value of t_f	Simulated values of t_f	Theoretical value of t_s	Simulated values of t_s
1	0.900	0.945	1.000	1.000	9.000	7.159	10.000	8.159
2	0.900	0.948	1.000	1.052	9.000	4.840	10.000	5.791
3	0.900	0.949	1.000	0.971	9.000	15.110	10.000	16.140
4	0.900	0.930	1.000	1.022	9.000	6.561	10.000	7.539
5	0.900	0.852	1.000	0.999	9.000	5.293	10.000	6.295
6	0.900	0.986	1.000	1.009	9.000	7.770	10.000	8.760
7	0.900	0.957	1.000	0.953	9.000	13.345	10.000	14.394
8	0.900	0.845	1.000	1.045	9.000	2.865	10.000	3.821
9	0.900	0.878	1.000	0.984	9.000	5.470	10.000	14.394
10	0.900	0.853	1.000	1.050	9.000	3.766	10.000	4.718
averages	0.900	0.914	1.000	1.009	9.000	7.218	10.000	9.001

Table 11.1. *Results for a busy period*

The corresponding values are shown in Tables 11.1 and 11.2. Regarding the dispersion of the results, we have $t_{f-sim} - \sigma_{tf} \leq t_f \leq t_{f-sim} + \sigma_{tf}$ and $t_{s-sim} - \sigma_{ts} \leq t_s \leq t_{s-sim} + \sigma_{ts}$, except for the value $t_f = 9$ of the first case, where the range is from 6.019 to 8.417. We must, however, remember that we only performed 10 simulations.

Simulation	Theoretical value of λ	Simulated values of λ	Theoretical value of μ	Simulated values of μ	Theoretical value of t_f	Simulated values of t_f	Theoretical value of t_s	Simulated values of t_s
1	0.500	0.456	1.000	1.041	1.000	0.764	2.000	1.725
2	0.500	0.469	1.000	1.072	1.000	0.584	2.000	1.516
3	0.500	0.496	1.000	0.935	1.000	0.943	2.000	2.013
4	0.500	0.479	1.000	0.990	1.000	0.779	2.000	1.790
5	0.500	0.502	1.000	0.997	1.000	0.964	2.000	1.966
6	0.500	0.504	1.000	0.991	1.000	1.146	2.000	2.156
7	0.500	0.514	1.000	0.955	1.000	1.187	2.000	2.235
8	0.500	0.498	1.000	0.951	1.000	1.329	2.000	2.381
9	0.500	0.515	1.000	0.937	1.000	1.054	2.000	2.121
10	0.500	0.488	1.000	0.970	1.000	1.177	2.000	1.266
averages	0.500	0.492	1.000	0.984	1.000	0.993	2.000	1.917

Table 11.2. *Results for a calm period*

11.3. Simulation of an M/M/S queue

We will use here, for time management for an M/M/S queue simulation, a different method from the previous one, taking a chronological point of view with a constant time interval. Indeed, unlike the case of an M/M/1 queue, the elements can leave in an order different from when they arrived.

The arrival parameters are always the rate λ of the arrivals (in elements per unit of time), the rate μ of the services at a station (the stations are assumed to be identical in terms of services), the number of stations S, the number of elements to enter into the system and the time step of the simulation.

The application requires a discretization of time which, by nature, is a continuous variable. It is therefore discontinuous by defining a time step; the dates will be integers 0, 1, 2, 3, etc. The time step is the measure of the time interval between two consecutive dates. It can be expressed in units of time (seconds, minutes, hours, etc.), as well as in tenths and hundredths of units of time. Thus, if we choose the minute as a unit of time, we can, if we choose a tenth of a minute, express the dates as follows: 0, 1/10, 2/10, 3/10, etc. The integers 0, 1, 2, 3, etc. then express tenths of a minute. The date 123 will be 12.3 minutes. This quantification of time obviously distances us somewhat from the Poisson hypotheses. A consequence of the discretization is the fact that several elements can leave on the same date. However, as shown below, the calculation is forced so that at a given date, only one element arrives in the system.

A simulation can perform the following actions.

11.3.1. *Calculation of arrival dates and service time for each element*

– Arrival date of element 1: da[1] = 0.

– Arrival date of element k: da[k] = da[$k-1$] + inter[k], where inter[k] is the time elapsed between the arrival of $k-1$ and the arrival of k. This random time interval, inter[k], is generated by the exponential distribution: $-(1/\lambda)\mathrm{Ln}(1-z)$, where z is a uniform random variable between 0 and 1.

In the same way, the service durations for each element, Ds[k], are obtained with the exponential distribution of parameter μ (thus of mean value $1/\mu$): $-(1/\mu)\mathrm{Ln}(1-z)$, where z is a uniform random variable between 0 and 1.

Since the results of the calculations are decimal numbers and the dates are integers, we round to the nearest integer. We then come across a difficulty because we can get a value of 0, which, for a service duration, is unacceptable. In our discrete system, the minimum value of the service duration must be 1. We are then led to take the value 1 when we obtain a value 0. It is the same for the time interval between two successive arrivals. We cannot accept that two elements arrive at the same time. We therefore warp our theoretical hypotheses by making this approximation. As a result, the average values of the service durations and the intervals between successive arrivals will be slightly greater than $1/\mu$ or $1/\lambda$.

The simplified algorithm in Figure 11.2 indicates the calculation of arrival dates and service durations for each element, where N is the number of elements to be entered into the system.

This gives two tables giving for each element i its arrival date da in the system and its service duration Ds.

The result of iterating the simulation is presented in a table where, for each element k, we have the following information: time interval between the arrival of element k and the arrival of element $k-1$, the arrival date of element k, service duration for element k.

```
For i = 1 to N
        If i = 1
                then    da[1] = 0              //arrival date of element 1
                        Ds[1] = genexp(μ)      //service duration of element 1
                        inter[1] 0             //inter-arrival time interval for 1
                else    inter[i] = genexp(λ)   //inter-arrival time interval for i
                        da[i] = da[i-1] + ti[i] //arrival date of element i
                        Ds[i] = genexp(μ)      //service duration for element i
        EndIf
EndFor
```

Figure 11.2. *General program*

11.3.2. *Iteration by successive dates of operations*

Date by date, arrivals and departures are processed to complete Table 11.3.

date	arrival	longF	station 1	station 2	...	station S	departures

Table 11.3. *Table to be filled in*

The iterative algorithm is shown in Figures 11.3–11.5.

```
// initialization
t = -1                  // t denotes the current date (increasing in steps of 1)
longF = 0               // longF denotes the length of the queue
For s = 1 to S Do
    occ[s] = 0          // all stations are unoccupied
EndFor
    ndep = 0            // number of departures
    As long as ndep ≠ N Make
        t = t + 1
        If there are no arrivals or departures for date t
            then   no event to note
        EndIf
        // processing of arrivals
        .........................................
        // processing of departures
        .........................................
    EndAsLongAs
```

Figure 11.3. *Initialization program*

```
//processing of arrivals
If there has been an arrival at t
    then   If LongF > 0   // the queue is not empty
            then    Insertion of element in the queue
                    LongF = LongF +1        //length of the queue
                    df[i] = t      //date of entry in the queue
            else    If there is a free station
                        then   occ[s] = i    //station s is occupied by i
                               ds[i] = t      //date of entry into service
                        else   Insertion of element in the queue
                               LongF = LongF + 1
                               df[i] = t      //date of entry in the queue
                    EndIf
           EndIf
EndIf
```

Figure 11.4. *Program for processing arrivals*

```
// Processing of departures
If there are departures at t
    then
        For every departure k Do
            ts[k] = date - da[k]      // time spent in the system for k
            Ds[k] = date - ds[k]      // service duration for k
            For s = 1 at nbs Do
                If occ[s] = k
                    then  occ[s] = 0  // release from s
                          ndep = ndep + 1  // number of departures
                          If longF > 0
                              then  choose j in the queue
                                    longF = longF - 1
                                    occ[s] = j
                                    ds[j] = t  // start date of service
                                    dd[j] = date + Ds[j]  // next departure date
                          Endlf
                Endlf
            EndFor
        EndFor
Endlf
```

Figure 11.5. *Program for processing departures*

In the iteration, the algorithm contains two parts: the processing of an arrival (Figures 11.4 and 11.6) and the processing of a departure (Figures 11.5 and 11.7).

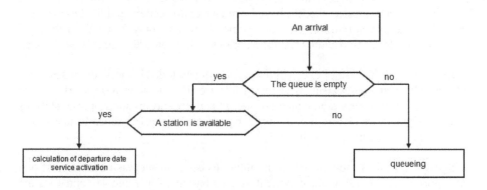

Figure 11.6. *Flow diagram of processing an arrival*

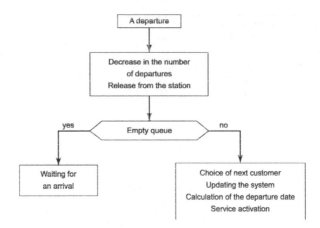

Figure 11.7. *Flow diagram of processing a departure*

11.3.3. *Synthetic results*

The different standard parameters characterizing a queue are calculated during the iteration: average number n_s of elements in the system, average number n_f of elements in the queue, average number n_u of elements in service, average number n_i of unoccupied stations, average time t_s spent in the system, average time t_f spent queueing, average time t_u of service. Times are expressed in units of time, regardless of the time step chosen. The calculations of all these parameters have been carried out so as to approach the steady state: only date values greater than 10 (or 100 or 1000 depending on the time step chosen) have been taken into account and the last 10 (100, 1000) dates have been removed, and the elements involved range from $S + 1$ to $N - S$ so as to eliminate start-up and termination periods and to consider a quasi-steady state.

Let us revisit the case of cars arriving at a highway toll. This toll comprises three stations which are equivalent in terms of service. Due to long-term works at the entrance of the toll, cars are channeled into a single queue. In addition, the stations work poorly and are slow due to computer problems (an easy excuse to justify the value of the service time we will take!).

Statistical studies show that the time intervals between successive arrivals of two cars approximately follow an exponential distribution of average $1/\lambda$ and that the service times approximately follow an exponential distribution of average $1/\mu = 3$ minutes.

The highway and the toll station have varying levels of traffic throughout the year. We consider three cases:

– in a normal period, the arrival rate of vehicles is 0.33 cars per minute ($\lambda = 0.33$, so $1/\lambda \approx 3$);

– during the spring holidays, the arrival rate of vehicles is 0.66 cars per minute ($\lambda = 0.66$, so $1/\lambda \approx 1.5$);

– during the summer holidays, the arrival rate of vehicles is 0.90 cars per minute ($\lambda = 0.90$, so $1/\lambda = 1.11$).

For each case, 10 simulations are carried out with 500 vehicles, and the tenth of a minute is taken as a time step. The synthetic results are shown in Table 11.4.

		Simulations										
		1	2	3	4	5	6	7	8	9	10	Averages
$\lambda = 0.33$ $\mu = 0.33$ $\Psi = 1$ $S = 3$	n_s	0.936	0.919	1.143	1.123	1.039	0.908	0.917	1.052	1.248	1.054	1.034
	n_f	0.043	0.013	0.063	0.065	0.051	0.025	0.013	0.046	0.115	0.047	0.048
	n_u	0.892	0.906	1.079	1.058	0.988	0.883	0.904	1.007	1.113	1.007	0.986
	n_i	2.108	2.094	1.921	1.942	2.012	2.117	2.096	1.993	1.867	1.993	2.014
	t_s	2.935	2.963	2,969	3.219	3.068	2.963	2.836	3.258	3.378	3.143	3.073
	t_f	0.135	0.042	0.164	0.186	0.150	0.081	0.042	0.140	0.312	0.140	0.139
	t_u	2.800	2.921	2.804	3.033	2.918	2.881	2.794	3.118	3.066	3.003	2.934

		Simulations										
		1	2	3	4	5	6	7	8	9	10	Averages
$\lambda = 0.66$ $\mu = 0.33$ $\Psi = 2$ $S = 3$	n_s	2.884	2.479	2.518	2.865	2.631	2.422	2.545	3.675	2.231	2.813	2.706
	n_f	0.833	0.492	0.675	1.061	0.659	0.551	0.565	1.729	0.441	0.884	0.789
	n_u	2.051	1.987	1.843	1.804	1.972	1.871	1.980	1.947	1.789	1.929	1.917
	n_i	0.949	1.013	1.157	1.196	1.028	1.129	1.020	1.053	1.211	1.071	1.083
	t_s	4.758	3.800	3.974	4.567	4.025	3.853	3.743	5.697	3.646	4.389	4.245
	t_f	1.362	0.746	1.057	1.688	1.009	0.871	0.832	2.650	0.712	1.404	1.233
	t_u	3.396	3.053	2.917	2.880	3.015	2.981	2.912	3.047	2.935	2.985	3.012

		Simulations										
		1	2	3	4	5	6	7	8	9	10	Averages
$\lambda = 0.90$ $\mu = 0.33$ $\Psi = 2.7$ $S = 3$	n_s	7.622	9.381	3.879	21.36	6.23	6.268	10.611	15.338	9.907	5.56	9.616
	n_f	5.132	6.768	1.497	18.501	3.662	3.742	8.164	12.499	7.153	3.032	7.015
	n_u	2.49	2.612	2.382	2.859	2.568	2.526	2.447	2.839	2.754	2.528	2.601
	n_i	0.51	0.388	0.618	0.141	0.432	0.474	0.553	0.161	0.246	0.472	0.400
	t_s	9.211	10.332	4,622	23.019	7.05	7.235	12.324	16.118	11.156	6.293	10.736
	t_f	6.195	7.423	1.758	19.898	4.128	4.294	9.442	13.085	8.036	3.408	7.767
	t_u	3.016	2.908	2.864	3.121	2.922	2.94	2.882	3.034	3.12	2.884	2.969

Table 11.4. *Results of simulations*

For all these results, there are "clear" values: the average service time is around 3 ($1/\mu = 3$), $t_u = t_s - t_f$, $n_u = n_s - n_f$.

Let us now compare the results to the theoretical values (Table 11.5).

The simulation results and the theoretical results are quite close. The biggest differences come from the last case (close to saturation, i.e. $\Psi = 3$), where rounding errors in calculations are largely responsible for the differences.

$\lambda = 0.33$ $\mu = 0.33$	$\psi = 1$	$S = 3$	$\lambda = 0.66$ $\mu = 0.33$	$\psi = 2$	$S = 3$	$\lambda = 0.90$ $\mu = 0.33$	$\psi = 2.7$	$S = 3$
Parameters	Simulated values	Theoretical values	Parameters	Simulated values	Theoretical values	Parameters	Simulated values	Theoretical values
p_o		0.364	p_o		0.111	p_o		0.022
n_s	1.034	1.135	n_s	2.706	2.889	n_s	9.616	11.021
n_f	0.048	0.135	n_f	0.789	0.889	n_f	7.015	8.321
n_i	2.014	2.000	n_i	1.083	0.889	n_i	0.400	0.400
t_s	3.073	3.168	t_s	4.245	4.377	t_s	10.736	12.246
t_f	0.139	0.138	t_f	1.233	1.347	t_f	7.767	9.247

Table 11.5. *Comparison with theoretical values*

12

Optimization and Simulation

CONCEPTS DISCUSSED IN THIS CHAPTER.– We will begin by presenting some optimization problems, such as the search for extremum of a function, and looking, in particular, at combinatorial optimization by quoting the "famous" problems: the traveling salesman problem, the vehicle routing problem and the knapsack problem.

A broad range of local methods is proposed by applying examples for the problems introduced above, such as the greedy algorithm, the gradient descent method, the simulated annealing method and the tabu method.

Finally, we describe and analyze, with examples, two methods that are increasingly used to approach optimal solutions: the genetic algorithms method and the ant colony method.

Recommended reading: [CON 06, DER 16, DOR 04, FAU 14, GOL 06, SIA 14].

12.1. Introduction

Optimization problems are an important class of operational research problems. They often do not have an exact analytical solution, at least not one which can be obtained in a reasonable time using computers. We are then led to look for approximations of the optimal solution(s) by using iterative algorithms.

EXAMPLE 12.1(1).– Search for the minimum of the function:

$$y = f(x) = 0.03(1.32x - 6)^4 + 0.1(x - 6)^3 - (1/3)(x - 6)^2 - x + 4$$

for x varying from 0 to 8.

All figures and tables are available in color online at www.iste.co.uk/cochard/stochastic.zip.

The problem is analytically solvable, in principle, by equalizing the derivative of
$f(x)$ to zero. However, the calculation is not simple and leads to the global minimum
($x = 1.89$, $y = -5.93$). Here, this example is just for educational purposes, because
knowing the solution, we can compare it to the solution produced by iterative
algorithms.

The representative curve in graph form is shown in Figure 12.1. It should be
noted that this function has two minimums in C and E and that a search by trial and
error could very well lead to the solution $x = 6$, which is not the optimal solution
sought.

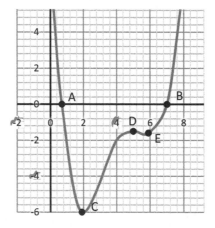

Figure 12.1. *Curve y = f(x)*

So, if we take the following simple algorithm:

Randomly choose an integer x between 0 and 8 (inclusive);

Evaluate $f(x)$:

$Min = f(x)$.

Do

$x = x + 1$;

Evaluate $f(x)$;

If $f(x) < Min$ then $Min = f(x)$.

While $f(x) > Min$.

If we initially choose $x = 1$, we will eventually obtain the optimal solution $x \cong 2$, but if we choose $x = 3$, we will get the wrong solution $x \cong 6$. This algorithm is therefore not suitable.

The problem of Example 12.1(1) is a problem that can be solved analytically, but with difficulty. Let us now look at problems with solutions that cannot be easily found in a reasonable amount of time by listing all possible solutions: combinatorial optimization problems.

EXAMPLE 12.2(1).– The traveling salesman problem (TSP): given a list of cities S and the distances between each pair of cities, find the shortest possible route that allows the traveler to visit each city once and return to the origin city.

Figure 12.2 shows a typical (but not necessarily optimal) path.

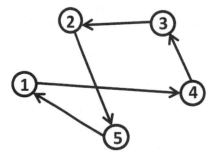

Figure 12.2. *Typical path*

The number of possible routes for S cities is $S!$, i.e. 120 for five cities, 3,628,800 for 10 cities and about 10^{157} for 100 cities. So, we quickly see the exploration limit for all the solutions.

It is still theoretically possible to do it (not by hand, but on a computer); however, it will take a lot of time if S is large. It is said to be an NP-complete problem (or NP-hard, where NP means "non-polynomial").

Other methods are therefore used to arrive at an approximation of the optimal solution that we will see later.

Figure 12.3. *Dutch mathematician Edsger Dijkstra (1930–2002) is best known for working on the search for efficient algorithms such as the shortest path. He was also a computer scientist and liked to make aphorisms such as: "The question of whether a computer can think is no more interesting than the question of whether a submarine can swim"*[1]

EXAMPLE 12.3.– Vehicle routing problem (VRP).

This is an extension of the previous problem. There are many variants to this problem. The simplest case is the one represented by a fleet of vehicles which, from a depot, must deliver to a set of customers.

In the classic problem, there are several vehicles taking routes in order to satisfy customers' needs.

Each customer must have their goods delivered by one single vehicle, which means that we must find disjointed routes (1 vehicle = 1 route) to satisfy all customers' needs.

Each of the vehicles therefore drives around a subset of customers, visiting them once per route. A route starts at the depot, denoted here as 0, and ends at the depot. Travel costs between the depot and customers and between customers are known.

Figure 12.4 shows an example of routes with three vehicles. All customers are visited: 1, 2, 3 by vehicle 1, 4 and 5 by vehicle 2, and 6 by vehicle 3.

---

1 The photograph of Edsger Dijkstra (credit: Hamilton Richards, source: Manuscripts of Edsger W. Dijkstra, licence OTRS) is from Wikimedia Commons: https://commons.wikimedia.org/wiki/Category:Edsger_Wybe_Dijkstra.

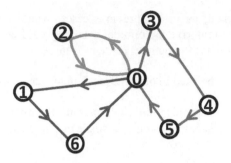

Figure 12.4. *Example of a possible solution*

However, we must satisfy customer demand. We therefore have a choice of routes for *m* vehicles (not necessarily identical) which have a given loading capacity *C* so as to minimize the total cost of transport and maximize the profit (the price of all customer deliveries).

Therefore, here we have two objectives, which are conflicting, but we can aggregate them into one by calculating the gain, the difference between the turnover and the transport cost, seeking to maximize this gain.

EXAMPLE 12.4(1).– The knapsack problem is one of the oldest problems studied in operations research. It is also an NP-complete problem. It involves filling a knapsack with a maximum given load using items which are all characterized by a weight and a value (Figure 12.5). The total value of the items in the bag must be as large as possible while respecting the weight constraints: the total weight of the items must be less than or equal to the maximum load of the bag.

Figure 12.5. *The knapsack problem*

The simplest method, as in the previous cases, would be to list all possible combinations and then to derive the optimal solution(s). Of course, this process can take time (and a lot of it!) if the number of items is large.

Other methods must be used to obtain a result in an acceptable period of time.

For some of these examples, we will present iterative algorithms to obtain optimal solutions (there is not necessarily a single or unique solution).

12.2. Local methods

Local methods consist, stating from an initial solution, of exploring the neighborhood of this solution. This neighborhood is obtained by elementary modifications of the initial solution. If, in this neighborhood, we find a better solution than the initial solution, then it takes its place and we continue with successive iterations up to a stop criterion.

EXAMPLE 12.2(2).– Let us take the example of the traveling salesman to illustrate the methods that follow in a practical way. The distance data are given in Figure 12.6. It is therefore a question of minimizing the total route starting from a node on the graph and returning to this same node, having only traversed the other nodes once. This type of path is called a "Hamiltonian path". We assume that the distance between two nodes is independent of the direction of travel of the arc connecting the two nodes.

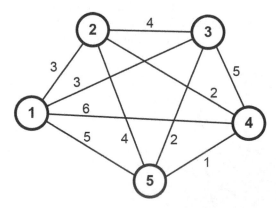

Figure 12.6. *Distances between cities*

First, let us give the exact solution by taking a small number of cities to visit so that this exact solution is obtained by examining all possible combinations. To do this, we can build a tree (Figure 12.7). There are 5! = 120 possible permutations of the nodes on the graph, but because we return to the starting point for each path, there are only 120/5 = 24 leaves in the tree. In addition, as a journey can be made in one direction or in the opposite direction, there are only 12 routes to examine.

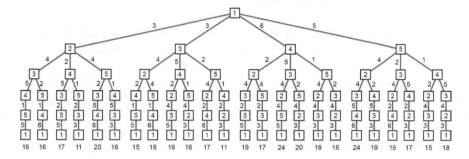

Figure 12.7. *Tree of possible solutions*

The optimum solution corresponding to the minimum path is 11 (Figure 12.8). Understandably, if the number of nodes increases, this exact solution will be more difficult to obtain. Hence, we need the methods of approximation, especially those that can be classified as "local search", which we will now examine in light of this example.

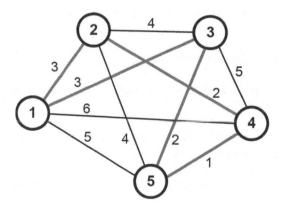

Figure 12.8. *The optimal solution*

12.2.1. *Greedy algorithm*

The first method is the greedy algorithm. It is so called in the processes where the maximum of a function is sought: at each stage, we choose the element that gives the function a maximum increase.

EXAMPLE 12.2(3).– In our example, the greedy algorithm should really be called a slimming algorithm, because we are looking for a minimum for the path.

Since the starting point does not matter, let us choose node 1, then look for the nearest neighbor. There are two: 2 and 3. Let us choose 3. So, we have the start of the path $1 - 3$. Now take the nearest neighbor of 3, which is 5. We now have the path $1 - 3 - 5$. Let us continue like this. We finally arrive at the path $1 - 3 - 5 - 4 - 2 - 1$, which corresponds to the exact optimal solution.

If we do not know the exact solution, can we say that the solution found is optimal? The answer is (unfortunately) no. To prove it, take the classic example of coins. Suppose that in an imaginary country we have coins of 1, 4 and 5 in local currency units. We want to pay the sum of 8 with the minimum number of coins. The greedy algorithm will begin by taking a coin of 5 and then three coins of 1, i.e. four coins in total. This solution is not optimal, because we could just use two coins of 4. The greedy algorithm is well adapted to certain types of problems and not at all to others. On the other hand, it can be useful when it comes to choosing an acceptable initial solution that can then be improved by other methods.

12.2.2. *Method of gradient descent*

The method of "gradient descent" consists of choosing an initial solution and making changes to it.

EXAMPLE 12.2(4).– For the traveling salesman problem, we could choose the initial solution with the greedy algorithm or choose it at random.

Take as initial solution A the path $1 - 2 - 3 - 4 - 5 - 1$ as shown in Figure 12.9. Its value is 18.

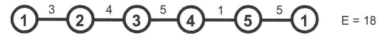

$E = 18$

Figure 12.9. *Initial solution A*

Let us make a local modification of this solution by swapping 2 and 3. We obtain the path B, $1 - 3 - 2 - 4 - 5 - 1$, of value 15 (Figure 12.10), which is much better than the initial path.

Figure 12.10. *Solution B*

Let us replace the initial solution with solution B and continue to make local modifications; for example, swapping 2 and 4, we obtain the path C, $1 - 3 - 4 - 2 - 5 - 1$, of value 19 (Figure 12.11).

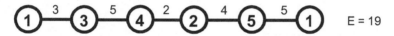

Figure 12.11. *Solution C*

We abandon C and return to B by swapping 4 and 5; solution D, $1 - 3 - 2 - 5 - 4 - 1$, of value 18, is obtained (Figure 12.12).

Figure 12.12. *Solution D*

We abandon D and return to solution B in which we swap 3 and 4, which leads to solution E, $1 - 4 - 2 - 3 - 5 - 1$, of value 19 (Figure 12.13).

Figure 12.13. *Solution E*

We abandon E and return to B, in which we swap 2 and 5, which gives the path F, $1 - 3 - 5 - 4 - 2 - 1$, of value 11 (Figure 12.14). This solution is much better than B.

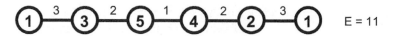

Figure 12.14. *Solution F*

We replace B with F (which is the exact solution).

We can continue in this way by trying to improve the solution at each step by making local modifications.

If the advantage of the method is its simplicity, its main disadvantage is coming across a local optimum rather than a global optimum. We risk falling victim to a "tub" or a "summit".

12.2.3. *Simulated annealing*

Simulated annealing comes from *annealing in metallurgy*. When a metal heated to high temperature is cooled, its crystalline structure tends to appear and when the metal is cooled, the crystalline structure is reformed. However, in this reconstruction of the crystalline structure, a defect may appear. To avoid this, the metal is heated (annealed) and then cooled again, in the hope that the defect will disappear.

In simulation, the simulated annealing method brings great improvement to the gradient descent method. It allows us to keep, under certain conditions, a non-optimal solution (the defect), to which a modification can give a better solution (the defect disappears).

In analogy with metallurgy, we are looking for a solution with minimal "energy". This is achieved by decreasing the temperature. For simulation, energy is the value of the function to be minimized (in the case of finding a minimum).

The algorithm below (called the "metropolis algorithm") describes the process (Figure 12.15). T_0 and T_{min}, respectively, denote the initial value and the final value of the temperature; N denotes the number of iterations, i.e. the number of times a solution is modified; c is the coefficient of lowering of the temperature; E represents the energy, i.e. the function to be minimized; $S0$ is the initial solution and $S1$ is the modified solution (of energy $E1$).

```
//algorithm of simulated annealing
While T > T_min
            For k = 1 to N
                        Calculate the energy E0 of S0
                        Make a modification of S0 --> S1
                        Calculate the energy E1 of S1
                        ΔE = E1 - E0
                        If ΔE < 0
                                    then S0 = S1
                                    else   p = rand(0,1)  //random number between 0 and 1
                                           q = exp(-ΔE/T)
                                           If p < q
                                                       then S0 = S1
                                           EndIf
                        EndIf
            EndFor
            T = cT  //decreased temperature
EndWhile
```

Figure 12.15. *Simulation program*

As we can see, the algorithm "keeps" solutions that seem bad (if $p < q$). A subsequent modification of this bad solution may give a better solution. This avoids staying close to a local minimum. The expression of q is an analogy with statistical physics.

A modification of a solution, in the case of Example 12.2, would consist of exchanging two cities.

It has been demonstrated that the algorithm actually converges to the optimal solution. However, the choice of the parameters T_0, T_{min}, N and c is crucial for the speed of convergence. Typically, c is taken at 0.9 or 0.99. N can vary between 100 and 1,000. The choice of T_0 is more delicate. We show that if we average ΔE on a large number of modifications of a solution, we can take T_0 such that:

$$e^{-\frac{\overline{\Delta E}}{T_0}} = \alpha$$

with α being between 0.2 and 0.5.

EXAMPLE 12.2(5).– Let us apply the algorithm to the traveling salesman problem with the previous data. Taking $\alpha = 0.2$, from which $T_0 = \sim 2$, $T_{min} = 0.5$, $N = 100$ and $c = 0.99$, we obtain the optimal solution (of energy 11) in 100% of the cases over 50 simulations.

On the other hand, with $T_0 = 10$, $c = 0.9$ and $N = 100$, the optimal solution was obtained only in 50% of the cases over 50 simulations, which shows that the choice of the parameter T_0 is crucial.

EXAMPLE 12.1(2).– The simulated annealing method can also be used to find the value of x that makes the function of Example 12.1(1) minimum. With $T_0 = 0.15$, $T_{min} = 0.05$, $c = 0.99$ and $N = 100$, after 10 simulations, we obtain an average of 1.91 close to the exact result (1.89). This example also shows that we have escaped the local minimum located near $x = 6$.

12.2.4. *Tabu search*

This method is deterministic and is less directly relevant to the subject of this book. However, being relatively well used, it is hard to ignore.

The method starts with an initial solution to a combinatorial problem and then examines the neighborhood of this solution. The neighborhood can be obtained by making simple modifications to the initial solution, for example, by swapping two terms. We then examine the "objective" function for each of the neighborhoods obtained. If the number of "neighbors" is very large, we can be content with a subset of the neighborhood. The new solution is then the one that corresponds to the best-placed neighbor.

The word "tabu" structure comes from the fact that we put the solutions that have already been explored in a memory (or "taboo"), so solutions do not overlap. We therefore avoid, in a neighborhood, choosing solutions of tabu memory.

We then start the process from this best neighbor. Note that during an iteration it is possible to obtain a solution that is worse than the previous one, but the point of the method is that we do not have to remain on a relative extremum.

12.3. Genetic algorithms

A genetic algorithm is an iterative algorithm for a population of individuals that are assumed to represent potential solutions to an optimization problem. It takes its name from evolutionary theory. In fact, the population of eligible solutions will have to evolve towards a population of optimal solutions.

As with real genetic inheritance, each individual (solution) is represented by a chromosome with genes.

The evolutionary process uses two main methods to obtain new individuals from a number of original individuals: crossover and mutation. Crossover usually consists of two "parents" selected to obtain two "children" by gene exchange. We will see the practical significance of crossover below. Mutation consists of modifying a few genes of a parent individual to obtain a child individual.

In this process, two special actions take place: the selection of individuals to participate in crossover and mutation, and the selection after crossover and mutation to choose the best individuals so as not to indefinitely increase the size of the population.

In most cases, starting from p individuals, this last action also gives p individuals, surplus individuals being eliminated after evaluation of their performance, which means we keep the *best p*. This evaluation consists of measuring the adaptation of individuals to the constraints of the problem, and in particular the value for each individual of the "objective" function to be minimized (or maximized). This adaptation is measured by a variable called *fitness*.

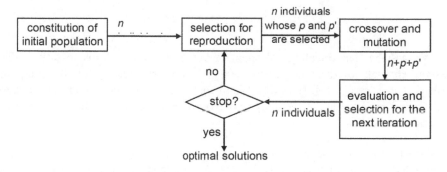

Figure 12.16. *Flowchart of a genetic algorithm*

The diagram in Figure 12.16 summarizes the iterative process. It is assumed in this diagram that p individuals are selected for reproduction and give birth to p children. Similarly, p' individuals are selected to produce p' mutated individuals. The population after reproduction is therefore $n + p + p'$. Evaluation after reproduction eliminates $p + p'$ individuals according to their *fitness*, and the population then returns to n individuals.

The choice of chromosome representation is quite crucial for success in obtaining optimal solutions within a reasonable period of time. Depending on the problem, it can lead to chromosomes whose genes can be represented by integers or real numbers.

EXAMPLE 12.5.– Take as a first illustrative example the traveling salesman problem shown in Figure 12.17.

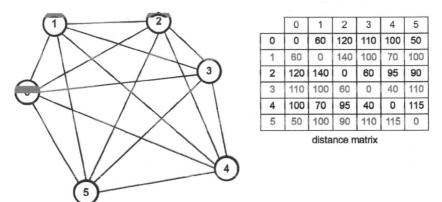

	0	1	2	3	4	5
0	0	60	120	110	100	50
1	60	0	140	100	70	100
2	120	140	0	60	95	90
3	110	100	60	0	40	110
4	100	70	95	40	0	115
5	50	100	90	110	115	0

distance matrix

Figure 12.17. *Problem to solve*

We assume that traveling salesman leaves city 0 and returns to city 0 after passing through all the other cities. We are therefore looking for the minimum path that they can travel. It can be found in one of the combinations of numbers 1, 2, 3, 4, 5 or 5! = 120. We actually only have to consider 60 combinations, as each path is reversible.

Clearly, we can find the minimum path without using a genetic algorithm (by simply listing combinations of 1, 2, 3, 4, 5 – tedious, but feasible – we get the solution 1 – 4 – 3 – 2 – 5 corresponding to a path of length 370), because the example proposed here is simple, and using a genetic algorithm would be like using a sledgehammer to crack a nut. However, it is only an educational example, the scope of which can extend to more complex problems (with hundreds of cities to travel through, for example).

We start by randomly choosing a set of 50 potential solutions; a potential solution is a solution of type *abcde*, where a, b, c, d and e represent a digit from 1 to 5, with all figures being different. By randomly drawing, according to uniform distribution, each of the five digits (verifying that they are all different), we obtain a potential solution that constitutes an "individual" of the population.

To start the crossover phase, the tournament method can be used to select the parents. This is only one method among many others, but it has the advantage of not automatically eliminating solutions that are uninteresting *a priori*, but which could be "improved" subsequently.

Suppose we choose 40% of the population as parents, i.e. 20 individuals. The procedure is as follows: 20 pairs of individuals are randomly selected and the lengths of the corresponding paths are compared in pairs; the winner of each tournament is the individual with the shortest path. Of these 20 pairs, we get 20 parents which we will match to produce children (two children per couple). We will get 20 children. The crossover process can be chosen as follows. For an *abcde* individual, we consider the left part *ab* and the right part *cde*. The crossover will be defined as the next exchange (Figure 12.18).

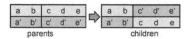

parents   children

Figure 12.18. *Crossover process*

The process has the advantage of being simple, but it still involves necessary corrections, because a child must also correspond to a potential solution. Thus, if we consider the case shown in Figure 12.19, we see that the result (the children) is not acceptable for a potential solution.

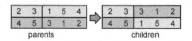

parents   children

Figure 12.19. *Case to modify*

It can be seen that for the first child as well as for the second, there are repetitions of certain digits. We must correct this situation by replacing, for example, "3" and "2" on the right-hand side of the first child with "4" and "5". Similarly, we replace "5" and "4" on the right-hand side of the second child with "2" and "3".

For the mutation operation, 10 individuals (i.e. 20% of the population) will be drawn from the population, each of which will give birth to 10 mutated individuals. The mutation will be defined as the permutation of the right-hand digit of the left-hand side with the left-hand digit of the right-hand side, as shown in Figure 12.20.

individual   mutated individual

Figure 12.20. *Mutation process*

Finally, the new population consists of 50 initial individuals, 20 children and 10 mutated individuals, or 80 individuals in total. The population size can be made constant (50) by sorting the 80 individuals according to the length of the paths and taking the 50 best ones.

Then, we repeat the previous operations in a second iteration and so on. After a certain number of iterations, we can hope, because of the increase in "quality" of the population, to approach the solution sought.

With only 10 iterations, we obtain (obviously, because of the random draws, the result can be different) a population made up, in descending order of the length of the paths, of 40 identical solutions of length 370, $1 - 4 - 3 - 2 - 5$ (or $5 - 2 - 3 - 4 - 1$), and a solution $1 - 4 - 3 - 2 - 5$ of length 435.

EXAMPLE 12.1(3).– To justify the universality of the method, let us examine a very different problem, that of the search for the absolute minimum of the function $f(x)$ mentioned in the introduction to this chapter (section 12.1). An analytical study shows that this minimum, for x varying from 0 to 8, is obtained for $x = 1.89$ with $f(x) = -5.93$. Suppose that we use a genetic algorithm to search for the value of x that makes the function f minimum with two decimals.

We need to get a number between 0.01 and 7.99. Let us use a binary encoding to represent a solution. This will be represented by 10 bits, the first three indicating the integer part of x, and the following seven being the decimal part (Figure 12.21).

1	2	3	4	5	6	7	8	9	10
x	x	x	x	x	x	x	x	x	x

Figure 12.21. *Coding a solution*

A solution appears as a vector with 10 components numbered from 1 to 10, as shown in Figure 12.21. Of course, this solution must be acceptable and satisfy the condition $0.01 \leq x \leq 7.99$. This means the left-hand side has to go from 000 to 111 and the right-hand side has to go from 0000000 (except 0000001 for the left-hand side 000) to 1100011. This last value corresponds in decimal to 99.

Thus, 100 random solutions will be randomly drawn as indicated above.

The process of crossover first requires the "parents" solutions to be chosen, which can be done, once again, by the tournament method: we draw at random two solutions from the population and we keep the one for which $f(x)$ is minimum. We start again 40 times to obtain 40 "parents" (which corresponds to 40% of the population). These parents will give birth to 40 children defined by the crossover process shown in Figure 12.22.

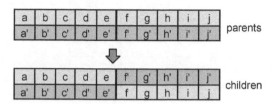

Figure 12.22. *Crossover process*

Of course, children must also be acceptable solutions, i.e. they must satisfy the conditions defined for each individual in the population. It can happen that one of the children is a combination 0000000000. In this case, it is modified by setting bit 10 to 1. It may also happen that the combination formed of bits 4 to 10 corresponds to a number greater than 99. In this case, it will be necessary to modify this child by setting bit 4 to 0.

We can now apply the mutation process to 20% of the initial population, so to 20 randomly drawn individuals. The exchange of bits 3 and 4 (Figure 12.23) must be performed as a mutation.

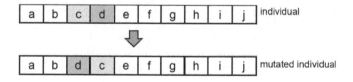

Figure 12.23. *Mutation process*

The same correction as that described above for children will also be carried out on mutated elements in order to obtain acceptable solutions.

The population has now increased to 40 children and 20 mutated elements and has therefore grown to 150 individuals. We classify these individuals according to the decreasing values of $f(x)$ and we keep the first 100 (so the best 100).

The previous chain of operations is then repeated a number of times. For 100 iterations, the results shown in Table 12.1 were obtained in 10 independent simulations.

Simulation	x
1	1.89
2	1.89
3	1.88
4	1.89
5	1.89
6	1.89
7	1.89
8	1.90
9	1.89
10	1.90
Average	**1.89**

Table 12.1. *Results*

At the end of iteration, each population consists of identical individuals.

EXAMPLE 12.4(2).– Let us look at a third example, the knapsack problem presented in the introduction to this chapter (section 12.1). Remember that this is about filling a knapsack with objects. The objects have the values and weights defined in Table 12.2. The knapsack can only contain objects less than or equal to 20 kg in weight. It is a question of finding objects to put in the knapsack while respecting the weight constraint, such that the sum of the values of the knapsack's objects is maximum.

Object	1	2	3	4	5	6	7	8	9
Weight (kg)	12	8	5	9	5	8	12	10	4
Value (€)	10	6	15	8	14	16	12	9	10

Table 12.2. *Data of the problem*

A group of objects can be represented by a 9-bit word, each bit corresponding to one of the nine objects. The value 1 indicates that there is an object in the bag; the value 0 indicates that the corresponding object is not in the bag. Thus, the following word (Figure 12.24) indicates that the objects 1, 2, 5, 6, 9 are in the bag and the others are outside.

1	1	0	0	1	1	0	0	1

Figure 12.24. *Coding a solution*

However, the weight constraint must be respected, which is not the case for the word in Figure 12.24, which does not respect it, because the weight of the objects is $12 + 8 + 5 + 8 + 4 = 37 > 20$. To constitute the initial population, we can successively choose at random each of the 9 bits of the word and reject it, if necessary, if the weight constraint is not respected.

In the simulation described below, the population is made up of 20 individuals selected as indicated above. For each of these individuals, the total weight W of the objects and the total value V of the objects are calculated.

Of the 20 individuals, 8 parents (40% of the population) are randomly selected with the tournament method, which is always very convenient to implement: we choose a pair of individuals eight times and we retain the part of the pair that has the highest value (sum of the values of the corresponding objects).

Then, we crossover these eight parents, the first with the second, then the second with the third, etc., to get eight children. The crossover process involves exchanging the last 5 bits between the two parents, as shown in Figure 12.25.

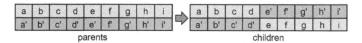

Figure 12.25. *Crossover process*

Of course, children must match compatible solutions, i.e. respect the weight constraint. If this is not the case, we proceed with the random draw of a bit, which we replace with 0. This continues until the solution is compatible.

Similarly, we can obtain a solution composed only of 0, which is not useful. We must check that the sum of the bits is not 0. If this is the case, we randomly select one of the bits and set it to 1.

These two modifications can also be used to choose the initial population. For every acceptable child, we calculate the total weight W and the total value V.

For the mutation operation, we choose to swap 2 bits randomly (Figure 12.26), always verifying that the weight constraint is respected. If this is not the case, once again, we modify as indicated previously.

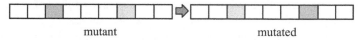

Figure 12.26. *Mutation process*

These operations are carried out on six individuals from the initial population (30%). For each mutated individual, we calculate the total weight W and the total value V.

The population of the initial 20 individuals has therefore increased by eight children and six mutated elements, which makes 34 individuals that can be classified by decreasing quality, i.e. by the values V. We retain the best 20 individuals, so as to keep the population constant.

Simulations	V			
	45	41	40	39
1	4 times	5 times	11 times	
2	20 times			
3	20 times			
4	20 times			
5	20 times			
6	14 times	6 times		
7	17 times	3 times		
8	9 times			11 times
9	20 times			
10	20 times			

10 iterations

Simulations	V	
	45	41
1	20 times	
2	20 times	
3	20 times	
4	20 times	
5	8 times	12 times
6	20 times	
7	20 times	
8	20 times	
9	20 times	
10	20 times	

20 iterations

Simulations	V
	45
1	20 times
2	20 times
3	20 times
4	20 times
5	20 times
6	20 times
7	20 times
8	20 times
9	20 times
10	20 times

100 iterations

Table 12.3. *Results for several iterations*

Then, we repeat the process a certain number N of times.

For this problem, we performed 10 simulations for three values of N: 10, 20 and 100 iterations. The result is given in Table 12.3.

12.4. Ant colonies

Like the previous method, this method is inspired by the behavior of living beings – in this case, ants. The corresponding algorithm is often called the AS algorithm, short for "ant system".

The social behavior of ants is specific. In searching for food and then returning to the anthill, each ant acts independently, in a self-deterministic way, but with the purpose of serving the colony. Going from anthill to food source, ants try to take the shortest path. They find this path based on the experience of the ants that preceded them. Ants rely on pheromones, which are *odorous substances* that ants deposit along their path. These pheromones are volatile and disappear by evaporating after a certain amount of time.

The significant presence of pheromones on a path therefore indicates a well-used path.

Imagine two paths leading from an anthill to a food source, as shown in Figure 12.27, with path B being longer than path A.

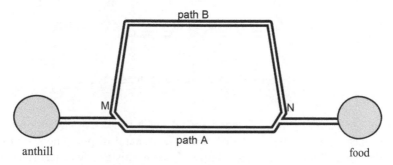

Figure 12.27. *Several paths lead from the anthill to the food*

Assume that the two paths have not been used yet. Imagine two ants simultaneously appearing at junction M, one taking path A, the other path B. we will also call these ants A and B. These ants leave pheromones along their path.

Ant A will reach the food source first, followed by Ant B. The first ant to return to the anthill is Ant A. In the meantime, the pheromones have partially evaporated. At junction N, ant A will resume the same path as ant B has not yet arrived at N and so has not yet left pheromones while the pheromones left by A are still notable. In addition, ant A leaves pheromones again.

When ant B reaches the food store and returns to the anthill, it will be able to "sense" at junction N that there are more pheromones on path A than on path B and will therefore choose to return via path A, also leaving pheromones. Thus, the path with the most pheromones will be path A, because it is shorter than path B.

From this situation, we can see that the probability of taking a path is proportional to the number of pheromones and therefore the passage of the largest contingent of ants.

Now suppose that the most-used path, A, is blocked by an obstacle (Figure 12.28).

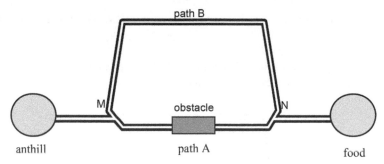

Figure 12.28. *An obstacle appears*

The ants on path A will turn around and take path B, leaving pheromones on this path, and then do the same on their return. The amount of pheromones on path B will increase and therefore the probability of taking this path will also increase, so path B will be the most used. As it is the only possible route, it becomes the shortest.

Finally, each path taken by an ant individually is a solution that enables the anthill–food journey. However, the optimal solution is the solution most used by the ant colony.

To solve a combinatorial optimization problem, we can take inspiration from the behavior of real ants by inventing virtual ants. These virtual ants are different from real ants:

– they travel in an environment that is not continuous and progress from state to state;

– we can endow virtual ants with memory, which allows us to trace their paths. In particular, a virtual ant knows the states it has already visited (and thus also those it has not visited);

– the deposit of pheromones by virtual ants is not necessarily immediate; it can happen after the exploration of a solution;

– a virtual ant can study the states according to the current state; in particular, it knows the "distance" to the immediately adjacent states, and it can also go back as needed.

EXAMPLE 12.2(6).– Given its origin, the ant colony method is particularly suitable for finding a minimal path, such as in the traveling salesman problem. Let us start by looking at this problem in view of the ant colonies. We will see later on that the method is not limited to this problem. So, let there be a graph like the one in Figure 12.17 that has $n = 6$ vertices.

In the initial configuration, we will randomly distribute a set of m ants on vertices 1, 2, 3, 4, 5 and 6 (for the purposes of the algorithm, we renumbered the vertices by adding 1). Each virtual ant has a memory, so it knows the vertices it has already visited. Initially, the memory contains only the starting vertex (1 or 2 or 3 or 4 or 5 or 6). Each ant will choose the neighboring vertex based on two criteria: the amount of pheromones on the corresponding arc and the distance between the initial vertex and the neighboring vertex. It will then move from vertex i to vertex j according to these two criteria. For each ant, the amount of pheromones will be updated at the end of a cycle (i.e. after returning to the starting vertex).

Let us explain the two criteria of choice.

At a given cycle t, the quantity of pheromones for a path ij is denoted $\tau_{ij}(t)$. It obviously depends on the cycle number t, because on the one hand, it can increase when ants use the path ij, and on the other hand, it gradually evaporates. It thus has the form:

$$\tau_{ij}(t + 1) = (1 - \rho)\tau_{ij}(t) + \Delta\tau_{ij}(t)$$

where ρ represents an evaporation coefficient of pheromones. It is between 0 and 1. If $\rho = 1$, the evaporation is fast and thus decreases the interest of being aware of the pheromones. If $\rho = 0$, the pheromones are persistent (no evaporation) and therefore this choice also reduces the interest of being aware of the pheromones. So we must choose ρ as $0 < \rho < 1$.

$\Delta\tau_{ij}(t)$ represents the quantity of pheromones deposited by all the ants on arc ij in cycle t. It is expressed in the form:

$$\Delta\tau_{ij}(t) = \sum_{k=1}^{m} \Delta\tau_{ij}^{k}(t)$$

where $\Delta\tau_{ij}^{k}(t)$ is the quantity of pheromones deposited by ant k on path ij in cycle t. It is customary to express it according to the length of the cycle traveled $L_k(t)$ by ant k:

$$\Delta\tau_{ij}^{k}(t) = \begin{cases} \dfrac{Q}{L_k(t)} & \text{if } i \text{ } j \text{ is part of the cycle} \\ 0 & \text{if not} \end{cases}$$

The greater the distance d_{ij} between vertices i and j, the less interested the ant will be. We can therefore measure the interest of an ant on the question of distance by taking the inverse $1/d_{ij}$, which we call "visibility" η_{ij}.

As a result, taking into account these two criteria, we can define the probability of ant k choosing path ij at time t by:

$$proba_{ij}^k(t) = \begin{cases} \dfrac{[\tau_{ij}(t)]^\alpha \eta_{ij}^\beta}{\sum_{l \in N_i^k(t)} [\tau_{il}(t)]^\alpha \eta_{il}^\beta} & \text{if } j \text{ is an unvisited vertex} \\[2mm] 0 & \text{if not} \end{cases}$$

In this expression, $N_i^k(t)$ represents the set of vertices that ant k has not yet visited in the current t cycle. The coefficients α and β define the relative importance of the two criteria (a) and (b) defined above (quantity of pheromones and visibility). Note that for $t = 0$, there are no pheromones and therefore the above probability is zero in all cases. For this reason, in order to initialize the process, we choose to take $\tau_{ij}(0) = c$, where c is a small positive amount, but not zero.

The AS algorithm is presented schematically in Figure 12.29.

//Initialization phase
Distribution of m ants on the n vertices of the graph
Initialization of the arcs with $\tau_{ij}(0) = c$
//Iterative phases
For t = 1 to N (*)
        For every ant k
                Construction of a path from the examination of probabilities $proba_{ij}^k(t)$
                and progressive filling of the set N_k of the vertices visited
                Calculation of the length $L_k(t)$ of the chosen path
                Calculation of the value $\Delta\tau_{ij}^k(t)$ for each section of the path
        EndFor
        Memorization of the best path from the $L_k(t)$
        Calculation of $\tau_{ij}(t)$ for each arc ij
        $N_k = \varnothing$
EndFor
(*): we can also stop the iterations if all the ants follow the same path
because the process then becomes stationary

Figure 12.29. *AS algorithm program*

The AS algorithm has been subject to many variations and improvements that we will not mention here. Let us apply the AS algorithm, in its standard version, to the traveling salesman problem, with visits to cities numbered from 1 to 6. The parameters of the model are chosen as follows, justified by experience: $\alpha = 1$, $\beta = 3$, $\rho = 0.5$, $Q = 100$ and $c = 0.01$. Remember that our problem here is very simple and would not justify such a significant development if it were not just for educational purposes. It is obvious that for a large number of vertices, it will take many ants and many iterations. It is advisable, in this case, to take a number of ants equal to the number of vertices: $n = m$. Since we plan to distribute the ants equitably but randomly on the vertices, and the number of vertices is small, we choose to take $m = 10n = 60$. We can also limit ourselves to 10 iterations, the convergence being quickly reached. The result, unsurprisingly, is the circuit $1 - 2 - 5 - 4 - 3 - 6 - 1$ (or any direct or inverse circular permutation) of length 370. The quantity of pheromones in the last iteration effectively shows the most-used path (Figure 12.30).

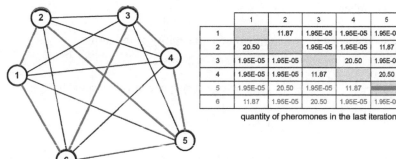

	1	2	3	4	5	6
1		11.87	1.95E-05	1.95E-05	1.95E-05	20.50
2	20.50		1.95E-05	1.95E-05	11.87	1.95E-05
3	1.95E-05	1.95E-05		20.50	1.95E-05	11.87
4	1.95E-05	1.95E-05	11.87		20.50	1.95E-05
5	1.95E-05	20.50	1.95E-05	11.87		1.95E-05
6	11.87	1.95E-05	20.50	1.95E-05	1.95E-05	

quantity of pheromones in the last iteration

Figure 12.30. *Results*

It is true that the quantity of pheromones is a good indicator of the circuit to be taken.

EXAMPLE 12.4(3).– The ant colony method can also be applied to other types of problems and is not a simple heuristic for the traveling salesman problem. To show this, let us apply the method to the knapsack problem explained in the previous section (section 12.3). It will involve, during successive iterations, each ant of a colony of m ants choosing objects up to the weight limit and noting the value of the objects in the bag. Each ant always starts every iteration with the same object.

So, we initially randomly assign an object to the bag of each ant belonging to a set of m ants. Then, each ant successively fills its bag by choosing an object while respecting the weight constraint, namely that the total weight of the objects of the bag, W, must not exceed W_{max}. The choice of an object is made by examining a probability that we will define later.

When the maximum weight limit is reached, the value of the objects in the bag is calculated and the ants deposit pheromones relative to their choice of objects. It will be considered that the pheromones are deposited on the objects themselves (contrary to the arcs of the previous example); it will be agreed that the dose of pheromones is proportional to the value V of the objects deposited in the bag, namely:

$$\Delta \tau_i^k (t) = \begin{cases} QV^k (t) & \text{if object } i \text{ belongs to the bag} \\ 0 \text{ if not} \end{cases}$$

the index k designating the ant, $V^k(t)$ the value of the objects in the ant's bag and t the iteration number.

An object i is chosen by ant k following a probability of the form:

$$proba_i^k (t) = \begin{cases} \dfrac{\left[\tau_i(t)\right]^\alpha \eta_i^\beta}{\sum_{j \in N^k(t)} \left[\tau_j(t)\right]^\alpha \eta_j^\beta} & \text{if } i \text{ is an object not yet chosen, but could be chosen} \\ 0 \text{ if not} \end{cases}$$

$N^k(t)$ represents the set of objects that have not yet been chosen by ant k. The denominator is intended to normalize the probability. The numerator has two components $\tau_i(t)$ and η_i, analogously to the probability of the previous example. $\tau_i(t)$ is the total amount of pheromones deposited on object i; η_i measures the appeal of object i, and we can simply take $\eta_i = p_i$ as the value of object i.

At each iteration, we update the doses of pheromones on each object, taking into account the contributions of each ant according to the relation:

$$\tau_i(t + 1) = (1 - \rho)\tau_i(t) + \sum_{k=1}^{m} \Delta \tau_i^k(t)$$

where ρ represents the evaporation coefficient of pheromones.

For a simulation, we will take $m = 120$ ants and 300 iterations. The other parameters are set to the values $\alpha = 3$, $\beta = 1$, $\rho = 0.5$ and $Q = 1$, and the initial quantity of pheromones is set at $c = 0.01$ for each object. Of course, the previous choice is debatable; it allows us to obtain an optimal solution rather quickly, but obviously other choices are possible.

At iteration 300, the result produces, for some ants, the optimal value of 45 for the value of the bag corresponding to the objects 3, 5 and 6. For other ants, we have other values lower than 45, which is normal since the initial object chosen is not necessarily in the set {3, 5, 6}. All of the ants that initially selected one of the objects in the set {3, 5, 6} chose the other two, which was not the case for the first iterations.

The balance of the pheromones deposited on each object at the last iteration shows the optimal choice, as the highest pheromone levels are on objects 3, 5 and 6 (see Table 12.4).

Object i	$T_i(300)$
1	728
2	960
3	3856
4	624
5	2790
6	7940
7	672
8	1100
9	2026

Table 12.4. *Pheromones deposited on the objects at the end of the simulation*

References

[BAR 01] BARTOLI N., DEL MORAL P., *Simulation et Algorithmes Stochastiques*, Éditions Cépaduès, Toulouse, 2001.

[BAY 00] BAYNAT B., *Théorie des files d'attente, des chaînes de Markov aux réseaux à forme produit*, Hermès, Paris, 2000.

[BER 07] BERCU B., CHAFAI D., *Modélisation stochastique et simulation*, Dunod, Paris, 2007.

[BOU 16] BOURBONNAIS R., VALLIN P., *Comment Optimiser les Approvisionnements*, Economica, London, 2016.

[BRE 09] BREMAUD P., *Initiation aux probabilités et aux chaînes de Markov*, Springer, Berlin, 2009.

[CON 06] CONSTANZO A., VAN LUONG T., MARILL G., Optimisation par colonies de fourmis, Report, Available at: http://www.i3s.unice.fr/~crescenz/publications/travaux_etude/colonies_fourmis-200605-rapport.pdf, 2006.

[DEH 82] DEHEUVELS P., *La probabilité, le hasard et la certitude*, Presses universitaires de France, Paris, 1982.

[DER 16] DEROUSSI L., *Metaheuristics for Logistics*, ISTE, Ltd, London and John Wiley & Sons, New York, 2016.

[DOD 08] DODGE Y., MELFI G., *Premiers pas en simulation*, Springer, Berlin, 2008.

[DOR 06] DORIGO M., BIRATTARI, M., STUTZLE T., "Ant colony optimization", *IEEE Computational Intelligence*, vol. 1, no. 4, pp. 28–39, 2006.

[DUP 05] DUPLANTIER B., Le mouvement brownien divers et ondoyant, *Séminaire Poincaré 1*, available at: http://www.bourbaphy.fr/duplantier 2.pdf, 2005.

[ENG 76] ENGEL A., *Processus aléatoires pour les débutants*, Cassini, Paris, 1976.

[FAU 79] FAURE R., *Précis de recherche opérationnelle*, Dunod, Paris, 1979.

[FAU 14] FAURE R., LEMAIRE B., PICOULEAU C., *Précis de recherche opérationnelle, méthodes et exercices d'application*, Dunod, Paris, 2014.

[FOA 04] FOA D., FUCHS A., *Processus stochastiques, processus de Poisson, chaînes de Markov et martingales*, Dunod, Paris, 2004.

[GOL 06] GOLDBERG D.E., *Genetic Algorithms in Search, Optimization and Machine Learning*, Addison-Wesley, Boston, 2006.

[HEN 09] HENRY M., "Émergence de la probabilité et enseignement", *Repères-IREM*, no. 74, January 2009.

[LEB 12] LE BELLAC M., VIRICEL A., *Mathématiques des marchés financiers, modélisation du risque et de l'incertitude*, EDP Sciences, Les Ulis, 2012.

[LES 14] LESSARD S., *Processus stochastiques*, Ellipses, Paris, 2014.

[PEL 97] PELLEGRIN C., *Fondements de la décision de maintenance*, Economica, London, 1997.

[PHE 77] PHELIZON J.-F., *Informatique opérationnelle*, Economica, London, 1977.

[ROS 93] ROSE J., *Le hasard au quotidien, coïncidences, jeux de hasard, sondages*, Le Seuil, Paris, 1993.

[RUE 89] RUEG A., *Processus stochastiques*, Presses polytechniques et universitaires romandes, Lausanne, 1989.

[SAP 11] SAPORTA G., *Probabilités, analyse de données, et statistique*, Technip, Paris, 2011.

[SIA 14] SIARRY P., *Métaheuristiques*, Eyrolles, Paris, 2014.

[VAL 07] VALLOIS P., *Modélisations stochastiques et simulations*, Ellipses, Paris, 2007.

Index

Other titles from

in

Information Systems, Web and Pervasive Computing

GHLALA Riadh
Analytic SQL in SQL Server 2014/2016

SOURIS Marc
Epidemiology and Geography: Principles, Methods and Tools of Spatial Analysis

TOUNSI Wiem
Cyber-Vigilance and Digital Trust: Cyber Security in the Era of Cloud Computing and IoT

2018

ARDUIN Pierre-Emmanuel
Insider Threats
(Advances in Information Systems Set – Volume 10)

CARMÈS Maryse
Digital Organizations Manufacturing: Scripts, Performativity and Semiopolitics
(Intellectual Technologies Set – Volume 5)

CARRÉ Dominique, VIDAL Geneviève
Hyperconnectivity: Economical, Social and Environmental Challenges
(Computing and Connected Society Set – Volume 3)

CHAMOUX Jean-Pierre
The Digital Era 1: Big Data Stakes

DOUAY Nicolas
Urban Planning in the Digital Age
(Intellectual Technologies Set – Volume 6)

FABRE Renaud, BENSOUSSAN Alain
The Digital Factory for Knowledge: Production and Validation of Scientific Results

GAUDIN Thierry, LACROIX Dominique, MAUREL Marie-Christine, POMEROL Jean-Charles
Life Sciences, Information Sciences

GAYARD Laurent
Darknet: Geopolitics and Uses
(Computing and Connected Society Set – Volume 2)

IAFRATE Fernando
Artificial Intelligence and Big Data: The Birth of a New Intelligence
(Advances in Information Systems Set – Volume 8)

LE DEUFF Olivier
Digital Humanities: History and Development
(Intellectual Technologies Set – Volume 4)

MANDRAN Nadine
Traceable Human Experiment Design Research: Theoretical Model and
Practical Guide
(Advances in Information Systems Set – Volume 9)

PIVERT Olivier
NoSQL Data Models: Trends and Challenges

ROCHET Claude
Smart Cities: Reality or Fiction

SAUVAGNARGUES Sophie
Decision-making in Crisis Situations: Research and Innovation for Optimal
Training

SEDKAOUI Soraya
Data Analytics and Big Data

SZONIECKY Samuel
Ecosystems Knowledge: Modeling and Analysis Method for Information and
Communication
(Digital Tools and Uses Set – Volume 6)

2017

BOUHAÏ Nasreddine, SALEH Imad
Internet of Things: Evolutions and Innovations
(Digital Tools and Uses Set – Volume 4)

Duong Véronique
Baidu SEO: Challenges and Intricacies of Marketing in China

Lesas Anne-Marie, Miranda Serge
The Art and Science of NFC Programming
(Intellectual Technologies Set – Volume 3)

Liem André
Prospective Ergonomics
(Human-Machine Interaction Set – Volume 4)

Marsault Xavier
Eco-generative Design for Early Stages of Architecture
(Architecture and Computer Science Set – Volume 1)

Reyes-Garcia Everardo
The Image-Interface: Graphical Supports for Visual Information
(Digital Tools and Uses Set – Volume 3)

Reyes-Garcia Everardo, Bouhaï Nasreddine
Designing Interactive Hypermedia Systems
(Digital Tools and Uses Set – Volume 2)

Saïd Karim, Bahri Korbi Fadia
Asymmetric Alliances and Information Systems:Issues and Prospects
(Advances in Information Systems Set – Volume 7)

Szoniecky Samuel, Bouhaï Nasreddine
Collective Intelligence and Digital Archives: Towards Knowledge
Ecosystems
(Digital Tools and Uses Set – Volume 1)

2016

Ben Chouikha Mona
Organizational Design for Knowledge Management

Bertolo David
Interactions on Digital Tablets in the Context of 3D Geometry Learning
(Human-Machine Interaction Set – Volume 2)

BOUVARD Patricia, SUZANNE Hervé
Collective Intelligence Development in Business

EL FALLAH SEGHROUCHNI Amal, ISHIKAWA Fuyuki, HÉRAULT Laurent, TOKUDA Hideyuki
Enablers for Smart Cities

FABRE Renaud, in collaboration with MESSERSCHMIDT-MARIET Quentin, HOLVOET Margot
New Challenges for Knowledge

GAUDIELLO Ilaria, ZIBETTI Elisabetta
Learning Robotics, with Robotics, by Robotics
(Human-Machine Interaction Set – Volume 3)

HENROTIN Joseph
The Art of War in the Network Age
(Intellectual Technologies Set – Volume 1)

KITAJIMA Munéo
Memory and Action Selection in Human–Machine Interaction
(Human–Machine Interaction Set – Volume 1)

LAGRAÑA Fernando
E-mail and Behavioral Changes: Uses and Misuses of Electronic Communications

LEIGNEL Jean-Louis, UNGARO Thierry, STAAR Adrien
Digital Transformation
(Advances in Information Systems Set – Volume 6)

NOYER Jean-Max
Transformation of Collective Intelligences
(Intellectual Technologies Set – Volume 2)

VENTRE Daniel
Information Warfare – 2nd edition

VITALIS André
The Uncertain Digital Revolution
(Computing and Connected Society Set – Volume 1)

KEMBELLEC Gérald, CHARTRON Ghislaine, SALEH Imad
Recommender Systems

MATHIAN Hélène, SANDERS Lena
Spatio-temporal Approaches: Geographic Objects and Change Process

PLANTIN Jean-Christophe
Participatory Mapping

VENTRE Daniel
Chinese Cybersecurity and Defense

2013

BERNIK Igor
Cybercrime and Cyberwarfare

CAPET Philippe, DELAVALLADE Thomas
Information Evaluation

LEBRATY Jean-Fabrice, LOBRE-LEBRATY Katia
Crowdsourcing: One Step Beyond

SALLABERRY Christian
Geographical Information Retrieval in Textual Corpora

2012

BUCHER Bénédicte, LE BER Florence
Innovative Software Development in GIS

GAUSSIER Eric, YVON François
Textual Information Access

STOCKINGER Peter
Audiovisual Archives: Digital Text and Discourse Analysis

VENTRE Daniel
Cyber Conflict

THERIAULT Marius, DES ROSIERS François
Modeling Urban Dynamics

2009

BONNET Pierre, DETAVERNIER Jean-Michel, VAUQUIER Dominique
Sustainable IT Architecture: the Progressive Way of Overhauling Information Systems with SOA

PAPY Fabrice
Information Science

RIVARD François, ABOU HARB Georges, MERET Philippe
The Transverse Information System

ROCHE Stéphane, CARON Claude
Organizational Facets of GIS

2008

BRUGNOT Gérard
Spatial Management of Risks

FINKE Gerd
Operations Research and Networks

GUERMOND Yves
Modeling Process in Geography

KANEVSKI Michael
Advanced Mapping of Environmental Data

MANOUVRIER Bernard, LAURENT Ménard
Application Integration: EAI, B2B, BPM and SOA

PAPY Fabrice
Digital Libraries

2007

DOBESCH Hartwig, DUMOLARD Pierre, DYRAS Izabela
Spatial Interpolation for Climate Data

SANDERS Lena
Models in Spatial Analysis

2006

CLIQUET Gérard
Geomarketing

CORNIOU Jean-Pierre
Looking Back and Going Forward in IT

DEVILLERS Rodolphe, JEANSOULIN Robert
Fundamentals of Spatial Data Quality